The King's Trial

The King's Trial

THE FRENCH REVOLUTION

VS. LOUIS XVI

Twenty-fifth Anniversary Edition
With a New Preface

DAVID P. JORDAN

UNIVERSITY OF CALIFORNIA PRESS

BERKELEY · LOS ANGELES · LONDON

University of California Press
Berkeley and Los Angeles, California
University of California Press, Ltd.
London, England
Copyright © 1979, 2004 by
The Regents of the University of California
ISBN 0-520-23697-1
Library of Congress Catalog Card Number: 78-54797
Printed in the United States of America

10 09 08 07 06 05 04
10 9 8 7 6 5 4 3 2 1

For Jonathan L. Marwil

Je boirai le calice jusqu'à la lie.
                    LOUIS XVI

Si on le juge, il est mort.
                    DANTON

L'époque de la condamnation de Louis
fut sans contredit la crise la plus
dangereuse de toute notre révolution.
                    ROBESPIERRE

Le meilleur a payé pour les méchants.
Les mauvaises causes ont leurs martyrs
comme les bonnes.
                    CARNOT

On ne peut point régner innocemment.
                    SAINT-JUST

Contents

Preface to the Twenty-fifth Anniversary Edition   xi

Preface to the 1979 Edition   xxv

Acknowledgments   xxxiii

Prologue   **The King's Longest Night**   1
The Tuileries, August 9–10, 1792

I   **The Question of the King**   11
May 1789–August 1792

II   **The End of the Monarchy**   34
July–September 1792

III   **The King Can Do No Wrong**   56
Paris, August 10–December 9, 1792

IV   **The Man of the Temple**   79
The Temple, September 1792–January 1793

V   **The Accusation**   101
The Manège, December 10–11, 1792

VI   **A Lawyer for the King**   117
The Manège, December 12–25, 1792

VII   **The King's Defense**   126
The Manège, December 26, 1792

VIII   **The King and Desperate Men**   141
December 27, 1792–January 13, 1793

IX   The First Two Votes   161
     The Manège, January 14–15, 1793

X   The Vote on Death   178
     The Manège, January 16–17, 1793

XI   The King Must Die   193
     The Manège, January 18–20, 1793

XII The March to the Scaffold   208
     Paris, January 20–21, 1793

XIII The Memory of a King   222
     January 21, 1793–January 21, 1973

Epilogue   231
Appendix The Third *Appel Nominal*   239
          A General Note on Sources and Authorities   249
          Index   269

Preface to the Twenty-fifth Anniversary Edition

NCE I SEND the corrected page proofs to a publisher and a book is out of my hands, my ardor cools; I lose interest and seek another love. When the first bound copies arrive, I thumb through a volume, read the preface, inscribe and send them to family and friends, and then shelve the book. I have no interest in reading what I have written. The invitation to do a new edition of *The King's Trial* disrupted this pattern. Here was an opportunity to reconsider what I had said and read all that had since been written on the subject.

I reread my book, now distant enough to seem the work of another author with habits of mind and style annoyingly like my own, and I read whatever I had missed of new work on the subject published since 1979. What has happened during this long interim is that Louis has found a new lawyer (Jacques Vergès), a modern scholarly biographer (John Hardman), and a team of revisionist historians that has turned up some new bits of evidence (Paul and Pierrette Girault de Coursac). There have also been essays on the meaning of the trial for French political thinking, the place of the trial in a Freudian reading of the Revolution, and even a monograph on Louis's reputation among nineteenth-century biographers, as well as much else.[1] Some old verities or assumptions have been jarred loose, and subjects I thought closed or uninteresting now seem to warrant revisiting. There was also a vast new literature on the French Revolution in which the king's trial played a part. Some strategic decisions had to be made. I have decided to set aside virtually all the general work on the Revolution, the ongoing controversies, debates, revisions of revisions—the origins of the Terror, the place of the Jacobins, the role of the war, among many others—despite its interest and its impact on Louis's trial. My original intention was to write a history of the king's trial, and so it remains. I have grafted none of the new work on the Jacobins, for example, onto my original characterization of them during Louis's trial, for I am not persuaded their behavior in the last months of 1792 is motivated differently from how I described it. Nor have I changed my mind about the place of the trial in the subsequent Terror. For better or worse, what I thought in 1979 remains my thinking today.

I will reiterate my arguments for continuing to think that the king's trial was not the beginning of the Terror in the French Revolution, that its outcome did not depend largely on legal procedures (which were numerous, if unorthodox), and that it did not set a precedent for either the Moscow Show Trials or the Stalinist purges in eastern Europe in the twentieth century.

The bicentennial of the Revolution was commemorated by a remarkable piece of public theater orchestrated by Jean-Paul Goude. I am interested here in only one small part of this national celebration: a televised reenactment of Louis's original ordeal. The ninety-minute program, the brainchild of the journalist-producer Yves Mourousi, was presented on TF-1 December 12, 1988. The program was a hit with television viewers, garnering a large audience. Mourousi and the participants mixed authenticity with anachronism, with professional actors playing historical figures and public notorieties such as Jacques Vergès—the flamboyant lawyer who defended Algerian revolutionaries and the Nazi torturer Klaus Barbie—playing themselves. In this production Vergès defended the king and was left unencumbered by the historical details of Louis's actual defense. There was a wholly unscientific telephone survey after the trial. Over half the participating viewers judged the king innocent of the charges, with 55% favoring acquittal and 17.5% preferring a penalty of exile. Thus almost three-fourths of the audience opposed the execution of Louis Capet. I had ended my book on a melancholy note: a memorial service for Louis XVI held in the old royal church of Saint-Germain-l'Auxerrois in 1973, mostly attended by the middle aged and the well dressed, where the monarchist newspaper *La Croix* was prominently displayed. Who could have guessed that fifteen years later millions would be drawn to watch a television reenactment and vote for acquittal? History had not been repeated; it had been restaged.

Unexpectedly, at least for a historian who originally wrote before the vogue of gender history and the apparent dominance of cultural history, more imaginative work has been devoted recently to the queen (and her trial) than to the king. Although Marie-Antoinette had no constitutional importance in the Revolution since she could not inherit the throne, her travail has attracted much attention. For the most part historians agree that the details of Louis's trial and its place in the Revolution are known. My book is now cited as an authority. One book, by Ferenc Fehér, took up the trial in the larger context of Jacobinism, and Michael Walzer answered him. I discuss this below. Otherwise, leaving aside Mourousi's clever televised entertainment, Louis's trial did not get much attention in the scholarly combats of the bicentennial.

The often polemical presentation of theses old and new during the bicentennial raised the heat under the cauldron of controversy. The French press regularly reported on the revisions to their national heritage; well-known academics appeared on television; and the intellectual periodicals turned their pages over to the dense controversy.[2] Steven Laurence Kaplan has chronicled these scholarly squabbles in his history of the bicentennial.[3]

In a less public, media-driven mode, scholars from around the world were assembled—with Keith Baker, François Furet, and Colin Lucas in one camp and Michel Vovelle, Jean-René Suratteau, and others in its opposing camp—to hold colloquia on the Revolution.[4] Several ambitious new interpretations of the Revolution appeared. The three best—by François Furet, William Doyle, and Simon Schama—will, in the case of Furet, dominate our thinking about the Revolution, in the case of Doyle, remain authoritative, and in the case of Schama, be the stylish embodiment of controversy for years to come.[5] None of these three diverges from my interpretation of the king's trial, and I am embalmed in the bibliographies of all three.

My rule of thumb is to consider here only those views that differ from my own, any new evidence that demands rethinking what I wrote in 1979, and only those arguments, approaches, and opinions that might cause me to modify what I then thought.

History, even when posing as a social science discipline, does not deal in replicable experiments, hypotheses that can be tested under controlled circumstances. Historians make arguments based on the available evidence. No matter how elegant or eloquent, those arguments are not and cannot be very durable, let alone definitive. The events we deal with are unique, unlike those in nature. The king's trial began, officially, November 13, 1792, and ended with his execution January 21, 1793. There was no other comparable trial, although it is possible to analogize Louis's trial with those of other overthrown leaders or make hypotheses that are counterfactual, what if the king had not been found guilty? being the most profound, plastic, and perennial.

Louis's trial, although delimited in time and place, is an event that reaches beyond both. It is momentous not because matters of life and death were decided but because of the defendant. Nor, I think, is it only the fact that the king was condemned and guillotined that gives the trial its impact. The murder of the Tsar's entire family by the Bolsheviks, a more chilling event, is oddly easier to metabolize because it happened in the midst of civil war and because it more resembles the St. Valentine's Day massacre than a national act of revolutionary justice. The very publicity of Louis's trial, as opposed to the hasty execution and burial of the Russian ruling family, is also responsible for its enduring fascination. More than 400 *opinions* or speeches were published by the deputies; there were four roll-call votes on Louis's fate (of the six during the Convention Assembly); the daily coverage in the press was extensive and supplemented the stenographic record kept by the Convention Assembly itself, not to mention pamphlets published in France and abroad; and the entire trial was conducted before the merciless gaze of Paris in revolution.

Nothing in the French Revolution was allowed to go, or has since gone, unnoticed. The Revolution published its utterances, decrees, and deliberations assuming its deeds and desires were of interest to all. The Court had whispered. The Revolution would shout. In the nineteenth century the ongoing cause of the Revolution was taken up by activists and thinkers from across the political spectrum. French socialists, anarchists, and revolutionists of all kinds proclaimed they were carrying on the work of the Revolution. Their foes insisted the Revolution was over. Alexis de Tocqueville spoke of a single revolution stretching from 1789 to his own day. Karl Marx, around the same time, linked the French Revolution to all subsequent uprisings, creating a paradigm that would be carried by the Bolsheviks into the twentieth century. The linkages between the two revolutions are many and varied. Let me cite only one. The first monument erected to Maximilien Robespierre was in the garden of Alexander, under the walls of the Kremlin, several months after the October Revolution. The decree was signed by Lenin himself, who therein describes Robespierre as a Bolshevik *avant la letter*, under whose leadership the Jacobins reached "one of the highest summits attained by the working class in struggling for its emancipation."

Louis's trial was borne on these currents of meaning and transformation. Linking the Bolshevik Revolution to the French Revolution, a largely rhetorical and interpretive enterprise, unexpectedly moved the question of political and revolutionary justice to the center of our anxieties when terror became so prevalent a part of the Russian Revolution. Many hearkened back to the king's trial or the Terror, which now became a foreshadowing of the Stalinist Show Trials. The twentieth-century lens became a new instrument of refraction.

The echoes of the king's trial have had a long life and have become remarkably familiar. All the issues, ideas, overtones, problems, paradoxes, and moral dilemmas that continue to claim our attention perplexed and provoked the king's accusers and judges in 1792. The 400-plus *opinions* published during the trial include multiple versions from some deputies who were unable to make up their minds. There were, additionally, many pamphlets on the trial written by those who were in and out of the National Assembly, and in and out of France. Arguably, no event in the French Revolution was so publicly debated. The vote itself, especially the third *appel nominal* on Louis's punishment, with its dozens of possible combinations and conditions, is a record of men wrestling with choices that were all unsatisfactory.

Questions of procedure and precedent, evidence and argument, morality and necessity, and politics and principle were obsessively debated, as was the meaning of the king's trial and death. They were not so much solved January 21, 1793, as brutally (but only momentarily) silenced. Recently, this unsettled judgment has been once again appealed, this time before the Committee for the Study of Louis XVI and His Trial founded under the presidency of the late Gabriel Marcel, a respected Christian philosopher. The organ of the committee is a quarterly review, *Découvert*, where Paul and Pierrette Girault de Coursac have published a number of their studies. These were conveniently brought together, augmented, and published in their 600-page *Enquête sur le procès du roi Louis XVI* (1984).

The Girault de Coursacs have set themselves a formidable task: the rehabilitation, both scholarly and moral, of Louis XVI. Their archival digging has turned up a few new or overlooked documents, and they have offered some quite original, not to say eccentric, reinterpretations. Almost none of this, it must be said, has attracted wide adherence or much notice among historians of the French Revolution.

The indictment against Louis, drawn up by Robert Lindet, took the form of a republican history of the Revolution in which the king was presented as a kind of malevolent deus ex machina whose interventions thwarted the Revolution at every important crisis. The Girault de Coursacs have responded by systematically investigating the charges against the king in chronological order. They have gone back to the sources whenever possible, having, for example, examined the raw materials that were sifted and edited by the various committees of the Convention Assembly in preparing the case against the king. Although presented throughout their work as neither a revolutionary nor even a warm friend of the Revolution, their Louis is not the counterrevolutionary indicted by the Convention Assembly. He is, rather, a French patriot who sought to save the kingdom from the excesses of the fanatical *clubistes* who followed the "metaphysical" effusions of the *philosophes.* The Girault de Coursacs' *Enquête* is too sprawling to be abbreviated, so I have chosen the flight to Varennes—when the king and his family fled Paris, June 1791, only to be captured at the town of Varennes, not far from lands under the control of the Austrian emperor—as an important episode that reveals their approach.

The story of the flight to Varennes I presented in 1979 was and remains conventional, consensual. The king, a virtual prisoner in the Tuileries since October 6, 1789, finally decided to quit his capital, make for the eastern frontier, and while there either negotiate with the Revolution or cross the border and join the *emigrés* who were raising an army to invade France and destroy the Revolution. The king's motives and goals were ambivalent, although he did leave behind upon his departure, in his own hand, a *Déclaration du roi adressée à tous les Français á sa sortie de Paris*, which declared his hostility to the Revolution from its beginnings. The revolutionaries assumed that Louis intended to leave France and return with a conquering army, but the king always denied this.

The Girault de Coursacs take the unique and extreme position that there were two escape plans, one engineered by the queen, the other by the king, with neither spouse aware of what the other was doing. Louis, they continue, did not determine to flee until after April 19, 1791, and had no plans to do so until the Parisians prevented him, on that date, from going to St. Cloud to take Easter communion. He then contacted General Bouillé, who had emigrated, to set in motion the machinery for his flight. This royal letter put Bouillé in no little difficulty. The General had hitherto operated on the assumption that his correspondence with Marie-Antoinette had the approval of the king (since the queen had gotten her husband to sign a couple of the letters and, according to the Girault de Coursacs, spoke in the king's name). Bouillé and Marie-Antoinette now concocted a scheme to have the flight fail so that her duplicity would not be revealed. The Girault de Coursacs propose this stunning and unsubstantiated hypothesis of betrayal by arguing that Marie-Antoinette thought originally to leave her husband behind. Now Bouillé plotted to have Louis captured at Varennes, while Marie-Antoinette and the Dauphin would escape. The queen, like her mother, Marie Theresa, in 1740, would rally her troops from horseback and reconquer the kingdom in the name of her son.

Fantastic stuff! But is it true? There is no way to know for sure. There are some letters that suggest Louis and Marie-Antoinette were making separate assumptions, maybe separate plans, and there is some evidence that the letters were tampered with. In a couple of these *"moi"* was scratched out and replaced by *"le roi."* The Girault de Coursacs argue that these slips of the pen indicate Marie-Antoinette was making her own plans, not those for the royal family. To my mind these new bits of evidence and the Girault de Coursacs' sinister and clever hypothesis neither overturn the view I have presented nor prove the queen planned to leave Louis to his fate. Politically, Marie-Antoinette appears more stupid and selfish than

cold-blooded and serpentine. Shifting blame for the Varennes deba-
cle to the queen helps little and would not have saved Louis's head.

The Girault de Coursacs present a complicated revisionist thesis:
the king had an independent politics, a middle course between the
extremists of the Court and those of the clubs, whose goal was to
save France from the latter. His trial was not just a miscarriage of
justice but a judicial murder carried out by the Jacobins and their
friends in order to destroy Louis's patriotic politics, thus destroying a viable alternative to political extremism. Evidence was suppressed; potential witnesses were murdered (in the prison massacres
in Orléans and Paris); and procedures were mangled, truncated,
and manipulated. The Girault de Coursacs offer a version of the
anti-Jacobin thesis, which arose during the Revolution and continues to our day.

This same anti-Jacobin thesis is taken up in another register by
Ferenc Fehér in the *The Frozen Revolution: An Essay on Jacobinism*
(1987). I can here neither recapitulate all of his arguments nor respond to them, something that has already been ably done by
Michael Walzer.[6] For my purposes it will be sufficient to address
Fehér's linkage of the king's trial to the terror in the French Revolution and, ultimately, to the eastern European purge trials of the
twentieth century. The former is explicitly forged by Fehér, the latter,
implicitly.

The king's trial, Fehér argues, was a dangerous compromise between future victims of the Terror and their future executioners.
Law was made from 1792 to 1793 in order to serve the particular
purposes of the Revolution, which were advanced and articulated
by the Jacobins, who both despised the law and saw it almost exclusively as an instrument of political power. The trial did not establish
the rule of law at this critical juncture of the Revolution but rather
made it a weapon of the faction. Jacobin arguments in the trial were
made with apparent disregard to circumstances and persons. In
truth they were made *in abstracto*. The most notorious moment was
Saint-Just's maiden speech November 13, 1792, the day Louis's trial
formally opened. The twenty-six-year-old unknown deputy, making no personal references to Louis XVI, declared the principle that
the king was guilty not for any acts he may have committed but because he was king. Saint-Just made political functions morally crim-

inal, and by implication and extension, social functions were also criminal. The crime was visible and needed no proof; one was king or an aristocrat or a part of some other anathematized group. Judicial procedures were mere chicanery for Saint-Just and the Jacobins.

It is this confusion of the real and the imagined king that creates much of the problem for Fehér. So long as the indictment and judgment were kept in the abstract, there was little problem. Saint-Just's brilliant speech and Robespierre's equally brilliant oration in December did just this. But once Louis XVI was introduced it became, Fehér argues, difficult to prove the crime. At this point, he continues, the Convention did not "waste much time in attempting to substantiate their accusation."[7]

The chilling result of the king's trial, Fehér concludes—and I have severely compressed his argument, squeezing out a good deal of the intelligence in the process—was the introduction of political justice into post-Enlightenment politics. The new maxim was that anybody can be crushed if those who have ruthless principles and hold sufficient power determine that their cause stands higher than the idea of traditional, conventional, or banal justice. The foundations for the Terror of 1793–1794 had been laid, as well as for other terrors well beyond the French Revolution.

The Girault de Coursacs and Ferenc Fehér represent not just the perennial interest in Louis's trial but also the two most fruitful critiques. The former make the argument from archival evidence to demonstrate their thesis; the latter concentrates on the theory and practice of Jacobinism. Both despise the Jacobins, attack them from different angles, and perhaps unexpectedly reach the same conclusions: Louis died on the scaffold because there was no rule of law in France from 1792 to 1793 that was insured by legal procedures. The staged television trial of the king is of another order, a kind of magical thinking whereby history can be reshaped to fit the needs of later opinions. Yet it too was anti-Jacobin and lifted the event out of its historical context.

In 1979 I argued—and I still stubbornly cling to the view—that the best way to understand the king's trial is to write its history. Remove the concrete realities of time, place, and circumstances from the trial, from any historical event, and almost any hypothesis is plausible. The Girault de Coursacs, Ferenc Fehér, and Yves Mourousi, in quite different ways, have done exactly this. They have denatured the trial, made it timeless. If we return to the Manège in the last months of 1792, with the prison massacres still a fresh memory, the victory at Valmy even fresher, the intoxication of declaring France a republic infecting all political judgments, and more than 700 newly elected deputies—chosen by the largest male electorate since 1789— determined to settle accounts with a king overthrown August 10 in a massive urban insurrection, things look different. At the time, there was almost no talk about the rule of law, although there was a great deal about procedures. The Jacobins were at the outset of their rise to preponderance. They did not dominate the Assembly, nor was it clear to many, perhaps most, that they would. The theorem that judging and condemning the king led to terror was unuttered because it was unthought.

In the course of the trial itself all these issues were vigorously debated. A national assembly where virtually every other man was a lawyer was deeply interested in how Louis was to be tried, nay, whether he could be tried. Mountains of seized papers were sifted through by the committees, often hurriedly and always with an ultimate political purpose in mind. This last, incidentally, was not a major cause for alarm to the deputies. We should remember that the American constitution makers allowed for impeachment, the legal attack of one's political enemies, and we do not think of them, or of an impeachment, as the work of terrorists or evidence that the rule of law has collapsed. Mistakes were made by the Convention Assembly, and tactics changed as the trial unfolded—in the form the indictment took, for example—but this is not equivalent to a deliberate and ultimately murderous systematic disregard for the law, for procedures, or for both. Nor is it an attack on the rule of law as a worthy principle. For all of their rhetorical fervor, the Jacobins, with the sole exception of Saint-Just—whose arguments were rejected by the Convention Assembly—made no attempt to abbreviate the trial and deny the defendant his days in court.

The issue that occupied the deputies, once they had determined whether they could try the king, which took several weeks of intense debate, was that of procedures. In this unprecedented trial the National Assembly made up procedures as they went along by modifying and supplementing those that existed in order to accommodate extraordinary circumstances. They did not truncate, redefine, or suppress procedures, as they would during the Terror. Louis got defenders, heard the indictment, answered it, and helped prepare his defense. His was indeed a political trial, but that was unavoidable if he was to be called to account for his actions. And in many ways the outcome was not a foregone conclusion. Certainly it was not so considered by those who sat in the Manège. There was long debate on each of the roll-call votes taken in the trial; the antiregicides had these four opportunities to vote against death. Everything was done publicly. No defendant during the Terror, perhaps no defendant in French history, enjoyed these benefits, albeit ad hoc at times, to such a degree.

History, runs the cliché, is constantly being rewritten. In the case of the king's trial, the verdict—on procedural, evidentiary, and philosophical grounds—is regularly appealed. I remain convinced there is not sufficient new evidence to exonerate the king while the other two categories for reconsideration remain virtually unchanged. Historical verdicts, for better or worse, are almost never overturned, except on television.

D.P.J.

Oak Park, Illinois
March 2003

Notes

1. Jacques Vergès has not written specifically on the trial. His extraordinary career is narrated by Bernard Violet, with the collaboration of Robert Jégaden, in *Vergès, Le Maître de l'ombre* (Paris, 2000). John Hardman, *Louis XVI* (London, 1993), is the biographer, and Paul and Pierrette Girault de Coursac, *Enquête sur le procès du roi Louis XVI* (Paris, 1984), the hagiographers. Susan Dunn, *The Deaths of Louis XVI: Regicide and the French Political Imagination* (Princeton, 1994), and Annie Duprat, *Le Roi décapité: Essai sur les imaginaires politiques* (Paris, 1992), explain their subject in their titles, as does Laurent Giraud, *Louis XVI au miroir des biographies romantiques* (Clermont-Ferrand, 2002), and Lynn Hunt, *The Family Romance of the French Revolution* (Berkeley, 1992), gives the trial a central place in her interpretative essay.

   I was first drawn to this subject by the compelling story that distilled into a few months so many of the anxieties of the Revolution. I pursued the story because a scholarly history of the trial had not yet been written. I then thought that the best way to understand the king's trial is as history and sought to unfold the events, paying close attention to time, place, circumstances, and character. Now that I have read a good deal of what has been written about the trial since I published my own book, I have been convinced anew that historical events are best understood historically. Those who would lift the trial out of its context—isolate its ideological dimensions, see in them harbingers of a murderous future, argue that the king was martyred—distort the story by removing the circumstances in which the trial took place.

2. *1789: La Commémoration* (Paris, 1999), made up of a collection of essays drawn from *Le Débat*, is indicative of the high seriousness of the ideological-scholarly controversies.

3. *Farewell, Revolution: The Historians' Feud, France 1789–1989* and *Disputed Legacies, France 1789–1989* (Ithaca, 1995).

4. The respective volumes engendered by these *colloques*, under the general title *The French Revolution and the Creation of Modern Political Culture*, were Keith Michael Baker, ed., *The Political Culture of the Old Regime* (1987); Colin Lucas, ed., *The Political Culture of the French Revolution* (1987); François Furet and Mona Ozouf, eds., *The Transformation of Political Culture, 1789–1848* (1989); and Keith Michael Baker, *The Terror* (1994).

5. My judgment is defensible exclusively on the grounds of personal taste. The books are William Doyle, *The Oxford History of the French Revolution* (Oxford, 1989), the most traditional of the three; François Furet, *La Révolution, 1770–1880* (Paris, 1988), the most "revisionist" view in the sense that Furet has something new and original to say about almost every aspect of the Revolution; and Simon Schama, *Citizens: A Chronicle of the French Revolution* (New York, 1989), a stylish general history. In addition there is François Furet's and Mona Ozouf's *Dictionnaire critique de la Révo-*

lution française (Paris, 1988), a collaborative work that is not strictly speaking a history of the Revolution, for its articles leave a number of subjects untreated, but whose intellectual vigor is unmatched. The Marxist historians, for their part, countered this scholarly assault, but feebly. There was no big interpretive history of the Revolution published by a Marxist historian to mark the bicentennial. Under the name of Albert Soboul, who had died some years earlier, Jean-René Suratteau and François Gendron edited a *Dictionnaire historique de la Révolution française* (Paris, 1989), which contained no contributions from Soboul. Michel Vovelle, the then incumbent of the prestigious chair consecrated to the Revolution, published a collection of his essays for the bicentennial, *Combats pour la Révolution* (Paris, 1993), and edited *Les colloques du bicentennaire* (Paris, 1991), a handbook of the hundreds of colloquia held throughout the world.

6. See Michael Walzer, *Regicide and Revolution: Speeches at the Trial of Louis XVI* (New York, 1992), with a new introduction by the author. Walzer, in an appendix, reprints Fehér's "Revolutionary Justice," chapter five from his *The Frozen Revolution: An Essay on Jacobinism* (Cambridge, England, 1987), and his own response, "The King's Trial and the Political Culture of the Revolution," which he presented at Oxford as part of the Furet-Baker-Ozouf-Lucas *colloque*.

7. These arguments are in Fehér, pp. 223–30.

Preface to the 1979 Edition

I N THE WINTER OF 1972 I went to Paris for an indefinite stay. This was to be the realization of a long-nurtured dream. France, and particularly Paris, were special places for me, even magical. I remembered the special smells of the city, the taste of a *café crème* in the morning, a Gitanes cigarette and a brandy in the evening, standing at the *zinc* of a neighborhood café, the odd sound of rubber-wheeled subways, the charm of old buildings set against a leaden sky. As always I found the city beautiful and exciting, even in December when the café tables retreat indoors, yielding up the sidewalk they invade during the warm months, returning it to the pedestrians. I wandered aimlessly through favorite neighborhoods, found an apartment, and settled into a pleasant, unencumbered existence. Whatever else I may have imagined doing in Paris, writing some history was not included.

One day I bought a book, *Le Procès de Louis XVI*, a collection of documents on the trial selected and presented by Albert Soboul. It is not a famous book, not an important book. Perhaps I was intrigued by the cover, a detail of a particularly repulsive contemporary print showing the king's severed head, complete with dripping blood, being held up to the crowd by the executioner. Anyhow, I took it back to my room, along with a couple of Georges Simenon novels, with their wonderful evocations of mundane and trivial social intercourse (could one be further away from the French Revolution than the world of Inspector Maigret?), and started reading.

I knew the general outlines of the king's trial: the monarchy had been toppled on August 10, 1792, by a revolution; the Convention Assembly had tried the king for treason, found him guilty, and condemned him to death; the sentence had been carried out on January 21, 1793. The trial was, for modern historians of the Revolution, a minor event. Georges Lefebvre, the doyen of twentieth-century historians of the period, gives but five pages to the trial in his text on the French Revolution. Modern students of the Revolution seemed more interested in what came before and after the king's trial. The king himself has suffered a similar disregard from historians. He has yet to find a scholarly biographer and we know him mostly through the eyes of authors interested in sentimentalizing the story and rendering his death a martyrdom or a tragedy. Indeed, we know a good deal more about the king's wife, Marie-Antoinette, a perennial subject for romanticizing biographers, than we do about the man who ruled France for nearly twenty years. The consensus among professional historians seems to be that Louis was an incompetent and weak man, a political bungler whose judgment was notoriously bad, who compensated for his personal disabilities by taking refuge in blind stubbornness, and who was a tiresome obstruction to the Revolution. Finally swept into the dustbin of history so that France could become a republic and get on with the important revolutionary work, Louis did not matter. This is a simplification, of course, but not a parody.

Reading the documents collected by Soboul I was enthralled, and gradually began to realize that this view of things was too simple, perhaps too simpleminded. The character of the king, Louis Agonistes during his trial, was a challenging puzzle. He was an unexpected mixture of pusillanimity and stubbornness, arrogance and simplicity, insight and blindness. He had, it seemed to me, a bad press. His enthusiastic champions, perhaps because they were enthusiasts, had done little to improve his historical reputation.

And if the defendant was interesting, the issues involved in the trial were even more interesting. Here was one of those rare moments in history when profound ideas and issues were distilled, by *la force des choses*, into a few months of feverish activity and in a single place, Paris from September 1792 to January 1793. The men who grappled with the enormous questions of sovereignty, regicide, and revolution, the men of the Convention, were themselves remarkable. Aside from the personal animosities that fueled so many of the debates, aside from the eccentricities of many of the actors, here were men with something important to say and they said it in the most compelling language I had ever read. History, I thought, had contrived to make an ideal subject for a book; and yet there were no books devoted to the history of the trial and death of the king.

Just to make sure, I checked the bibliography Soboul had included at the end of the documents. There were the works I was familiar with, a few monographs on this or that aspect of the trial, E. Seligman's old but excellent two volumes, *La Justice en France pendant la Révolution, 1791–1793* (Paris, 1901, 1913)—the most comprehensive treatment of the subject, but putting the trial in the larger context announced by his title—and the classical historians of the Revolution, Jaurès, Michelet, and Mortimer-Ternaux particularly. Then I checked the catalogue room of the Bibliothèque nationale and the published bibliographies of the Revolution. Still nothing. Hundreds of pamphlets from the time of the trial and soon afterward; several contemporary collections of speeches from the trial; numerous biographies and hagiographies of the king; but no history of the trial itself. Here, for reasons I still do not understand, was an important event, a crucial event in the Revolution, in search of a historian.

I aspired to be that historian. I decided to write a history of the trial, beginning on August 10, 1792, and ending on January 21, 1793, from the fall of the monarchy to the execution of the king. The materials were abundant and accessible, the subject inherently dramatic. The cast of characters was fascinating and ideas seemed to share the stage with men contending against the impersonal forces of history. The time of the trial, coming as it did at the very beginning of the Convention's career, promised well; I might be able to grasp, in its infancy, the components of Jacobin triumph over the National Assembly and their subsequent command of the Revolution.

I did not want to write Louis's biography. I did not want to write an analytical study of the constitutional and political issues involved in regicide (a book that has now been written by Michael Walzer). I did not want to study the political behavior of the Convention and its deputies by analyzing their backgrounds and voting patterns (a book that has now been written by Alison Patrick). I did not want to write a history of the first months of the Convention, or of Paris in revolution. I wanted, quite simply, to tell the

story of the king's trial, to write a narrative history of the kind that
has fallen out of favor with historians in recent years. I wanted to
try my hand at what used to be thought the major task and challenge of a historian: to tell an important story, to tell it accurately,
and to tell it with some concern for style. And I had my ideal reader in mind. He—"it" sounds ridiculous and "he/she" clumsy—
would be interested in history (and probably history as narrative),
have some general historical culture, and be willing (could I hope
anxious?) to read a history on an important subject, a history deliberately unencumbered with a scholarly apparatus. A serious history book without footnotes!

This then is an old-fashioned book, written in an old-fashioned
way and with an old-fashioned goal in mind. Such a book, addressed to such a reader, would have to be reliable as well as
readable. I wanted to strike a balance between the skills and con-
cerns of a professional historian and what I imagined to be the interests of nonprofessional readers. I take accuracy and reliability to
mean that a narrative is made from the sources and is *au courant*
with the most recent research.

To begin with I made two decisions: my book would have no
footnotes to interrupt the narrative flow; and I would read all the
sources for the trial before I read any secondary authorities. Both
decisions were an overreaction to the current state of academic historical writing and I'm not willing to die in a ditch to defend them.
But once taken I stuck to these commitments. At the end of this
volume I have provided, chapter by chapter, a general guide to the
sources of my information. Where there are difficulties with the
sources—as with some of the memoirs of revolutionaries—I have
indicated them. Where there are outright contradictions, I have
indicated them. Where there are several versions of an event, or
variant readings for a text, I have told the reader and explained,
where I thought it appropriate, why I have preferred one to another. Where I have diverged from an accepted opinion I have told
the reader and tried to mention a representative expression of the
traditional view. Where I have followed the views of distinguished
historians I have tried to give credit.

In deciding not to use footnotes I reasoned that any student of
the French Revolution would be familiar with the sources for the

king's trial, since I have discovered nothing new in the archives and have, in fact, relied almost exclusively on printed sources, whether published at the time or later collected by scholars. Hence elaborate references and citations would be redundant for these readers. On the other hand, my imaginary reader would probably be grateful to be spared the cumbrous machinery of scholarship, so obtrusive in a narrative, and would probably be satisfied with the general indications I have provided of my diligence. All the details of this story, whether of dress or speech, gestures or manners, food or weather, furniture or activity, are derived from the sources. In addition, I have tried, whenever possible, to tell the story using the words of those who lived it. I believe this lends verisimilitude; I believe also that the words of Robespierre and Louis, Danton and Vergniaud, and a dozen others, are more poignant, more immediate (even in my translations) than any summary or paraphrase could be; and lastly, I love these contemporary resonances, this formal homage to the past.

My second decision, to read the sources before reading the authorities, was purely personal, taken with no concern for my imaginary reader. I began at an arbitrary beginning, August 10, 1792, and I began with the published proceedings of the Legislative Assembly and then the Convention Assembly, working through this material in chronological order. I wanted, if possible, to experience the story unfolding in time as it unfolded during the Revolution. I read the pamphlets of the day in the same way, ditto for the newspapers. Then I read the recollections, the memoirs, the letters of those who had been there, and I sought, in the great collections of the Bibliothèque nationale, Département des estampes, the light that drawings and etchings, paintings and woodcuts of the period could throw on the trial. Then, and only then, when the story was clear in my mind, when I had made judgments about the characters and issues involved, when I had decided what was important and what was not, did I turn to the authorities on the Revolution. First the classics, Jaurès, Michelet and Mortimer-Ternaux; then more recent or scholarly works. Sometimes I was persuaded by their reading of the evidence, sometimes not. But it was interesting to approach the subject with as few preconceived notions as possible, to have the illusion of making up my own mind. This process of reading the sources in chronological order took me fourteen months, and by a happy coincidence, which I probably contrived, although subconsciously, I reached the climax of the trial (January 21, 1793) almost exactly on that day, but 181 years later.

There are, in addition to the narrative approach and the absence of footnotes, a number of other idiosyncrasies in this book. Like anyone else who has devoted a considerable amount of time and energy to a subject, I think my subject important and tend to think it has been undervalued by other historians. I hope this is a rather harmless byproduct of intense concentration on a short scene in the past rather than an obsession. At any rate: I argue, usually implicitly, that the king's trial is fundamental to an understanding of the later political development of the Revolution. Most historians, I am aware, see the events of 1793—the purging of the Convention, the ascendancy of the Mountain and Robespierre, the creation of the machinery for terror, and the emergence of the Committee of Public Safety in an attempt to reestablish the executive principle in government—as more significant than what came earlier. I do not disagree that the year following the king's trial is important. I do think, however, that certain important threads of those momentous developments were spun from the trial itself. And in a curious way it is gratifying to study such problems in their earliest, embryonic manifestations. The enormous question of food, and its relationship to Paris radicalism and the political factions, is basic to the history of the trial from its beginning. The murderous struggle between Jacobins and Girondins, which had much to do with the subsequent political development of the Revolution, is the center of gravity of the entire trial, pulling all the scattered elements toward it, and often deforming them in the process. The confused quest for an executive authority once France had become a republic informs many of the debates on the king's fate. The Terror and the *sans-culotte* movement, the Commune of Paris and diplomacy, even the war—for the victory at Valmy on the eve of the sitting of the Convention made the trial possible— are all a part of the king's trial, as much as they are a part of the Revolution's subsequent history.

And as these larger issues cannot be separated from the course of the trial, so also does the trial prove an ideal vantage point for observing the emergence of new political leaders. For example, Saint-Just's maiden speech, and one of his greatest, was delivered during the trial. Or consider the significant change that Robespierre's politics undergo in the course of the trial. Attacked by the Girondins, singled out, along with Marat, as the spokesman and instigator of urban violence, that lonely and complex man devoted his energies to making a coherent and consistent ideology for the Mountain, which he sought to mold in his own image. And just as some dominated, others lost their hold on the minds and hearts of the deputies.

My view of the Jacobin-Girondin struggle is not especially original, although it may be a bit out of fashion. I have moved the struggle back several months and argue that Girondin ineptitude, both in terms of tactics and strategy, not only lost them control of the initiative in the trial, but also put into the hands of their antagonists, the Mountain, the means for their destruction. Their persistent and intemperate attacks on Paris, their inability to separate personal hatreds from revolutionary politics, their parliamentary irresponsibility, their disdain for or fear of "the people"—which sprang from their moderation, especially on social questions—all resulted in radical and ill-conceived political experiments which had a disastrous impact on the trial and on the course of the Revolution, and eventually cost the Girondins their heads.

The king's trial is the most extraordinary trial in French history, if only because the defendant is the most extraordinary ever put into the dock. Yet throughout the trial I was struck by how seldom Louis appeared, how easily he was swallowed up by what the *conventionnels* obviously thought more important issues, especially the Jacobin-Girondin struggle. Louis appeared before his accusers only twice, first to hear the indictment against him (December 11, 1792), then to present his defense (December 26). He spent a total of six or seven hours confronting his judges. I suspect that many of the defendants hauled before the notorious Revolutionary Tribunal, even at the height of the Terror, had a more extensive day in court than did the king. Louis, unlike Charles I of England, was not the central character in his own trial. But if he was not there in person, if he drops from sight after August 10, only to appear when summoned, he is present in spirit. Like Samuel Beckett's

Godot, Louis is constantly being talked about without being on stage.

Then there is the question of the scope of this book. It begins at the end of a long and complex historical development and ends at the beginning of another long and complex historical development. We are always being advised to begin at the beginning, which seems good advice. But the beginning—unless perhaps you are Thomas Mann beginning his Joseph tetralogy in the Garden of Eden—is usually an arbitrary point. I have tried to tell the reader something about events and issues and men prior to August 10, 1792, but I could not sincerely apologize for the sketchiness of these descriptions unless I had intended to write another book than the one I have written. The same is true of the asides and remarks that point to the future history of the Revolution. In both cases I made a practical decision: August 10 is the logical place to begin; January 21 the logical place to end.

The first draft of this book was written in Paris some months after the research was completed. This was not due to the belief that it was necessary to be in the place where the events I was describing happened in 1792–1793, but because I wanted to be in Paris, where I most enjoy working. Since then this book has gone through several metamorphoses. It even had a brief life as a cross between a drama and a narrative, with the story forced into acts and scenes. It has now returned to a form closely resembling its first emergence from the cocoon.

Chicago   D.P.J.
March 1978

Acknowledgments

Nearly everyone who writes history these days goes into debt, intellectual and emotional debt. I am no exception; and it is a pleasure to acknowledge my creditors here.

The patience, encouragement, suggestions, and criticisms of my dear friends Jonathan L. Marwil and Richard S. Levy were above and beyond the call of duty. I cannot thank them adequately here without falling into sentimentality. They both read the manuscript several times, in several versions, each time decorating it with comments and suggestions—not to mention the numerous discussions on Louis and his trial, on history and how it ought to be written, on style—and whatever merits the book has of clarity, of precision, of style, of concept, are present because of them.

Several other friends had a hand in the making of this book. They read the manuscript in whole or in part, in one version or another. I hope they will accept the mere listing of their names as a symbol of my gratitude: Stanley I. Mellon, of the University of Illinois at Chicago Circle, my teacher and friend; Stephen R. Graubard, the editor of *Daedalus*; Norman F. Cantor, of New York University; John Clive, of Harvard University, and Stuart Pierson, of Memorial University, St. John's, Newfoundland.

Alison Patrick, of the University of Melbourne, kindly answered a number of queries by mail. My friend Chips Sowerwine, also of the University of Melbourne, and his wife Aude, rented me their lovely Paris apartment, where this book was written. M. Jean Adhémar, former conservateur en chef du Département des estampes at the Bibliothèque nationale, guided me through the collections of the BN and gave me an eighteenth-century collection of revolutionary pamphlets whose frontispiece serves as the frontispiece of this book. The map of revolutionary Paris was lovingly drawn by Anders Nereim. Mr. Alain L. Hénon, Associate Editor of the University of California Press, gave this orphan of a book a home. The American Philosophical Society gave me a grant, from the Johnson Fund (in 1971), which helped defray the expenses of doing research in Paris.

And finally two unique debts, one to the past, the other to the present. From the time I first read the late Garrett Mattingly's *The Armada* I aspired to write a book like it, though I despaired of doing it as well. This is the narrative inspired by my reading, an attempt at the book I imagined.

The King's Longest Night

THE TUILERIES, AUGUST 9–10, 1792

ALLOW WAS in short supply in Paris but the Tuileries, the king's château since 1789, was ablaze with candles on this hot, clear night. All the windows were open to let in what little air was stirring. The public rooms were crowded with troops and armed men nervously awaiting an attack from the people of Paris.

In the royal apartments on the second floor the king and his family also waited. Only the royal children, the dauphin, age seven, and his sister, Madame Royale, age fourteen, were oblivious to the excitement: they were sleeping, watched over by their governess, Madame de Tourzel. The king, Louis, the sixteenth of his name, was passive, even lethargic. He was dressed in violet, the traditional color of mourning for French kings, but he showed no signs of distress, no awareness of danger. Marie-Antoinette, whose selfishness and stiff public manners had long ago alienated the affections of her subjects, was more agitated than her husband. Two years of revolution had affected her profoundly. The once beautiful queen, her faced lined, her hair graying, looked older than her thirty-seven years. The king's sister, the pious Madame Elisabeth, and the queen's friend and companion, Madame de Lamballe, completed the royal entourage.

Around 12:45 A.M. the sounds of the tocsin, the alarm bells

1

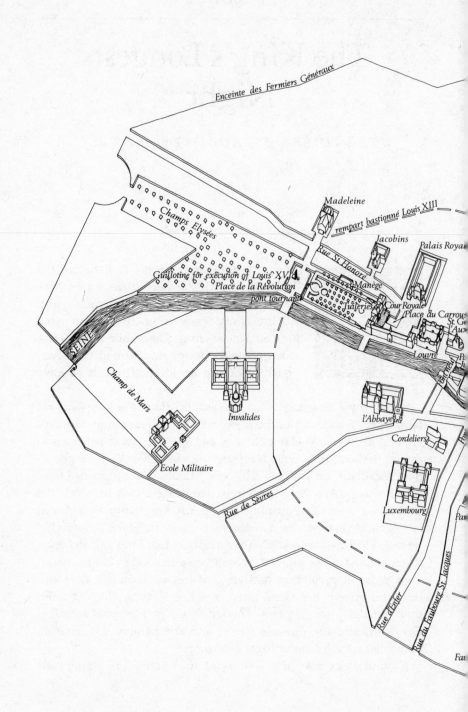

Enceinte des Fermiers Généraux

Champs Elysées

Madeleine

rempart bastionné Louis XIII

Jacobins

Palais Royal

Rue St Honoré

Guillotine for execution of Louis XVI.
Place de la Révolution
pont tournant

Manège

Tuileries

Cour Royale
Place du Carrousel

St G
l'Au

SEINE

Louvre

Champ de Mars

Invalides

l'Abbaye

Cordeliers

École Militaire

Rue de Sèvres

Luxembourg

Rue d'Enfer

Rue du Faubourg St. Jacques

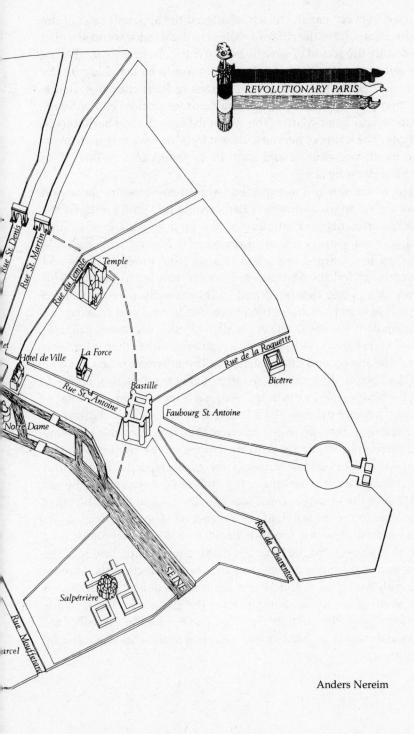

REVOLUTIONARY PARIS

Rue St. Denis
Rue St. Martin
Rue du temple
Temple
Hôtel de Ville
La Force
Rue St. Antoine
Bastille
Rue de la Roquette
Bicêtre
Faubourg St. Antoine
Notre Dame
Rue de Charenton
SEINE
Salpétrière
Rue Mouffetard
arcel

Anders Nereim

housed in every parish church, shattered the apparent calm of the night. Everyone in the château rushed to the windows and strained to identify the sound of specific bells. Which churches were ringing the call to arms, which neighborhoods would be marching on the Tuileries? Some shouted out the names of Paris churches, insisting they recognized the unmistakable tones of the bells of Saint-Antoine and Saint-Marcel, the two most feared neighborhoods in the city. The hours of nervous, almost hysterical waiting were over. The tocsin was ringing and soon Paris would answer the call to march against her king.

The attack was not unexpected. Almost two months earlier, on June 20, an angry and armed Paris crowd had easily entered the royal apartments and intimidated the king and his family. June 20 had been a dress rehearsal for August 10. Both attackers and attacked had learned important lessons from June 20. Louis and his commander, the Marquis de Mandat, concluded that the Tuileries was poorly defended and could probably not withstand a siege. Louis himself had little interest in tactics, and Mandat, an unimaginative if loyal officer, had made the necessary preparations. The château itself, built as a residence rather than a fortress, would be the second line of defense. The insurrectionists must be checked before they entered the grounds of the Tuileries. By holding the bridges across the Seine, Mandat hoped to make the attackers pay a heavy price in blood before they reached the château. If, he reasoned, they managed to cross the river from the left bank and attempted to join up with the troops on the right bank, they would then face seasoned troops strategically placed in and around the château. At the east end of the Tuileries gardens stood the old château of the Louvre, which was heavily defended. All the other entrances to the château had been sealed off. The stone-walled terraces surrounding the grounds could be held against attack by a handful of men, and the Pont Tournant, a mechanical bridge at the west end of the grounds, was locked. The insurrectionists, Mandat thought, would have to fight on his terms. He had strengthened the garrison, nearly doubling its size. The château and its grounds were bristling with soldiers and the Cour Royale, the largest of the three courtyards in front of the Tuileries itself, was defended by artillery.

Mandat's preparations were thorough and competent. Now it was up to the king; only he could set the defensive machinery in motion. Louis had to decide to fight or surrender, defend the monarchy or abdicate. But Louis hated decisions. The fate of the martial Bourbon house rested with a vacillating and pacific king. In the midst of the excitement the king remained inert, seemingly indifferent to what was about to happen.

Madame Elisabeth, who had been leaning out a window to hear the sounds of Paris in insurrection, left her post and walked over to Pierre-Louis Rœderer, the representative of the Department of Paris. The mayor of Paris, Jérôme Pétion, had refused to defend the château, as had the Legislative Assembly. By default of municipal and national authorities, Rœderer was left with the responsibility of defending the king and the monarchy. It was not an obligation he sought. Rœderer was a bland and timid man who preferred bureaucratic obscurity; but events had thrust him into prominence. Almost as much as the king Rœderer hated decisions.

When Madame Elisabeth approached he was sitting at a table reading the law of August 3, 1791, which dealt with the declaration of martial law. "What is that you have in your hand?" the king's sister asked. "Madame, it is the law dealing with the use of public force." "And what are you looking for?" "I was trying to find out if it was true that the Department had the authority to proclaim martial law." "And is it true?" "Madame, I don't believe so." It was not an answer to inspire confidence.

Rœderer had earlier told one of the king's ministers that martial law could only be proclaimed when the public tranquillity was habitually threatened, and he was unsure whether the Department, whose jurisdiction overlapped that of the municipal government of Paris, had the authority to run up the red flag of martial law. Besides, this, he had explained, gesturing vaguely toward the Carrousel where a crowd was gathering, "is a completely different thing than a simple disturbance of public tranquillity. It is a revolt stronger than martial law." Rather than exceed his authority, rather than compromise his political future, Rœderer wanted Louis to leave the Tuileries and seek refuge in the Legislative Assembly, which was in session just across the garden from the château. Rœderer stubbornly insisted he could not and would not proclaim martial law: Louis, just as stubbornly, refused to leave the Tuileries. The king retired to his bedroom, Rœderer went on reading the laws.

Around 2:30 A.M. a messenger arrived to report to the king that there were no signs of the sections of Paris marching. They were having trouble collecting their contingents. Perhaps the tocsin would go unanswered. The news, as it spread through the château, dissolved the sense of danger. There would be no attack; the revolutionaries would skulk back to their mean homes and submit to their rightful leaders; the monarchy would endure and triumph.

This optimistic interlude disappeared with the dawn. Paris was not marching but the sections remained agitated. The streets of Saint-Antoine and Saint-Marcel were lit with torches, armed men were assembling. At around 4:00 A.M. the sound of a coach, probably carrying Mayor Pétion to the city hall, the Hôtel de Ville, rattling over the cobblestones of the Cour Royale roused the château. In the royal apartments Madame Elisabeth was the first up. She went to the window. The dawn was dark red, as if nature had conspired to prefigure the events about to unfold. She shook Marie-Antoinette awake to see the beautiful sunrise. But politics interested the queen more than panoramas. She went over to Rœderer, who had spent the last couple of hours dozing in a chair, and asked him what was to be done. The king and his family, he answered, must seek safety in the National Assembly.

"Monsieur, there are troops here. It is time to know who will triumph, the king and the constitution, or factionalism." Rœderer responded dryly that if the queen was determined to fight, the king would have to concern himself with preparations for resistance. During this exchange Louis emerged from his bedroom. He was still drowsy with sleep. His carefully curled and powdered hair was flattened on one side where he had slept on it. His violet suit, rumpled from being slept in, complemented his lopsided coiffure. The disheveled king repeated what he had said some hours earlier: he had no intention of leaving the Tuileries. He had no faith in the Legislative Assembly. He seemed determined to fight for his crown. Rœderer managed to persuade the king to send a representative to the Assembly to see if they were willing to defend

THE TUILERIES UNDER ATTACK, AUGUST 10, 1792. An anonymous engraving, in color. The conception is static and even hieratic, but the engraving, contemporary to the event, conveys some of the excitement of the fall of the monarchy. The puffs of smoke coming from the château are from the Swiss defenders firing muskets. The Cour Royale is the center of the three courtyards; and the royal apartments were on the second floor. The open area in front of the three courtyards where the attackers are standing is the Carrousel. The attack, as depicted here, is much too orderly; but it makes clear the important role of artillery, and the château itself is accurately presented. *Bibliothèque nationale*

LOUIS AS REVOLUTIONARY.
A popular engraving (artist unknown) commemorating the invasion of the Tuileries on June 20, 1792. Louis was forced to put on the "Bonnet de la liberté" by the crowd (the caption insists, euphemistically, that the cap was presented to the king by the nation). This is one of the few portraits of the king where revolutionary and monarchical symbols are juxtaposed. *Bibliothèque nationale*

LOUIS IN HIS GLORY. Lithograph by Delpech, after a semiformal portrait of the king. The signature is a facsimile of the king's. He is bedecked with the ribbons and medals of the *ancien régime*, but appears here without his robes of monarchy. *Bibliothèque nationale*

the monarchy. Etienne-Louis-Hector DeJoly, the minister of justice, volunteered and set off across the garden.

Louis had momentarily thrown off his lethargy. He buckled on a ceremonial sword, put his hat under his arm, gathered his family together, along with several ladies of the court, and went to inspect his troops. It was around 6:00 A.M. The troops in the château itself, mostly professionals with a leaven of devoted courtiers, were passionately loyal to the king and greeted their commander-in-chief with enthusiasm. Louis then ordered his family to remain behind while he descended to the courtyard. The Swiss mercenaries he met on the way acclaimed him with shouts of "Down with the factions!" "Down with the Jacobins!" But once in the courtyard, where the guns were manned by members of the Paris National Guard, the artillerymen shouted "Long live the nation!" "Down with the veto!" "Down with the traitor!"—taunts he had not heard since June 20. Louis kept his composure but reviewed the troops perfunctorily, then returned to the château, unable or unwilling to rally his defenders.

At about the same time Louis reentered the château and mounted to the royal apartments, DeJoly returned from his mission to the Assembly. He had found the deputies—or at least those who remained since the supporters of the king and of General Lafayette's constitutional monarchists had abandoned their seats—frightened, confused, and unwilling to act. The only decision the Legislative had been able to take was to sit tight and remain in session so that the sovereignty of the nation, embodied in the Assembly, would not be compromised. The national authorities were of the same mind as the municipal and departmental authorities: to oppose revolutionary Paris was unthinkable if not impossible. Let events run their course.

Rœderer, who had left the château to find out what had happened to DeJoly, intercepted the excited minister as he was about to enter the Cour Royale. "The Assembly hardly listened to us. There are not enough members to make a decree; at the most there are 60 or 80." In addition DeJoly reported having seen armed men pushing into the château gardens by way of a gate near the Manège, the former riding academy of Louis XV where the Legislative met. Some

of the artillerymen had unloaded their guns; others had turned
their guns on the château itself, defying orders. And in the Carrousel, just in front of the château, DeJoly reported seeing an enormous crowd armed with pikes, swords, even sticks.

Rœderer escorted DeJoly to the king, who received the report
along with a rumor that the municipality of Paris had ordered 5,000
musket balls distributed and another that the Commune (the city
government) was disorganized—a euphemism for the coup d'état
at the Hôtel de Ville—the mayor under house arrest, and Mandat,
who had earlier been summoned to report to the Hôtel de Ville,
either arrested or dead. The insurrectionists were on the march.
Still Louis would not hear of leaving the château. The king was
seated at a table next to the entry to his reception room. His hands
rested inert on his knees; he was oblivious to his surroundings.
His earlier decision to fight had evaporated. He listened to the
reports and rumors listlessly, almost in a daze. Gathered around
him were the queen, Madame Elisabeth, the remaining ministers,
and the ladies of the court. "Sire," Rœderer pleaded, "Your Majesty has not five minutes to lose. You will be safe only in the National
Assembly. The opinion of the Department is that you go there
without delay. You do not have enough men to defend the château. They are no longer well disposed toward you. The artillerymen have unloaded their guns."

The king looked up blankly at Rœderer: "But I haven't seen a
large crowd at the Carrousel." "Sire, there are twelve pieces of
artillery and a huge crowd is arriving from the *faubourgs*." Louis
stared at the floor. Gerdret, one of Rœderer's colleagues, loudly
supported his superior's plan. "Don't raise your voice here with
us," snapped Marie-Antoinette. "Let Monsieur the *procureur-
général-syndic* speak." She turned to Rœderer, reminding him that
the château was full of armed and determined men. "Madame, all
Paris is marching."

The king looked up and glanced with disinterest around the
room. Then he slowly got up and turned to his wife: "Let us go."
He stood rooted, waiting for someone to tell him what to do next.

Madame Elisabeth asked Rœderer if he would be responsible for
her brother's safety: "Yes, Madame, on my life, I will march immediately in front of him." DeJoly asked if the ministers could join

the royal family; the queen asked on behalf of Madame de Tourzel and her daughter. Rœderer agreed to both requests. Then he explained to the king that representatives of the Department would surround the royal entourage and, escorted by some National Guardsmen, they would all walk to the Manège. "Yes, it will be just as you say," Louis muttered. Rœderer opened the door to the reception room and announced that the king and his family were going to the National Assembly. He sent for the officer in charge and gave instructions.

As soon as the escort arrived the royal party marched through the reception room. The crowd watched mutely. The king said, to no one in particular, "I am going to the National Assembly." As they passed through the *œil-de-bœuf*, the foyer leading to the royal apartments, Louis took the cap of one of his escorts and exchanged it for his own plumed hat. The astonished guard stuck the royal hat, with its large white feather, under his arm and continued marching. The royal entourage descended the Great Stairway, passed through the Central Pavilion and out into the Cour Royale. Louis noted once again that there were not so many people gathered in the Carrousel. Rœderer reiterated that all Paris was marching. When they reached the terrace, which was crowded with National Guardsmen, they were greeted with revolutionary slogans: "Long live the nation!" "No more veto!" "No women, no women, we want only the king, the king alone." The royal fugitives kept marching.

They crossed the gardens without incident. Louis, about to lay down his crown, a crown that Bourbon apologists traced back almost a thousand years to Hugh Capet, was heard to remark: "The leaves are falling early this year." In front of the Manège they were met by a delegation from the Legislative Assembly, who surrounded them and marched them into the hall. Louis had not stood in the midst of the nation's elected representatives since the autumn of 1791 when he accepted the constitution under which he still governed.

Once inside the Manège he was confronted by a constitutional difficulty: by law the king could not be present in the hall when the Assembly was in session. Louis seldom concerned himself with such questions of etiquette. He was usually surrounded by lackeys

who looked after these details. But now he was without his courtiers and in the midst of men sensitive to the issue of separation of
powers. He could sit neither on the benches reserved for ministers
of the crown nor in the places reserved for the deputies. While
Louis stood there the deputies debated the issue. They decided
that the king and his family could take refuge in the Logographie,
a tiny room behind the rostrum reserved for the reporters of the
Assembly's debates. An iron grill separated the Logographie from
the floor of the Assembly. The fugitives could see and hear all that
was going on, but the constitution had not been violated. The
room was stuffy and cramped. The children were cranky, Marie-
Antoinette anxious and nervous. She fidgeted, clasping and un-
clasping her hands in her lap. Only the king appeared composed.
He said little to his family.

Earlier that morning, when Louis was determined to fight, he
had issued his only order: force was to be met with force. The
order had not been rescinded when he abandoned the château.
The king's loyal defenders, without their commander-in-chief,
were left with a situation in which the king's order had little meaning, since Louis was no longer in need of defense. But the order
stood. Two hours after Louis XVI reached the Manège fighting
broke out across the gardens. The dreaded attack on the Tuileries
had begun.

CHAPTER I

The Question of the King

MAY 1789–AUGUST 1792

 HE KING WAS a problem for the Revolution from its beginning. The march that led Louis across the Tuileries gardens to lay down his crown had begun at least as early as the calling of the Estates-General in 1789, the first representative body to meet in France since 1614. For 175 years the kings of France had ruled under the legal maxim "the king can do no wrong"; they had said, as Louis XVI said when a subject challenged the legality of his actions, "it is legal because I wish it." This view of government and society could not live in harmony with its antithesis, a representative national assembly elected by manhood suffrage; and the French traditionally date their Revolution from the first week in May 1789, when the Estates-General gathered at Versailles, the home of the French monarchy since the seventeenth century. There they were received by the king, marched in procession, and celebrated mass before sitting down, on May 5, to begin deliberating.

The fundamental question confronting the nation was how France was to be governed and by whom. The monarchy, having yielded to the pressures of a rebellious aristocracy and bankruptcy, sought to control the Estates-General it had called into existence by insisting on a strict observance of the traditional forms. Following the old order of things the representatives of the nation had been elected and sat according to the rules of 1614. The deputies repre-

sented not the collective wishes of their electors, but rather the
corporate interests of the old feudal state, which was divided into
three orders or estates: clergy, nobility, and everyone else. Each
estate had been elected only by voters belonging to that estate, and
the three estates were to meet by order except when called together
by the king. And they would vote by order, not by head: one
order, one vote. The voting, again following tradition, would be
done in the order of relative importance in society: the clergy
would vote first, the nobility second, the Third Estate last. Thus
the first two orders of society, clergy and nobility, would have a
majority on any issue, assuming, as most observers did, that the
first two orders had similar if not identical interests.

The abbé Sièyes in his rousing and influential pamphlet *What Is
the Third Estate?* estimated the Third Estate at 97 percent of the
population and argued, correctly, that they were a nullity in politics. Their aspirations were to *be* "something." What "something"
meant was variously explained by the hundreds of pamphleteers
and petitioners who flooded the presses in 1789 with their theories
and hopes. Proposals ran the gauntlet of political possibilities, but
all stopped short of republicanism. The consensus was that France
would be best governed by a constitutional monarchy, somewhat
on the British model. The Third Estate aspired to play a significant
role in this imagined constitutional monarchy, but the traditional
hierarchies—king, aristocracy, and commons—would remain un-
touched. In other words, France would be reformed politically but
the social structure would remain intact. It proved an impossible
vision.

The first two estates were internally split. The upper echelons of
the clergy, largely descended from the noble houses of France,
were theoretically aligned with the nobility. Both enjoyed a privileged position in society, both were reluctant to give up their
privileges, both hated the liberals in their midst and feared the
commons, yet both believed, in general, that the powers of the
monarchy must be curbed. There was a contradiction at the heart
of the aristocratic view: the privileged had enormous social power
and prestige, but little political power. They wanted the balance
adjusted in their favor. All three estates agreed that reform was

necessary and that reform meant redistributing the power accumulated by the monarchy over the centuries. The question was which of the orders would be the major beneficiary of this weakening of the monarchy. The aristocracy, of course, did not appreciate the irony of having begun a revolt against the monarchy, a revolt it could not control, could not manipulate or exploit.

The king, deliberately putting himself beyond faction, deliberately trying to represent all of France, was caught in the cross-fire. Before 1789 his authority had been unquestioned; no institution in France could, in theory at least, check his power. Louis was not opposed to reform, but he was opposed to any reordering of society. He had no intention of sharing his authority with his subjects, whatever their estate, high or low. All reform must emanate from the crown, and he was anxious to have the support of all three orders in his reformation of his country.

France needed reformation. So much was clear to all three estates. But could reformation be accomplished within the complex traditional framework of the *ancien régime*? Those who were skeptical prayed they were mistaken; those who were optimistic disregarded or underestimated the difficulties. The interests and aspirations of the three estates and the king were different, probably irreconcilable. It was the Third Estate that took the initiative, in June 1789. Having suffered the humiliation of being treated as social and political inferiors since the opening of the Estates-General, fearful of rumored plots against them by the court and the nobility, and isolated from the political life of the nation centered in the court, the commons realized that if the Estates-General continued to meet and deliberate by orders and vote by orders, they were doomed. They were weak and would remain weak while the first two orders remade the state in their own image. On Saturday, June 20, 1789, the commons reached for power in a single daring move. That morning, they found the doors of their meeting hall locked and guarded by soldiers. They took over the royal Tennis Court and swore an oath that they would not disperse until they had given France a constitution. It was a great moment, for the commons declared *themselves* to be the nation, the representative embodiment of the national will, the National Assembly rather than the most insignificant and impotent of the traditional orders of society.

The king could neither tolerate nor ignore the commons' assertion of supremacy. He, not some elected representatives, was the embodiment of national sovereignty. He decided to crush this novel presumption. On June 23 he appeared before the three estates, assembled together as the Estates-General, in a *séance royale*, to reassert his prerogatives and return his subjects to obedience. Nowhere is the distance separating the king from his subjects more evident. All the trappings of royalty, all the punctilios of court etiquette, were exploited on this occasion to impress upon the Estates-General the majesty of the crown. "Gentlemen," the king declared, "I believed to have done everything in my power for the good of my people when I decided to call you together. It would seem that you have only to complete my work; and the nation awaits, with impatience, the moment when, by the harmony of the beneficent views of its sovereign with the enlightened zeal of its representatives, it can enjoy the well-being that such harmony will produce." No king, Louis thought, could have done more, indeed no French king had; and he sat back in his chair while a secretary read out to the Estates-General the *Déclaration du roi*, a summary of the royal will.

The fifteen clauses of the *Déclaration* represent Louis's position on the question of the monarchy and the Revolution. The traditional order of society would be maintained, the three estates would deliberate and vote by order. He refused to recognize a National Assembly without distinctions of rank, just as he refused to recognize a society without privileges. Any actions taken unilaterally by any one of the three orders he chastised as "unconstitutional," as "contrary to the letters of convocation" (which had called the Estates-General into existence), and "contrary to the interests of the state." The three orders were invited to deliberate on the national crisis, but they were forbidden to tamper with "the ancient rights . . . of the three orders," with "feudal and seignorial property," or with "the rights and honorific prerogatives of the first two orders." Nor could the Estates-General concern itself with the established church, the clergy, ecclesiastical discipline, or questions touching worship. These subjects, fundamental to the constitution of the *ancien régime*, were reserved for the king alone. Louis viewed the Estates-General as a species of royal council whose advice he sought but might not take.

Following the reading of the *Déclaration* the king spoke again: "I may say, without deluding myself, that no king has done as much for any nation." Any who would thwart the realization of his plans for his people, he warned, "would render themselves unworthy of being considered Frenchmen." Then, in an additional series of thirty-five clauses, again read by a secretary, the king outlined his intentions. He was willing to reform the tax system of France and would accept proposals from the Estates-General "if they accord with the royal dignity and the dispatch essential to public service." But all property must be respected, especially "all rights and prerogatives, useful or honorific, attached to lands and titles or belonging to individuals." And the king would continue to regulate titles, their inheritance and the privileges attached to title. But some of the most detested abuses of the *ancien régime—lettres de cachet* (which could imprison indefinitely without cause), the *corvée* (forced labor on the roads), and the *mainmorte* (a feudal encumbrance on property)—would be suppressed. In addition the king announced his willingness to revise the hated Salt Tax, to reform the administration of justice, to rationalize the criminal and civil law codes, and to create new censorship laws as long as they did not affect "the respect due to religion." He promised provincial estates throughout France as the organ for local initiative, but specified that half their representatives must come from the first two estates, and he promised to eliminate internal customs duties. "Reflect," he told the representatives before taking his leave, "that none of your resolutions, none of your projects, can have the force of law without my approbation. Thus I am the natural guarantee of your respective rights, and all the orders of the state can take comfort in my equitable impartiality."

Louis was right. The estates, whether sitting by orders or as a National Assembly, could not legislate without the king's cooperation; and Louis had detailed exactly how far he was willing to cooperate. If his subjects insisted on going farther they would go into

rebellion. The lines were drawn. In the last clause of his intentions
the king had been careful to add that control of the army would
remain in his hands.

No group, probably not even the court party, found Louis's proposals acceptable. The question now, and until August 10, 1792,
when France became a republic, was how to preserve the principle of monarchy and the need for an executive authority and yet
reform France fundamentally. For the moment the king seemed to
have the advantage, and he followed up the *séance royale* by mass-
ing troops at Versailles and dismissing Jacques Necker, his first
minister and a man thought sympathetic to the commons. Paris,
fearing an attack, was thrown into panic which took the form of a
frantic search for weapons in the city. The spontaneous movement
culminated on July 14 in the first great act of revolutionary violence:
the capture and destruction of the Bastille, the forbidding royal
prison in Paris. The very next day, as the victorious Parisians set
about reorganizing the government of the city, replacing royal ap-
pointees with men sympathetic to the Third Estate, the first wave
of emigrants left France, among them the king's brothers. News of
the fall of the Bastille, the symbol of royal arbitrariness, traveled
quickly, and municipality after municipality threw off the yoke of
absolutism. By early 1790 the government of most of the cities of
France was in the hands of revolutionaries.

At approximately the same time a movement of rebellion, the
largest in more than a century, exploded in rural France. The Great
Fear, a jumbled theory of conspiracy which said that the court and
the nobles were planning to subjugate the countryside by force,
destroy the harvest, and inflict terror on the population, captured
the popular imagination. As the rumor spread along the roads
peasant communities responded by taking up arms. The peasantry
rose to defend themselves against imagined brigands; but the rebellion quickly turned into an attack on feudalism. Few châteaux
were burned and few landowners were killed, but the hated documents of feudal obligation were destroyed. These two spontaneous
revolutionary movements saved the commons. Instead of calling
out the forces of law and order, instead of demanding that the
municipal and rural riots be put down, instead of rallying to the
crown, the Third Estate seized the opportunity to blackmail the

crown and strengthen their cause. The king, they argued, must bow to the national will, must treat with his subjects constituted as the National Assembly, without division of rank or privilege.

Unable, or unwilling, to move against his rebellious subjects, the king first temporized and then submitted. On August 4, 1789, in another moving demonstration of revolutionary enthusiasm, the Assembly abolished feudalism. This blow, made possible by rural and urban uprisings, destroyed Louis's vision of a rejuvenated France under his leadership. The country had passed to revolution and the Assembly began restructuring France. On August 20 it started work on the Declaration of the Rights of Man and Citizen, a statement of the principles of a new France and the revolutionary response to Louis's view of the state and society enunciated at the *séance royale*. On September 11 it decreed that the king would have only a suspensive veto: he could delay the enactment of legislation for anywhere from two to six years, but he could not veto it outright, he could not amend it. At a single vote the king's power was circumscribed.

Once again, while the Assembly deliberated and the king schemed to save his authority, the people of Paris took to the streets. Food shortages and the persistent fear of attack, effectively played on by street-corner orators and radical journalists and pamphleteers, caused the Women's March to Versailles (October 5). The king and his family—"the baker, the baker's wife and the baker's son"—were forcibly brought to Paris on October 6. There they remained, in the Tuileries, under the watchful care of revolutionary Paris. The National Assembly soon followed the king, settling into the Manège on November 9. Just before deserting Versailles, soon to become a relic of the absolutist past, the Assembly had ordered the nationalization of all church property (November 2). This enormous landed wealth, which had given the church worldly power, was to be used to support the revolutionary paper money, the *assignats*, that was ordered printed. By early 1790, then, all the power and institutions Louis had forbidden his subjects to reform had been attacked and radically altered: the powers of the monarchy had been curbed, the church nationalized, the nobility virtually done away with (although the formal decree did not come until June 19, 1790).

Edmund Burke, the British conservative who devoted his last years to excoriating the French Revolution and defending British institutions, was already at work on the first great book to be inspired by the Revolution, his *Reflections on the French Revolution*. As early as 1790 it was clear to Burke, and to other thoughtful observers, that the *ancien régime* was dead, attacked in its vital organs, murdered, as Burke saw it, by the people up in arms and the lawyers in the Assembly who had been seduced by metaphysical schemes for a new society and who lusted after the power they had been so long denied. The king's failure to impose his reformation on the nation meant many things for Burke, but most significantly it meant that the Revolution would run its dreadful course and that the world he venerated, the world of the king, the church and the nobility, was doomed.

Stripped of most of his authority the king was left with few weapons in his struggle with the Revolution. He was forced to fight with delay and duplicity and watched passively from the Tuileries as the Assembly decreed the *ancien régime* into oblivion. Another king might have exploited what resources he had to better advantage. Louis's support among his subjects, although he had done little to cultivate it, remained strong; there were large sections of the population and public opinion which deplored what was happening as much as he did. But Louis had always been aloof from his people, isolated at Versailles, hostile to most advice, even that of family and friends. When he announced his will to the nation in the *séance royale* he publicly declared that he would remain isolated from the antagonistic factions. It was a role he had chosen for himself, one he would live out with the conviction or stubbornness of a man convinced he is right.

On May 21, 1790, the Paris Municipal Law was passed, virtually removing the capital from royal control and reorganizing the city into sections for the purposes of electing the new municipal government, called the Commune. Originally sixty in number, these sections were electoral districts like our city wards. Participation in the sections was to be controlled by the constitution's distinction of "active" and "passive" citizens. The former, distinguished by their ability to pay a certain amount of tax, could vote and stand for

office; the latter could not. And the sections were to meet only
when permitted to do so by the National Assembly. Further to insure that the sections did not get out of hand and challenge the
authority of the National Assembly, they were burdened with a
hopelessly complex series of procedures for carrying out their primary function, the election of the 148 members of the Paris municipality, the Commune.

But the sections were not content to remain occasional elec-
torates. Their number was soon reduced to forty-eight and they
met frequently. The sections decentralized the government of
Paris, and they were armed and had been since the fall of the Bastille. The National Assembly might now rule France but Paris, the
largest, wealthiest, and most unruly city in the kingdom, was ruled
by its Commune, which in turn was ruled by the sections. In place
of the single royal will that had prevailed Paris now had forty-
eight wills. The sections became the real springs of revolutionary
activity in Paris, functioning with the self-assurance, even the arrogance, of independent republics. The Assembly had, unwittingly,
created a competitor for power. No government could dominate
France without first dominating Paris.

The Assembly next turned its attention to the first two orders of
the old society. On June 19 the nobility was officially abolished. On
July 12, on the eve of the first celebration of the Fête de la fédération (as Bastille Day was then called), the Assembly passed the
Civil Constitution of the Clergy. The Civil Constitution, the logical
outcome of the confiscation of church property, rendered the
church essentially a department of government. Later the same
year (November 12) the Assembly devised an oath to the state that
clergymen would have to swear before being allowed to perform
their duties.

The emergence of Paris and its semiautonomous government
not only shifted the center of gravity of national politics, it also
changed the nature and course of the Revolution. Paris had been
abandoned by Louis XIV and his two successors: now it would
have its revenge. As the National Assembly was busy dismantling
the *ancien régime* numerous clubs and debating societies were
springing up in the capital. These extraparliamentary groups varied in political persuasion, from monarchists to advanced demo-

crats. Some were holdovers from prerevolutionary days, although now they became basically political in nature and sought to influence the Assembly, and some were of new growth. Some catered to a general public with nominal admission fees and offered debating in public as an attraction; some catered to the rich by demanding a substantial entrance fee. Two particular societies concern us here because they became formidable revolutionary clubs and because their emergence expresses the changing nature of politics.

The Club breton had originally been founded at Versailles by deputies to the Estates-General from Brittany. When the Assembly moved to Paris the club enlarged itself, changed its name to the Société des amis de la constitution (Society of the Friends of the Constitution), and established correspondence with a number of provincial societies. The Society rented the former premises of the Dominican monks, on the rue Saint-Honoré, and gradually came to be known by the nickname once carried by the monks, the Jacobins. Their annual subscription was small enough to give their nightly meetings a popular following. By October 1791 the Jacobins were debating publicly, and their galleries were perpetually crowded with both devoted and curious onlookers.

The Société des amis des droits de l'homme et du citoyen (Society of the Friends of the Rights of Man and Citizen) also took its nickname from its meeting place, a former Franciscan monastery on the rue Cordeliers, hence the Cordeliers Club. Subscriptions at the Cordeliers were even lower than those at the Jacobins, and the club attracted people of lower social status. It was to counteract the opinions nightly broadcast at these two clubs that the conservative and aristocratic revolutionaries founded a series of societies of their own. Paris was seething with revolutionary talk, whether in the clubs and societies or in the myriad cafés. The Assembly, as well as the court, viewed the proliferation of these bodies with apprehension; but there was little they could do.

And if the political clubs were one of the most characteristic products of revolutionary Paris, the newspapers were the other. They quickly became the most original source of revolutionary ideas and rhetoric. Freed of the threat of royal and ecclesiastical censorship, the Paris press spawned dozens and dozens of exotic growths. Their names alone declared the enormous range of opinion they catered to: *Patriot français*, *Le Point du jour*, *Révolutions de Paris*, *L'Ami du peuple*, *L'Ami du roi*, *Journal du diable*, *Journal royaliste*, *Révolutions de France et de Brabant*, and this is only a random sample. Some died quickly, to be just as quickly replaced; some became permanent features of the Revolution. Most of these newspapers were originally put out, singlehandedly, by self-taught journalists. But soon the deputies to the National Assembly themselves went into the newspaper business. The amount of capital needed was small by modern standards, and no man with political ambitions could afford to be without an organ for his ideas. Public opinion, contemptuously disregarded by the *ancien régime*, was now aggressively courted by the press. We do not know how widely read these many newspapers were, but their numbers alone indicate that the newspaper-reading public was substantial and that it took some effort to avoid being informed of what was happening in Paris and France.

Ironically enough the Revolution had not gone far enough in dismantling the *ancien régime*. The king had been made a mere magistrate but he remained at the center of politics because he could suspend or ratify legislation. Consequently, the Assembly needed his cooperation; the conduct of political business still required the deputies to solicit royal support. The Assembly, afraid that this situation might create a great parliamentary manager who would carry the king's policies through the Assembly, decreed on November 7, 1789, that all deputies were excluded from ministerial office. The decree did not prevent the king from trying to influence or coerce the Assembly through attracting ambitious men to his party, sometimes by bribes, nor did it prevent would-be parliamentary leaders from seeking court patronage, but it did wreck the schemes of Honoré Gabriel Riqueti, comte de Mirabeau, who devised the first comprehensive plan for reestablishing monarchical authority in the Revolution.

To many, Mirabeau's pock-scarred face seemed the image of his soul. A man of immense intelligence and energy, his physical appetites competed with his intellectual appetites, and both yielded to his ambition. His bohemian life prior to the Revolution was a scandal to his family and the nobility generally. On the eve of the

Revolution, Mirabeau was near personal and financial ruin. He could not, with his reputation, stand for a seat in the second estate, but he secured a seat in the commons. He threw his massive energy and intellect into dominating the Assembly. Through a series of highly dramatic confrontations—"Go and tell those who sent you that we cannot be moved hence save by force of bayonets!" he had shouted at the king's representative on one occasion—and his genius for oratory, Mirabeau had established his ascendancy over the Assembly.

But Mirabeau was not content merely with popularity. He had a scheme for channeling the Revolution in the direction he thought best and this necessitated having the complete support of the king. Mirabeau was in many ways a representative noble of his generation, urbane, frustrated politically, and corrupt. In May 1790 he had accepted a stipend from the court, along with an agreement that his substantial debts would be paid. In return, he agreed to give the court political advice and to work for the king in the Assembly. The deal was secret, not discovered until after Mirabeau's death. He threw himself into his new task with his usual zest. On June 1, 1790, began a remarkable series of fifty "Notes" to the court which, taken together, form one of the most rigorous and compelling treatises on practical politics ever written. Here was the first substantial answer to the question of what to do about the king, for the Assembly's solution was only partial.

Mirabeau's analysis of the politics of the Revolution is brilliant; his advice to the king, although complex and cynical, was realistic. Louis, he reasoned, still had most of his prestige intact, and he still controlled the traditional symbols of patriotism. Moreover, there were basic antagonisms in France that Louis could exploit. The financial interests of Paris were antithetical to the commercial and agricultural interest of the provinces. The king could play provincial France off against his ungovernable capital. In addition, the king was isolated in Paris. He had no money in the treasury and no competent ministers. He must flee Paris, establish himself in some provincial capital—Mirabeau suggested Rouen, the capital of Normandy—and make an appeal to the nation in the name of "the peace and safety of the state, and the indivisibility of king and people." He wanted to make Louis a patriot king.

The plan had much to recommend it; it might have worked. But Mirabeau, like those after him seduced by the same vision of reestablishing the monarchy in power and then guiding it themselves, had failed to take into account the character of the king. Louis would have none of it. He distrusted Mirabeau and he detested not only the people Mirabeau advised him to cultivate, Lafayette in particular, but also the politics of force and fraud that Mirabeau proposed as the only salvation for the monarchy. Besides, Louis had his own plan; and Mirabeau's death, providentially at the height of his popularity (April 2, 1791), freed the king from any obligations he might have felt toward his political mentor. Louis was preparing to insure his own salvation, and events fixed the time for putting his plan into action.

For personal and political reasons Louis had insisted, at the *séance royale*, that religion not be tampered with. His wishes were ignored. It proved to be the church settlement that precipitated civil war in France rather than provincial antagonisms toward Paris, which Mirabeau prophesied. At the end of 1790 the Assembly had decreed that the clerical oath be enforced by the executive. Thousands upon thousands of men and women in religious orders suddenly found themselves faced with an impossible choice. If they refused to take the oath they were suspect and liable to punishment from the civil authorities. If they took the oath they risked endangering their immortal souls by recognizing the supremacy of the state. On March 10, 1791, the pope removed all doubt: in the papal bull *Charitas* he condemned the Civil Constitution of the Clergy and threatened all those who swore the oath with excommunication.

The clergy now split into juring and non-juring priests. Those who had earlier joined the Third Estate, identifying with those of their class rather than with those in the church hierarchy who were noble, now had to decide if they were willing to risk excommunication. They had joined the Third Estate to express their discontent with the hierarchy, their desire for reform of the church, the state, society. But the Revolution had gone too far and the pope, tardily to be sure, had forced them to choose. Some fled, some went into hiding, some continued to minister to their flocks, at great personal risk. The Revolution, having deprived the king of church support,

having broken the church's monopoly on education, having expro-
priated all its worldly wealth, had now also deprived itself of
church support. Countless clergy were driven into the arms of the
counterrevolution. The king was deeply troubled by the Assembly's attack on the church. He was himself a pious man, a Christian
king. The pleading of his reactionary brothers, his former ministers, his aunts (who had fled on February 20, 1791), even his wife,
had not stirred Louis to action. Now he decided to flee.

The flight to Varennes is one of the momentous events of this
period of the Revolution, not only for the king himself and for
France, but for Europe. The crowned heads of Europe, everyone
knew, were hostile to the Revolution. Fortunately for France they
were involved elsewhere in Europe with their own problems, their
own schemes. Carving up Poland or strengthening their hold on
their own people and domains were more important than inter-
vening in French affairs. In addition, the other European courts
were not displeased to see the French monarchy, long a disturber
of European peace, weakened or distracted. They had doubtless
welcomed news of the decree renouncing wars of conquest (May
22, 1790). They had no reason to suppose Louis would be toppled
from his throne or that the Revolution would spread, by force of
arms, outside France. For the revolutionaries the international situation was a blessing; France could concentrate on domestic affairs.
The king's flight shattered this international complacency and precipitated the conflict that was to engulf Europe and revolutionize
the Revolution.

The idea of flight was not new. Louis's advisers, urged on by
Marie-Antoinette, had been telling the king for months to leave
Paris. The plan had been concocted by the Baron de Breteuil,
former minister of the royal household and a confidante of the
queen; the Marquis de Bouillé, a rude, energetic old soldier, former
commander of the royal armies in the north and the man who had
savagely put down the mutiny in Nancy; and Count Fersen,
Swedish ambassador to the French court and suspected of being
Marie-Antoinette's lover. The royal family, incognito and carrying
forged passports, would leave Paris and travel east. Once close to
the frontier they would be met by armed escorts sent by Bouillé.

They would cross the border and, out of the reach of the Revolution, assemble the forces of counterrevolution.

For a gamble of such importance the plan of flight had been poorly worked out. Its success depended on a tight timetable of rendezvous for the king and his waiting escort, but it failed to take into account Louis's reticence about leaving, his general indecisiveness. Louis was several hours late in leaving the Tuileries, and once on the road he exasperated his family and friends by descending from the coach at every change of horses to talk with the hostlers. The plan also was not a very well-kept secret. Marat had been bruiting it about in his newspaper for weeks, and there had been a dress rehearsal for flight on April 18. The king and his family, under the pretext of going to St. Cloud to celebrate Easter, were stopped and returned to Paris. The St. Cloud affair convinced the Paris authorities, as Marat had not, that the king was thinking of fleeing the country. It was General Lafayette's responsibility, as commander of the National Guard, to see to security at the Tuileries, and he personally checked the château.

On the night of June 20 Bailly, the mayor of Paris, concerned about the possibility of escape, sent Lafayette to the Tuileries again. He reported, *incredibile dictu*, that all was secure; this at the very moment when Louis was making his escape! The royal family apparently fled through the single door left unguarded, at Lafayette's orders, to allow Count Fersen free access to the queen's apartment. Accompanied by their children and a governess, the royal couple left the château around 2:00 A.M. The escape was accomplished without incident or detection. Marie-Antoinette had brought along a considerable amount of food to make the journey more pleasant. The party, resembling in many ways a family out for a picnic, mounted the heavy and sumptuous coach awaiting them and drove out of Paris.

On the morning of June 21 Lemoine, the king's valet, found his master's bed empty. The news spread quickly in Paris and threw the city into panic. Who was in complicity? Who was negligent? These questions were never answered. Only the few republicans in Paris, isolated from power and with little hope for the future, welcomed the king's flight. Madame Roland added a hasty postscript to a letter she was about to send: "The king and queen have fled. I am writing you in haste, to the sound of cannon, and in the greatest excitement. That's it; war is declared!" The king was now a renegade. For Madame Roland and her friends the flight was providential: Louis, by his own actions, had played into the hands of his enemies in a single dramatic and ill-considered action.

The royal fugitives were captured in the little town of Varennes, a few miles from the border. They had only to cross the bridge over the Aire River to be out of France; but the king's dallying had caused them to miss their escort. Revolutionary romanticism has created a charming and plausible story of the king's capture. Jean-Baptiste Drouet, a local functionary, is said to have recognized the disguised king from a coin, a louis d'or, and alerted the authorities in Varennes, who blocked the bridge. The king surrendered rather than risk his family's safety in a skirmish. The king and queen were ordered returned to Paris. The National Assembly sent a deputation to accompany the prisoners back to Paris, which they reached on June 25. Drouet marched at the head of the procession while the Parisians, who lined both sides of the route to see their captive king, defiantly kept their hats on their heads. The National Guardsmen insulted the king by pointing their muskets to the ground. The fragile complex of reverence, hope, and tradition that had bound the French to their king was destroyed.

The National Assembly acted quickly and radically, suspending the king and his veto, and issuing orders to the crown's ministers. The Assembly became the executive and legislative authority in France, transforming the country into a de facto republic long before August 10, 1792. But there were difficulties. The Assembly's actions were illegal. France still did not have a constitution and hence no body had the right to suspend the king. In addition the suspension of an anointed king split the Assembly itself irrevocably. Royalist deputies, and there were many in the National Assembly, could not accept the suspension and retired to the Aventine, refusing to participate in an Assembly that had removed the king. And the flight to Varennes was the prelude to war, the king's capture the immediate pretext of invasion. The flight to Varennes marks the beginning of a seemingly inexorable, if tortuous, drift into republicanism in the Revolution.

A majority of the deputies to the National Assembly, perhaps a majority of Frenchmen, were not yet ready for a republic in June 1791. They wanted to preserve the monarchy at any cost. The new constitution was ready for acceptance. The great work that was to justify the Revolution and give France new foundations had been designed to include a constitutional monarch. The Assembly needed Louis's cooperation lest the republicans triumph or France be reduced to civil war. Conservatives and moderates alike—in fact everyone except the royalists on the one hand and the advanced democrats on the other—were determined to find a compromise that would save the monarchy and the constitution.

On July 15 the compromise was struck. Louis, the Assembly said, had been abducted. The Marquis de Bouillé, who was conveniently in exile, was made the scapegoat. Lafayette was thus tacitly exonerated; the Assembly had no interest in discovering who had helped the king escape. If Louis would accept the constitution he would be reinstated. The fiction of an abduction was reluctantly swallowed by a majority of the Assembly. Royalists and republicans, for different reasons, went into opposition. While the factions regrouped Louis accepted the constitution on September 14, and on September 30 the National Assembly dissolved itself to make way for the Legislative Assembly, the first representative body to be elected and sit under a constitution.

The new constitution was a cumbrous and often confused document, the creation of many hands, many political opinions. The king was the executive authority and had a suspensive veto, hence his cooperation would be essential if France were to be a constitutional monarchy. In addition, the National Assembly, shortly before its dissolution, had passed a "self-denying ordinance" that excluded deputies from membership in the new Legislative Assembly. This meant that no men with previous parliamentary experience could sit in the Legislative and that those who had won a political following in the National Assembly must look elsewhere for support of their politics. War was imminent, the old political alignments were a shambles, and on the throne was a man who had declared his hostility to the Revolution. It is doubtful that the new constitution could have worked, even with a more coopera-

tive king. Louis's contempt for the constitution he had been forced
to accept only made failure certain; he devoted his energies to
undermining it.

Louis saw the constitution as a direct attack on his most cherished values, an affront to his person and his historical prerogatives. Its principles made a mockery of his life and his divinely
instituted magistracy. The prospect that his son might succeed to a
paper throne was unbearable. Had Louis had more political sense
he might have kept these profound reservations locked in his
heart. But he broadcast them when he fled to Varennes, leaving
behind, in a conspicuous place, his "Declaration of the King Addressed to All the French on His Departure from Paris." Written
by the king himself, almost two years to the day after the *séance
royale*, it is a revealing document and a piece of political folly. Louis
had not been changed at all by the experience of two years of revolution.

The "Declaration" breathes the spirit of another age, another set
of values and assumptions. After explaining his reasons for hating
the Revolution—its government was metaphysical and hence impossible on this earth, the king was deprived of the power to do
good, the natural leaders of society were spurned and humiliated,
the traditional order of society had been upset—Louis sums up his
views in an irenic and Christian credo. If only his subjects will
submit,

> What pleasure it would give [the king] to forget all his personal injuries
> and to see himself once again in the midst of you, when a constitution,
> that he will have freely accepted, will cause our holy religion to be re-
> spected, will cause the government to be established on a stable base
> and made useful by his action, when the goods and the estates of each
> will no longer be interfered with . . . and when, at last, liberty will be
> grounded on a solid and unshakeable foundation.

With such ideas and ideals, which for Louis were articles of faith,
he could not be reconciled to the Revolution. The executive authority could not function. The rupture between king and Revolution—in political terms, between legislative and executive—was
beyond healing. It only remained to be seen which of the two
would triumph, and when.

The Legislative Assembly, filled with new and inexperienced

men anxious to further their own careers and direct the course of the Revolution, and heavily factionalized, could not and did not act consistently. In fact the Legislative hardly acted at all, paralyzed by political fragmentation, bereft of a single group powerful and persuasive enough to impose its will on the body. The king opted for isolation, withholding his support from most of the legislation sent to him, not only because he found much of it too radical but also because he hoped the factions would tear each other apart and thus clear the way for his return to power. Some of the former deputies to the National Assembly, denied reelection to the Legislative, sought a political base in the clubs and societies. From this time the Jacobins particularly became an increasingly important forum for radicals. Only another crisis, most people felt, could clarify the muddle into which the Revolution had fallen. A new faction, gathered around J.-P. Brissot, sought to dominate the Legislative and create the needed crisis which would ultimately destroy the monarchy and the constitutional settlement and thus prepare the way for a republic dominated by Brissot and his friends.

Brissot was born in the cathedral town of Chartres, the thirteenth in a family of seventeen. From an early age he had to make his way in the world, fixing on journalism as his path to recognition and success. Brissot could hardly have picked an occupation less congenial to his gifts and inclinations, but young men on the make in France had few choices. Brissot's major fault was his facility. He wrote quickly and easily and was usually satisfied with a superficial knowledge of whatever subject he took up. He had a vivid imagination which he fed on travel literature; a nearly theatrical personality which grew on him until he was unable to be his natural self; a penchant for taking up quixotic causes, writing a book, and then dropping the subject to pursue another with equal energy and naiveté. Before he was thirty he had published more than half a dozen works on a variety of subjects, thrown himself into countless schemes. But though he spread himself too thin, and became the self-declared expert on literally dozens of complex subjects, his enthusiasm and high spirits were infectious, and many were willing to overlook his priggishness and self-conceit to appreciate his undeniable virtues—intelligence, honesty, loyalty, and conviction.

Brissot aspired to the same role that had seduced Mirabeau: to be the controlling will of the Revolution. He had, however, no desire to mediate for the court and preserve the monarchy, for in Brissot's grab-bag of political ideas was republicanism. Almost from the opening of the Legislative he challenged the court. On October 20, 1791, he called for military action to disperse the émigrés; on November 9 the Legislative voted the decree; on November 12 Louis vetoed it. On November 29 the Legislative voted a decree against non-juring priests; on December 19 Louis vetoed it. On December 16 Brissot, exasperated with the court's intransigence, threatened the king with an insurrection. But Brissot's great scheme was for war, a massive republican crusade launched against monarchical Europe.

On March 1, 1792, Emperor Leopold II of Austria died. He was succeeded by his more warlike brother, Francis II. The French were frightened, although their fears turned out to be exaggerated. Still, the Austrians did finally commit themselves to supporting a Prussian invasion of France shortly before the French declaration of war reached Vienna. Brissot played, brilliantly and irresponsibly, on these fears of war from abroad. "We need treachery on a grand scale," he preached, "our salvation lies that way, for strong doses of poison remain in the body of France, and strong measures are necessary to expel them." Or, on another occasion: "War is actually a national benefit . . . A people which has won its freedom after ten centuries of slavery needs war; it needs war to banish from its bosom the men who might corrupt its liberty."

War, Brissot reasoned—and he had many supporters—would destroy the monarchy at home by forcing Louis to join in the crusade against his fellow monarchs or be exposed as a counterrevolutionary. War would also destroy the factions, create a republic of talent and virtue (which would, incidentally, welcome and reward Brissot and his friends), cow the foreign enemies of the Revolution, and unleash revolutionary enthusiasm on Europe. War was to be the panacea for all the ills of France. Even the possibility of insurrection at home would be eliminated in Brissot's scheme, for the people in arms, so potentially dangerous in Paris, would be sent to the front.

There were few men willing or committed to opposing the war.

Even the court welcomed it. "The fools! don't they see that they are serving our purposes," Marie-Antoinette wrote to Fersen. Indeed the king's analysis of the situation, for once, was more realistic than that of his subjects. The revolutionaries were unprepared for war, the king was still seen by many as the natural leader of France, and the defeat which he expected, the inevitable result of incompetence, would reestablish the throne in all its prerevolutionary glory. Brissot had reasoned that the war would rally all Frenchmen around the revolutionary flag which he and his friends were waving; Louis reasoned that a national crisis would bring Frenchmen under the white flag of the Bourbons. Only victory, a smashing and swift victory, a far-fetched possibility in the spring of 1792, could save the war party. Louis would triumph both from defeat and delay. War was declared on April 20; France suffered her first defeat on April 28. The prospects for victory looked bleak.

The war, although it did not accomplish all that Brissot had prophesied, profoundly changed revolutionary politics. The drastic and dangerous simplification of politics created by a war, the need for increased centralization (which increased the importance of Paris), the excessive burden the war put on the economy, and the social revolution set in motion by calling the citizens to arms and mobilizing the nation—all exploded the traditional political world of court, club, and Assembly. The war released the Revolution from the thralldom of clumsy constitutional institutions; it spawned new leaders who sought their support in the streets of Paris rather than in the Legislative. It gave the sections of Paris a new boldness and importance. Yet Brissot's insistence on creating a crisis to reshuffle the balance of power in France left a baleful legacy: if spontaneous revolutionary violence was not forthcoming at the right moment—as it had been in 1789—it could be artificially generated by ambitious or frustrated individuals or factions. And Brissot's scheme also encouraged the belief that the best course of action was a violent one.

The court was right. Brissot and his friends were incapable of running a successful war. But instead of their incompetence destroying the war party it made them more desperate. It was all too easy to blame defeat on the generals inherited from the old royal army or on the king's duplicity. What was now needed, the war party decided as news of the wretchedly ineffective revolutionary armies reached Paris, was another show of force in the capital. The king must be intimidated into supporting the war, retracting his recent vetoes, and recalling Brissot and his friends to the ministerial posts from which they had recently been dismissed. The people of Paris, egged on by the war party, its journalists, and street orators, prepared to move. They petitioned the Commune for permission to demonstrate, under arms, on June 20 at the Tuileries.

Neither the municipal government, the Department of Paris, nor the National Assembly was willing to deny the petition or protect the king and the Tuileries. All expected to benefit from the proposed action. Louis had few troops at the Tuileries and the château was not fortified. His bodyguard had been dismissed, by order of the Legislative, on May 30. The demonstrators, a motley collection of men, women, and children—the presence of so many women and children meant that the demonstrators expected there to be no fighting—badly led and badly armed, invaded the royal apartments and threatened the king and his family. Louis, calling on his remarkable resources of personal courage and dignity—he had at least some of the makings of a popular king, the patriot king imagined by Mirabeau—rode out the demonstration and yielded nothing. The blow of June 20 missed the king, but not the crown. The American ambassador, Gouverneur Morris, wrote that evening in his diary: "The constitution has this day I think given its last groan."

Now events moved quickly toward a climacteric. At the end of June, Lafayette, as part of his bid for personal power, tried to close down the Jacobin Club and failed. He fled to his estates. Both Jacobins and Cordeliers became more brazen. The Legislative, in response to the news of the Prussian entry into the war, which reached Paris on July 6, passed decrees (July 11) for proclaiming *la patrie en danger*, thus mobilizing the country. Patriotic volunteers from throughout France began flocking into the capital to participate in the third Fête de la fédération and then move on to the front. The forty-eight sections of the city, disregarding the old municipal law which had limited their membership and sittings, threw themselves open to everyone and sat in permanent session.

The National Guard was called up and it too threw its ranks open to "passive" citizens. Volunteer battalions were formed in the city itself. Paris, convinced that it would be invaded and that Louis was preparing a coup d'état against his people, became egalitarian; and the city was armed. The more radical sections plastered the walls of Paris with inflammatory revolutionary posters. On July 15 all the regular troops in the city, amid enormous public and patriotic enthusiasm, left for the front. The patriots—thus did they refer to themselves—whether provincial or Parisian, stood shoulder to shoulder and cheered their comrades on their way to war.

The king saw it all and went doggedly ahead with his plans to arm the Tuileries. On July 30 the soon-to-be-legendary volunteers from Marseille, bent on dethroning the king, marched into Paris singing their great fighting song, "La Marseillaise." They carried a severe flag, topped by the red revolutionary cap. Both the battle hymn and the patriotic banner were immediately embraced by the Revolution. The old National Guard flags, with their emblems derived from the monarchy, disappeared. The next day section Mauconseil repudiated its allegiance to the throne, starting the chain of events that would drive Louis to the Manège. On August 3 a majority of the forty-eight sections demanded the king be deposed and made an ultimatum that would come due on August 10.

"What sublime sentiments of patriotism I saw . . . during the discussions of the fall of the king!" wrote Anaxagoras Chaumette, one of the new revolutionary fire-eaters who were thrust into prominence by the impending revolution. "What was the National Assembly," he continued, "in comparison to the united representatives of the sections of Paris." Indeed it was nothing. Paris was preparing to dethrone Louis as its definitive solution to the problem of the king.

CHAPTER II

The End of the Monarchy

JULY–SEPTEMBER 1792

 HE ATTACK against the monarchy would have two distinct aspects: the original Commune of Paris, still dominated by moderates, would have to be overthrown in order to deny the king any help from the National Guard, officially under the Commune's control; and at the same time the insurrectionists of the sections, the federals and the volunteers, would have to be organized into two attack forces, one marching from the left bank of the Seine, the other from the right bank. They would converge at the Tuileries and attack the isolated king.

Military preparations began on July 26 when representatives of the federal troops still in Paris met with sectional leaders at an inn near the entry to the radical faubourg Saint-Antoine, in the east end of the city. All the military leaders and street fighters who were to play a decisive role in the coming revolution were there: Fournier the American, an adventurer and experienced street fighter; Santerre, a wealthy brewer capable of rallying his neighborhood; Alexandre, a former money changer who was influential in Saint-Marcel, the other radical neighborhood of Paris; Claude-François Lazowski, the revolutionary son of an important Polish family; François-Joseph Westermann, a former riding master with considerable military talent; and Jean-Louis Carra, onetime librarian and archivist turned popular journalist. None of these men had yet played a significant role in national politics. They conspired to organize the two attack forces; Danton organized the coup d'état against the Commune.

This was not another demonstration, not another spontaneous mass movement. It was a major military operation. The king's normal bodyguard of 300 Swiss mercenaries and 600 National Guard had been beefed up with an additional 4,000 men at the Tuileries itself, not counting the National Guard detailed to hold the bridges across the Seine. Taking the Tuileries would be difficult and bloody. Alexandre respected the professional troops he would be fighting and was particularly worried about his ability to force the Pont-Neuf and the Pont Saint-Michel, the two strategic bridges separating the right from the left bank. He made an incognito tour of the proposed battle sites on the night of August 9 and concluded that it might be impossible to take the Tuileries. But his appraisal of the situation was purely military. He left out of account Danton's proposed coup d'état at the Hôtel de Ville: it proved to be decisive.

The revolutionaries had conspired carefully: the tocsin was to sound at midnight and set the troops in motion. At the same time Danton and his friends would seize power at the Commune. But the revolutionary timetable was upset. It was not until the early hours of the morning of August 10 that the troops were assembled in Saint-Antoine and Saint-Marcel and Danton had enough strength to overwhelm the Commune. Between 6 and 7 A.M. Danton led "the assembly of the representatives of the majority of the sections, united to save the public welfare" to victory. The first meeting of the new Revolutionary Commune was presided over by Sulpice Huguenin, a lawyer from Nancy with impeccable revolutionary credentials. The mayor, Jérôme Pétion, was put under house arrest; the Marquis de Mandat, Louis's commander, was summoned from the Tuileries, intimidated by Danton, and arrested (he was murdered on his way to jail, probably by Jean-Antoine Rossignol); and the cannon guarding the bridges were ordered disarmed and returned to the artillery park. The last existing authority in Paris, the Commune, was in the hands of the revolutionaries. The Revolutionary Commune issued its first decree: "The people, placed between death and slavery, foreseeing the ruin of the country, seize once again its rights. The sovereign has spoken." The brewer, Santerre, was made commander of the right-bank troops; Alexandre took charge of the left-bank troops. As soon as news of Danton's successful coup d'état reached the sections they set off for the Tuileries. At the same time, the contingents gathered at the Jacobin Club and the Cordelier Club started marching.

Both Santerre and Alexandre expected fighting before they reached the château and planned accordingly. They would be marching through several sections of the city that had not supported the ultimatum or were suspected of having royalist sympathies. The women were expressly ordered to stay behind. But there were no confrontations, the march to the Tuileries was unopposed. When Alexandre reached the river he prepared to storm the Pont-Neuf. The defenders of the bridge, stripped of their cannon, offered no resistance: Alexandre crossed the undefended bridge. At almost the same moment the Marseillais crossed the Pont Saint-Michel without a fight. The entire left-bank force reached the Tuileries without having fired a shot. They ranged themselves and their cannon in front of the Tuileries, "in complete order, occupying the elevated parts of the place." When Santerre's right-bank force arrived, again without firing a shot, the insurrectionists had about 7,000 men and outnumbered Louis's defenders. Attackers and defenders, both waiting for orders, stared at each other through the gates of the Cour Royale. The nature of the battle was prefigured by the massacre of a patrol of National Guard, accompanied by a few onlookers, who had been sent out from the château to reconnoiter the perimeter. Throughout the night the artillerymen of the National Guard, stationed at the Tuileries, had been deserting and by early morning the château was virtually without crews to man the cannon. But it was the king's move, his departure for asylum with the Legislative, that broke the stalemate.

When they saw Louis depart the revolutionaries opened or forced the gate protecting the Cour Royale, believing that the king's departure meant the château had surrendered without a fight. What had been planned as a military operation seemed to be turning into a political demonstration. The insurgents entered the château and some began climbing the Great Stairway, calling upon the Swiss to join them. Some of the Swiss threw down cartridges, apparently as a peace offering. Then came the order to fire, and fraternity was replaced by discipline. The volley of musket fire created panic. The insurgents tripped down the stairs, falling over dead and wounded men, to reach the courtyard. But there was no cover in the cobbled Cour Royale and the disciplined Swiss had their choice of targets. The courtyard was strewn with dead and dying men when the victorious Swiss descended from the château and calmly retrieved the artillery left abandoned by the National Guard. They had won an easy victory.

Neither Santerre nor Alexandre were at the Tuileries for this first action. It was the street fighters, Westermann and Fournier, along with the commanders of the Brest and Marseille federals, Moisson, Garnier and Desbouillons, who rallied the insurgents and threw them against the Swiss in a frenzied suicide charge. The enormous energy of the attack and the superior numbers of the insurgents carried the day. The musket fire of the Swiss was murderous but inadequate. Alexandre returned from the Hôtel de Ville in the midst of the fighting. He saw ferocious hand-to-hand fighting going on everywhere. The Marseillais bore the brunt of the attack and they fought "not like lions, but like tigers."

As soon as the king, a prisoner in the Logographie, learned that the château had been forced, he hastily scribbled a note to the Swiss to cease fire and march to join him at the Manège. General d'Hervilly, a Swiss, carried the king's orders back to the besieged château, risking his life. The Swiss formed up for an orderly retreat. The insurgents refused to accept surrender or retreat. The battle ended, the massacre began.

Everyone found in the château, everyone found wearing a red uniform, the uniform of the Swiss, was slaughtered on sight. Two Brestois federals, whose uniforms unfortunately resembled those of the Swiss, were butchered. The Swiss themselves jumped out of windows to escape the slaughter. Surrender meant summary execution. A few lucky ones managed to get out of the château, across the gardens, and into the surrounding streets. They desperately looked for places to hide. A few were protected by humane Parisians, most were butchered and their bodies stripped. "The Champs-Elysées and the Tuileries," wrote an eyewitness, "were covered with corpses and blood, and these naked corpses were a

spectacle of horror which it will be difficult to forget . . . I don't
think there was a street which had not seen, at least, a head carried
on the end of a pike."

By around 3:00 P.M. the château had been secured by the revolutionaries. The federals retired, leaving the grisly mopping-up
operations to the men of the *faubourgs*, many of whom had not participated in the fighting. The women took upon themselves the
ghoulish job of stripping the bodies of the dead. The butchery continued into the night; a fire started in the château could not be
brought under control until 2:30 A.M. because the firemen could
not get close enough. On the morning of August 11, with the château still smoking, the Tuileries was thrown open to visitors interested in seeing this monument to popular vengeance against the
monarchy. John Moore, an Englishman living in Paris, was among
the visitors. He climbed the Great Stairway "to see the ravage that
was made in all the rooms by the action of yesterday." He was
halfway up "when I heard the shrieks of some one above, and
soon after the body of a man was carried down. I was told that he
had been detected in the act of stealing some of the furniture belonging to the palace, and was instantly put to death by the people
around him."

It is difficult to provide an accurate body count. There are seldom
reliable statistics kept on atrocities. About 600 Swiss were killed,
either in the château, the gardens, or the surrounding streets,
along with many National Guard and some ladies and gentlemen
of the court. In all there were about 800 dead. The insurgents lost
324 men, mainly from the radical faubourgs Saint-Antoine and
Saint-Marcel. Sixty Marseillais were also killed. The victory was a
triumph of the provincial federals and the *menu peuple* of Paris. Except for Danton and his friends at the Hôtel de Ville the nationally
known leaders of the Revolution were conspicuously absent.

"Never," wrote Barbaroux, one of the leaders of the Marseillais,
"has the majesty of the people showed itself with more grandeur
than on this day. The fall of the Bastille, in the judgment of the
Parisians, was nothing in comparison." Robespierre celebrated it
as "the most beautiful revolution that has honored humanity, that
of equality, of justice and of reason." But August 10, the second
French Revolution, never passed into legend as did the fall of the

Bastille. It remained not a day of joy and celebration, but one of solemn anger. The revolutionaries felt themselves betrayed, first by Louis, who had armed the palace against his own people, and then by the Swiss, who had fired on them. The significance of the victory, of course, was enormous: it made France a republic and, almost inevitably, brought Louis to trial. But the resentments surrounding the event, the hatreds it created, could not be laid to rest. The massacre of the Swiss was insufficient to satisfy the Parisians. They demanded further vengeance. The captured Swiss must pay with their heads, so too the king's advisers, and the king himself. Only a Carthaginian peace was acceptable to the revolutionaries. The political leaders might celebrate the victory in heroic words or hope to take advantage of it to establish their own power, but they would have to give Paris its revenge. No political group or leader could succeed if they forgot who had fought and won at the Tuileries, or if they disregarded the bloodthirsty demands of the revolutionaries.

The sections, the federals, and the advanced democrats had triumphed. Yet even the bourgeoisie had a place in the successful revolution. The sudden collapse of the old forces of order, expressed in the desertions at the Tuileries and the unopposed march of the insurgents, meant that the middle class had withdrawn its support from the monarchy. If August 10 was an expected revolution, it was also a desired revolution. France had seen her king in action as an absolute and as a constitutional monarch, and repudiated both by repudiating the monarchy.

An hour after the fall of the Tuileries the Revolutionary Commune sent a declaration to the Legislative Assembly claiming Louis as its prisoner. The king was the most important spoil of victory and the Legislative's hope was to keep him as its hostage—the only political leverage the disgraced and despised Legislative could hope for. But the Commune insisted, and the Commune was armed. On August 13—the king and his family had spent the past few days in the Logographie and the nights at the nearby Feuillants—the royal prisoners were taken by the Commune to the Temple, the former château of the Templar knights in Paris. The procession carrying Louis to prison crossed Paris at a funereal pace. Madame de Tourzel, who sat in the coach with the prisoners, the mayor, and representatives of the Commune, complained that "all these gentlemen had their hats on their heads, and treated their majesties in the most revolting manner."

The Commune's imprisonment of the king made it clear, if it had not been before, that Paris had assumed leadership of the Revolution. The Legislative remained nominally in power until a new, republican, assembly could be elected. It passed some decrees legalizing the victory of August 10, suspended the king, issued a call for new elections, and set up an interim Provisional Council of six ministers and a standing committee of twenty-one deputies to govern France. It also prepared a pamphlet to be distributed throughout the country, which explained what had happened, the causes for the revolution, and, incidentally, its own part in the overthrow of the monarchy.

The Commune simply ignored the Legislative and in a series of decrees and proposals, expressed in a fierce, aggressive, patriotic, and utopian rhetoric, set about organizing its victory, solidifying its power. The citizens were ordered armed and gunpowder was deposited in each section. Hundreds of pikes, made out of the gates and grills of churches, were ordered and distributed. The Commune acted as an independent republic and even seriously considered such proposals as replacing "the feudal expression vous [polite 'you']" with the "natural word TOI," or tearing down the bell tower of the church of Saint Germain-l'Auxerrois, from which it was said the call to massacre Protestants on St. Bartholemew's Day (1572) had been issued.

On August 18 the victims of the attack on the Tuileries were buried. Charles-Philippe Ronsin, of the Revolutionary Commune, delivered the funeral oration, a ferocious call for revenge against the king, his court, and the Swiss. A day earlier the Legislative, pressured by the Commune, had set up a special criminal court, the Tribunal of August 17, to deal with the survivors of the Tuileries. The Tribunal handed down the first purely political death sentences since 1790, against several of the king's former ministers, but these were insufficient to satisfy the demands of Paris. And the war was going badly, which further pushed the city to the edge of hysteria.

On August 19 the Prussians invaded France. The next day the fortress of Longwy capitulated. The Brunswick Manifesto, a tough and impertinent declaration which threatened the city with destruction by fire and sword, soon followed. On September 2 news of the fall of Verdun, the last fortified city on the road to Paris, reached the city. The Prussians were only 140 miles from Paris and seemed unstoppable. Danton roused the Revolution, called the country to arms. He was superb, heroic:

> All are roused, all are up in arms, all are burning to fight . . . The tocsin which is about to sound is not a signal of alarm, it is a call to charge upon the enemies of the country. To vanquish them, Gentlemen, we must be audacious, and more audacious, and ever audacious, and France will be saved.

"To arms, to arms, Citizens, the enemy is at our gates" was the response of the Commune who took upon themselves the national defense. Revolutionary Paris was galvanized. The gates to the city were closed, an armed citizenry patrolled the streets, houses were searched for weapons. The threatened Prussian attack synthesized all the scattered, but related, elements of a city in crisis into a theory of conspiracy similar to the one that had sent the peasantry into rebellion in 1789. The city's hysteria focused on the prisons, stuffed as they were with hundreds of Swiss and political prisoners. Here was the Prussian's fifth column, ready to put Paris to the sword as soon as her defenders left for the war zone. Paris must be purged.

The press was filled with lurid descriptions of what the prisoners would do, and these nightmare visions pandered to the growing obsession that the prisoners must be killed. The murders began on September 2, around 2:00 P.M., when some twenty prisoners, including several non-juring priests, were dragged from the cart transferring them to the Abbaye prison and butchered. The massacres quickly spread to the other Paris prisons and lasted, with diminishing ferocity, until September 7. Perhaps 1,300 prisoners, men, women and children, were massacred, or about half the prison population.

It is impossible to fix blame for this grotesque episode in the Revolution, or rather there is enough guilt to go around. But almost immediately the September Massacres became a political issue and would continue so at least till 1793. It was impossible for ambitious men and their followers to use August 10 as a stick with which to beat their opponents. That revolution established the republic and had about it, despite the massacre of the Swiss, an unmistakable grandeur. But the September Massacres were not an act of foundation and horrified most men. If the moderates could prove that the massacres were instigated by the radicals rather than being a spontaneous or irrational outburst of popular vengeance, they might be able to wrest control of the Revolution from the allegedly bloody hands of their opponents.

The September Massacres immediately became a political issue, and two distinct views of what had happened and what it meant became fundamental to the political struggles of the Revolution. In general the radicals tried to connect the September Massacres to the revolution of August 10, since then the massacres would be beyond criticism, as were the few lynchings that had followed the fall of the Bastille. They argued, consequently, that the massacres were spontaneous in origin, born of anarchy and hysteria and danger, an almost legitimate response to the failure of the national government to punish the betrayers of August 10. The massacres thus became the just retribution of a revolutionary people. It was best, the radicals insisted, to draw a veil of obscurity over the episode and get on with the business of making France a republic. The moderates, in general, argued that the massacres were the result of a conspiracy by the radicals to murder them under cover of the prison massacres and thus to pave the way for a radical seizure of power which would be the prelude to a general leveling of society. Far from being the inevitable conclusion to August 10, the September Massacres were the work not of the people but of a few hired assassins unleashed on Paris by the radicals. These murderers and their employers, the *septembriseurs* as they were called, could be identified, the moderates said. They must be punished for their crimes before the republic could be created.

In one form or another the question of the September Massacres bedeviled the debates during the early months of the republic. The moderates refused to let go of so useful a weapon and the radicals were forced to defend the massacres as a way of defending themselves. A revolutionary force, similar to a force of nature, beyond the control of any man, had swept through the streets of Paris in the first week of September. Men were awestruck before it yet could not let the episode be, could not accept their own share of the guilt for failing to act when prisoners were being butchered on the streets of Paris after being hauled before popular sidewalk tribunals. The grim truth of the entire bloody week was tough to swallow: hundreds of victims of the massacres, of all ages and both sexes, had died not because they were part of a fifth column of counterrevolutionaries; they had died simply because they were in prison, like the unfortunate prostitutes of La Force prison. The September Massacres too were a part of the complex legacy of the revolution of August 10.

The interim period between August 10 and the sitting of the Convention Assembly on September 21 is basic to all that came later. The monarchy, the constitution, and the national government fell together on August 10 and France had, technically, no legitimate government until the Convention met. Yet somehow the Revolution survived the crisis. The doddering Legislative and the ferocious Commune improvised a government, kept the bureaucracy going, provisioned Paris, supplied the army, held the Prussians at bay, and then, on September 20, at Valmy, defeated them. This was the first important victory of the revolutionary armies and the beginning not only of the Prussian retreat from French soil but also of the revolutionary wars of aggression which would continue, unabated, into the Napoleonic era. Valmy saved France and saved the Revolution. The king's fate was sealed. Theoretically at least the establishment of a republic did not demand that the king be tried. A number of men, royalists and revolutionaries alike, thought Louis might be spared. The victory at Valmy eliminated this option. Not only did it give the Revolution some breathing space, the leisure to conduct a trial, Valmy also eliminated the need to keep Louis alive as a political pawn and made it easy to argue that Louis himself was the cause of the war, that it was the king who had called the foreigner onto French soil to save his throne. The victory at Valmy was a defeat inflicted not only on the Prussians, but on the monarchy as well. Now the king must pay for his treasons.

The Legislative, imitating the earlier National Assembly after the flight to Varennes, merely suspended the king instead of dethroning him. Valmy insured that the throne would remain empty. For the first time in French history France was to be a republic. The defeated foreigner could not restore Louis, nor could any deal concocted in secret among the political leaders. August 10, the September Massacres, and Valmy had solved the problem of what to do about the monarchy: there now remained the problem of what to do about Louis himself. The solution would rest with the most extraordinary parliament in French history, the Convention Assembly, which was elected by universal manhood suffrage.

The Convention met on Friday, September 21, in the Salle des Tuileries. The newly elected deputies, or those who had arrived in Paris, were joined by members of the defunct Legislative for the opening address. Then, surrounded on both sides by double rows of applauding citizens, the *conventionnels* marched solemnly across the Tuileries gardens to the Manège, following approximately the same route Louis himself had taken on August 10, to declare France a republic.

The Revolution has left its mark on almost every aspect of French life, every law, every institution, even the language itself, but not on architecture. All the landmarks of the Revolution in Paris have a long history of their own, antedating the Revolution. The business of the Revolution was done in buildings created by kings to celebrate their glory.

The Manège had been Louis XV's riding academy. The place was so ill-suited to its revolutionary function as a legislative chamber that it remained a maddening reminder of the *ancien régime*'s contempt for deliberative bodies. Men complained frequently and bitterly about the wretched hall, but France would be made a republic and the king would be tried and the deputies would struggle for control of the Revolution, in the Manège.

In the shape of a long, stretched-out rectangle, the converted Manège was stifling in the summer and cold in the winter. The only windows in the place ran along the top and provided little light and less air. In winter the only heat came from a single porcelain stove, a model of the destroyed Bastille, in the center of the hall. The floor area had been a racing oval; the benches, six ranks of them, ran up at a sharp angle from the ground. Above these benches, reserved for the deputies, was an enclosed balcony for spectators, the so-called tribunes, which held about 300 and were often overcrowded. The length of the hall was divided into two approximately equal parts by a speaker's podium (also called the tribune) and the bar of the Convention, where petitioners stood to address the deputies. This was on one side of the hall. On the other side was the president's elevated chair, and just below him the secretaries' table. The deputies faced each other across a narrow gangway or aisle, and the placement of the president's chair automatically divided the hall into a right and left side. The traditional separation of politics into Right and Left had begun while the National Assembly was still meeting at Versailles, in another hall, similarly divided. For the meetings of the Convention the president's dais had been moved to the opposite side of the hall, hence what had been the Left in the Legislative now became the Right. At the opening of the Convention the deputies were reluctant to sit in places previously occupied by royalists or *feuillants* lest they be contaminated. The most radical deputies, who came to be known as the Mountain because they preferred the highest ranks of benches, were, ironically, on the president's right. The largest section of the hall was occupied by deputies uncommitted to either Right or Left. They were referred to as the Plain, or more contemptuously, the Marais (swamp).

The Manège with its foul air, poor light, wretched acoustics, and cramped space not only made debate and deliberation difficult and

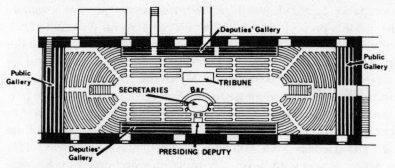

GROUND-PLAN OF THE MANÈGE.
From M. J. Sydenham: "The French Revolution."
Reproduced by Permission.

frustrating, it also encouraged, as a number of deputies pointed out, factional strife and hatred. From its opening session it was clear that the Manège would be the scene of a bitter, protracted, and eventually destructive struggle for political power. But before plunging into the debates we should take a closer look at the deputies and their politics.

There were 749 deputies, excluding those from the overseas colonies who had not yet arrived in France. They had been elected by more than a million Frenchmen, and not a single one of them had stood for election as a royalist. The legal age for deputies was 25 and the youngest of them, Saint-Just, was only a few days over the minimum age. The oldest deputy, Louis Lonqueue, a professor at the Collège de Chartres, was 74. As in all revolutions, however, young men predominated. Only 10 percent of the deputies were between 25 and 31; but 75 percent were between 31 and 50—a generation of men who had come to maturity during the last years of the reign of Louis XV or the early, hopeful years of Louis XVI. In cultural terms as opposed to political they had come to maturity during a period that historians of ideas and intellectual movements have dubbed the High Enlightenment. Plutarch and Tacitus and Cicero, the favorite authors of an extraordinary revival of antique republicanism, supplemented by Voltaire, Montesquieu, Diderot, Rousseau (to name only a few), seemed also present in the Manège, for the revolutionaries persistently cited chapter and verse from this rich intellectual heritage common to all.

Almost every other man was some kind of lawyer, or listed his occupation as *avocat, conseiller, procureur, notaire, juge*, or *homme de loi*. To this preponderance of lawyers (47 percent) we can add another 10 percent of the deputies, who had held official posts in the past and had had some legal training. No other profession or group was similarly represented. Merchants, businessmen, manufacturers, and tradesmen taken together accounted for only 10 percent of the membership. Doctors and churchmen made up 6 percent, as did professors, teachers, and other representatives of the arts and sciences. Men with military experience, very important for a nation at war with most of Europe, only accounted for 8.5 percent. Landlords and the landed interest in a country that was more than four-fifths agricultural accounted for only 6 percent. But even this small number were considerably more than representatives of of the peasantry or the working class. Only two deputies of the 749 could legitimately be classed as workers (*ouvriers*), with another six coming from working-class origins. Perhaps ironically the *ancien régime* had the same number of deputies as the working class: seven marquis and one prince of the blood.

The *conventionnels* were men of the middle class, and they were men deeply attached to their natal districts. It is remarkable how many of them lived and died in the same district, often in the same town, as had their fathers before them. The majority had been elected because they had distinguished themselves at home, because they were men of local standing whose political sentiments, in many cases, seemed to be in harmony with August 10. Socially and economically there was not much difference between the deputies. Their political differences sprang not so much from their place in society as from their previous political experience, especially in national politics, their openness to new ideas, their personalities and temperaments, and in a few cases their geographical origins. Almost 37 percent of them had had some kind of political experience in either the National Assembly (83 men) or the Legislative (194 men). Unlike earlier assemblies the Convention did not have to flounder over procedures or waste weeks and even months learning the routines of government. This 37 percent also meant that many deputies came to the Convention with some political ideas, perhaps even some attachment to a faction.

Most of the deputies, of course, were men new to national politics. A few, like the precocious Saint-Just, immediately thrust themselves and their genius into national prominence, but for the most part the Convention was dominated in its early months by men who had already distinguished themselves, men who had clearly-defined politics or behaved as if they had. Leadership was thus provided by familiar activists, and many of the personal animosities and issues and differences in ideology that had crippled the Legislative were carried, unresolved, into the Convention. This was certainly true of the two major factions of the republic.

Revolutionary antagonists obviously come in pairs: Cavaliers and Roundheads; Whigs and Tories; Mensheviks and Bolsheviks;

and in France Jacobins and Girondins. And with the Jacobins and Girondins comes an enormous baggage train of controversy that began during the Revolution and has grown in bulk ever since. The struggle between Jacobins and Girondins ended, as such conflicts usually do, with the destruction of one group by the other.

The Jacobin triumph, which meant the purging, proscription, and eventual death of most of the Girondins, has colored our view of their enemies and made even the identity of the Girondins a controversial matter. Historians tend to see the past through the eyes of the victorious rather than the vanquished. In the spring of 1793 the Jacobins drew up a series of exclusion lists to be used in purging the Convention. These have been usually taken as evidence of who was and who was not a Girondin. But this is the beginning of the difficulties. The several exclusion lists do not all carry the same names, and inclusion on one of these lists does not necessarily mean a man was a Girondin, only that he was considered an enemy by the Jacobins. The Girondins, and the Jacobins too for that matter, were not a political party in any sense in which we understand political parties. They had no party machinery, no party funds, no party discipline on voting, and in many cases no party platform. They were at best loosely-connected groups of men who had been friends, who shared political ideas, or who were thrown together on specific issues.

That the Girondins have passed into history as a coherent group or faction is largely the result of Jacobin propaganda during the Revolution. Even their collective name, although contemporary with the Revolution, was not often used. The men of the day preferred to identify political groups by the names of their leaders. In a bewildering series the names march through the newspapers and pamphlets and memoirs and speeches of the Revolution—Brissotins, Rolandists, Robespierrists, Maratists, Dantonists, and many more. The name Girondins, derived from the Department of the Gironde, whose major city is Bordeaux, is in many ways inappropriate. Only a few of the Girondins came from the Gironde; and by no means did all the leaders of the group—the so-called "inner sixty"—come from this region.

But amid the confusion, before the historians take up the terms and the problem and reshape it, we can see two identifiable factions in the Convention, holding two identifiable points of view, and struggling for control of the Revolution. And it is not unfair to identify them using these familiar names, Jacobins and Girondins. From a study of voting patterns, published speeches and pamphlets, friendships, and the proscription lists we can identify nearly 200 Girondins, of whom a smaller group, the inner sixty, provided leadership, held office in the Convention, were politically active. The remainder were supporters. The Jacobins were a smaller group, perhaps 110 deputies who sat and voted with the Mountain. Neither group then had a majority in the Convention. Both had to depend on the votes of the deputies of the Marais, which is one of the reasons speech-making played so important a role in the Revolution. The majority of uncommitted deputies had to be persuaded or seduced into supporting either Jacobins or Girondins.

In social and economic terms there was little difference between the two groups. Both were of the same generation and came from the same social class, the provincial, professional bourgeoisie. Both shared a common intellectual heritage, came from all over France, and were republicans. Both groups were blessed with leaders of remarkable capacity, even of genius, and both eventually died for what they believed. Both groups had had political experience in earlier national assemblies and both had orators capable of moving men's hearts and minds. It would be convenient to have some clearcut sociological distinction that might explain why the Jacobin-Girondin struggle was so murderous, but alas, such does not exist. The political elite in the Revolution, at least during this period, represent an ideological split in the bourgeoisie which manifested itself over particular issues. The Jacobins consistently supported Paris, its radical sections and Commune, and consistently championed the *sans-culottes*, the *menu peuple*, in a word the Paris population, excluding the very rich and the very poor, as "the people." The Jacobin "people," the vanguard of the Revolution for their self-appointed representatives, may have been a fiction, a useful revolutionary myth, but for the most part the Jacobins consistently celebrated and pushed the egalitarian aspirations of their constituents. They saw themselves as an elite vanguard of egalitarianism, which they associated with republicanism and whose central characteristic was virtue, which might be rendered as civic pride, patriotism, and responsibility. At any rate, the Jacobins self-consciously tied their political fortunes to "the people" and assumed they spoke for "the people."

The Girondins, on the other hand, were terrified of egalitarianism, which they saw as potential anarchy and social revolution ultimately issuing in the leveling of French society. They were equally terrified of the headquarters of this movement, Paris. They consistently berated the popular movement, the sections and the Commune, which they insisted was nothing more than a bloodthirsty and undisciplined mob, cynically manipulated by the Jacobins. The September Massacres were, for the Girondins, proof of what "the people" of Paris could and would do. The Commune they saw as composed of a bunch of socially and intellectually inferior ruffians who delighted in violence and, as Pétion put it, "trampled under foot all ideas of morality and humanity." The Jacobins were no better than the men they claimed to represent, and probably a good deal worse. Here is Brissot's lurid vision of a Jacobin France, a nightmare calculated to terrify the bourgeoisie:

> The disorganizers are those who want everything levelled, property, freedom of movement, the price of commodities, the diverse services rendered to society, etc. They want the field worker to receive the compensation of the legislator; they even want to level talents, knowledge, virtue, because they lack all these qualities.

The Jacobins, of course, wanted nothing of the sort. They were as devoted as their enemies to maintaining a society with distinctions of wealth and talent, a society based on private property. And the Girondins too had their "people," their own myth of republicanism. The true republicans, they argued, were not the *canaille* of Paris, they were the millions of Frenchmen who lived in the provinces, obeyed the laws, worked hard, and wanted not egalitarianism so much as they wanted liberty. In general the Girondins were more socially conservative than the Jacobins and probably less convinced that the revolutionary government must be increasingly centralized.

And if fundamental political differences set Jacobins and Girondins against each other, the personal hatreds that often obscure ideological differences made reconciliation impossible. Camille Desmoulins hated Roland and his wife with only slightly less passion than did Marat; Louvet despised Robespierre while Barbaroux found his vanity disgusting; Madame Roland had a long list of men she detested, chief among them being Danton, and she infected all her many admirers, especially Buzot and Guadet, with her rancor; Brissot thought the Jacobins the spokesmen for the *loi agraire* which would destroy all private property. And this list of antipathies could be extended almost indefinitely. The hatreds and recriminations of Jacobins and Girondins alike are poisonous, vile, and endless. Neither group had a monopoly on vituperation and neither group deserves any distinction or praise for such behavior. The last time Jacobins and Girondins had been able to act in concert was during the weeks following August 10, when they gleefully cooperated in hounding into prison or exile the remnants of earlier revolutionary factions. In the Convention men attached to one or the other faction seldom spoke to each other, even men who had once been fast friends. Danton made at least one attempt to reconcile the factions at the end of November, but with no success. Guadet rejected the compromise. "You don't know how to sacrifice your resentment to the country," Danton told him, "you are stubborn and you will perish." Danton's failure meant the struggle would be fought to the death.

An episode early in the trial puts the Jacobin-Girondin struggle into focus and lets us see, in a concentrated moment, their differences of personality and politics. On October 29 J. B. Louvet, one of the inner sixty, came to the tribune to accuse Robespierre. Robespierre responded on November 5. Both men spoke as representatives of opinions that were more than personal, and both men spoke about the Revolution and its meaning. Here are two self-conscious statements of political philosophy, two position papers on the Jacobin-Girondin trial of strength.

Louvet had first achieved recognition as the author of frivolous and licentious romances. His *Aventures de Faublas* (1786–1789) was a notorious book in its day. During the Revolution Louvet's local political activities in Paris had attracted the attention of Madame Roland, always on the lookout for bright young men (he was thirty-two in 1792) whom she might attract to her cause. Louvet became Madame Roland's lapdog, obsequious and officious. He scurried around the Roland salon and eventually became the editor of Roland's newspaper, *La Sentinelle*. Like so many men of the Revolution who came to politics by way of literature or an intellectual life, Louvet was unsuited for his new role. He lived a much happier life in his own romances, where extravagant love, improbable situations, and happy endings were the rule. In this world of his imagination Marguerite Dennelle, his ugly, small, heavily pockmarked wife, became the beautiful and sensual Lodiska. Louvet himself became a robust, handsome lover rather than the thin, balding, bilious little man with awkward manners he was in real life.

But if Louvet was an unlikely choice to do combat with Robespierre—and the Girondins seemed to have a knack for picking the wrong men at crucial moments—he had energy and a nervous exuberance that sometimes seemed to resemble courage. He took it upon himself to accuse Robespierre while celebrating his own political friends. The accusation, his *Robespierride* as it came to be known, had circulated among the Girondin chieftains long before it was delivered before the Convention. The *Robespierride* carried the imprimatur of the faction. On October 29 the right moment came to deliver the speech that was burning a hole in Louvet's pocket. Robespierre had just descended from the tribune, challenging anyone to accuse him of misconduct, if he dared. Louvet dared. The accusation apes the style of Cicero's *Catiline*, a faithful French echo of antiquity's most famous accusation. In the *Robespierride* Louvet denounces Robespierre as the leader of a longstanding conspiracy whose goal is to destroy the Girondins and seize political power. "Robespierre," said the new Cicero about to launch his attack, "it is from the ensemble of your actions that the accusation will emerge."

Louvet accuses Robespierre of arrogance and egotism, issuing in a disgusting personal cult fostered by himself. He accuses Robespierre of having destroyed the Jacobin Club by turning it into a shrine consecrated to himself. He accuses him of cowardice on August 10, of seducing the Commune after August 11 when he presented himself as the ideologue for Parisian radicalism, and of forming a triumvirate with Danton and Marat as the first step in

establishing a dictatorship. He accuses him of driving the true patriots out of the Jacobin Club and of having had a hand in instigat-
ing the September Massacres as a cover for the murders of the Girondin leaders. He insists throughout that Robespierre and Marat
worked together and that consequently Robespierre supported
and encouraged Marat's bloodthirsty solutions to the revolutionary
crisis. He concludes by calling for the impeachment of Marat and a
committee to investigate Robespierre. The speech contains most of
the major assumptions of the Girondins: their fear of social revolution, their hatred of radical Paris and its Commune, their insistence that the Jacobins and the *septembriseurs* are one and the
same, and their belief that the Jacobins are a bunch of demagogues
shamelessly manipulating the Parisians. It also contains some of
the Girondin antidotes for this Jacobin poison: purging the Convention of the radicals, punishing the *septembriseurs* (who happen
to coincide with the Jacobin leadership), and reducing the influence of Paris.

Louvet says in his *Mémoires* that the *Robespierride* "produced the
greatest effect." Indeed it was well received, as an oration. The age
loved formal oratory, and Louvet's Ciceronian conceit was appre-
ciated by his audience. Politically the speech had less impact.
Louvet preached successfully to the converted. The heathen majority, apparently, remained unmoved, waiting for Robespierre's
response before acting. The English poet William Wordsworth was
in the gallery the day Louvet delivered his *Robespierride*, and in *The
Prelude* he celebrates the event:

> The streets were still; not so those long arcades;
> There, 'mid a peal of ill-matched sounds and cries,
> That greeted me on entering, I could hear
> Shrill voices from the hawkers in the throng,
> Bawling, "Denunciation of the Crimes
> of Maximilian Robespierre"; the hand,
> Prompt as the voice, held forth a printed speech,
> When Robespierre, not ignorant for what mark
> Some words of indirect report had been
> Intended, rose in hardihood, and dared
> The man who had an ill surmise of him
> To bring his charge in openness; whereat,

>When a dead pause ensued, and no one stirred,
>In silence of all present, from his seat
>Louvet walked single through the avenue,
>And took his station in the Tribune, saying,
>"I Robespierre, accuse thee!"

Robespierre's response was equally dramatic. A large number of spectators had spent the night of November 4 at the doors of the Manège hoping to get a seat. The *Chronique de Paris* estimated that 700–800 spectators, mostly women, jammed into the galleries to hear Robespierre. The *Thermomètre du jour* added the colorful detail that a couple of men "held a piece of tripe in their hands, waving it about and saying that the morsel had been dipped in acid and it was for the enemies of Robespierre and Marat to eat."

After some trifling thrusts at Louvet's rhetorical excesses and his questionable morals as a writer of popular romances, Robespierre went to the heart of the matter: moderate versus radical revolution. He defends the revolutionaries of August 10 as the saviors of France. He admits there may have been some excesses, but in the heat of battle public safety takes precedence over "the criminal code." If the Commune acted illegally in destroying the monarchy, which Louvet had implied, then so too did the men who stormed the Bastille. Revolutionary acts are "as illegal as liberty itself." Robespierre then connects the September Massacres to August 10, lamenting that terrible episode but insisting that it could neither have been avoided nor stopped. All revolutions are violent, and one cannot celebrate the fall of the Bastille and condemn the fall of the monarchy. "Citizens," he implored his hearers, "do you want a Revolution without a revolution?" At the end of Robespierre's response, amid much applause for the speaker, Louvet demanded a chance to defend himself. But the Convention moved to the order of the day, a decision supported by several prominent Girondins. Robespierre had won the day, and any further confrontation would be useless and probably damaging to their cause. The Girondin chiefs had had enough and Louvet was left to deliver up his final refutation of Robespierre in a pamphlet, *To Maximilien Robespierre and His Royalists*.

Robespierre's oratorical triumph marks a new phase in his career, although his intellectual ascendancy over the Convention would not come for some months. He defended himself by defending the Revolution and in doing so deliberately put on the mantle of ideologue of the Revolution. The *Moniteur*, the semi-official newspaper of the Revolution, recognized the importance of the occasion by recognizing, for the first time, the national significance of the Jacobin Club. The meeting of the Jacobins for Monday, November 5, at which Robespierre was eulogized, was the first to be reported in the *Moniteur*. These reports would become a regular feature of the newspaper.

Jacobin and Girondin had clashed head-on. Their diametrical views were given eloquent words by the two protagonists, and if Robespierre and the Jacobins won the oratorical trial of strength, it remained to be seen which faction would win the final battle.

CHAPTER III

The King Can Do No Wrong

PARIS, AUGUST 10–DECEMBER 9, 1792

 OST OF THE revolutionaries would have been happier had Louis died defending the Tuileries. The monarchy and the monarch would have fallen together, the troublesome question of what was to be done with "Louis the Last" would have been answered. A number of deputies lamented the king's survival, resented having to bring him to trial. The decision to try Louis was not reached until December 3, and then only reluctantly when all the other options had proved impossible and pressure from Paris became irresistible. The trial got off to a bad start because of the ineptitude of the Legislative and then became inextricably entwined in the Jacobin-Girondin struggle, which only further complicated an already delicate and difficult situation.

In its decree suspending the king the Legislative stipulated that all papers and documents found at the Tuileries be confiscated and all the papers of Louis's former ministers be impounded. A commission was set up composed of sixteen men representing the sections, the Commune, and the Legislative. They inventoried the confiscated papers and prepared a report on their contents. The work was hurried and ill-conceived but it gave official sanction to the view, never questioned throughout the trial, that the king would have to answer to the nation.

On August 15 the Legislative heard the first report concerning these seized papers, the so-called Delaporte papers because the majority of them belonged to this former minister. Charles Basire explained to the Legislative that the papers contained records of money sent by Louis to *émigrés*. Here was evidence that Louis had supported the counterrevolution, and the papers were ordered printed and sent to all the departments of France and the armies. The Legislative's goal was to turn public opinion against the king and further justify the revolution of August 10. A second report, delivered that evening, produced evidence that Louis had continued to pay his bodyguards after they had fled France and joined the counterrevolutionary forces in Coblenz. Publication of these papers was a propaganda move rather than a serious attempt to prepare a case against the king. It would have been better to wait until a substantial case could be put together, but the Legislative was still smarting from its loss of power and insisted on doing something.

Nothing more was done about the king's trial until the first meetings of the Convention Assembly, although Louis's punishment was an important issue in the election of the Paris deputies to the Convention. Throughout the period separating the fall of the monarchy from the sitting of the Convention men talked incessantly about the problem of the king. Two assumptions dominated: the king was guilty and he would have to answer to the nation. But here was the end of consensus. Should the king be tried, could the king be tried? And if he were to be tried who would try him, when would they try him, how would they try him? Danton believed, and apparently so did many other deputies, that if the king came to trial he was doomed. Here was the dilemma: not only was a royal trial unprecedented, not only were there no generally-accepted procedures for such a trial, but there were many who had no desire to send Louis to the scaffold, even if they welcomed the fall of the monarchy.

The complicated question of procedures dominated the early weeks of the Convention; and more substantial questions of the meaning of sovereignty or the legacy of August 10 and the September Massacres, not to mention the constant political infighting that marked all the debates and the persistent pressures from Paris, were often lost sight of. The legal maxim that the king can do no wrong had protected the monarchy under the *ancien régime*. In the constitution of 1791 the king had been declared "sacred and invio-lable" and hence immune from prosecution. The available prece-dents made a trial impossible. The Revolution had to find a way out of this impasse. French kings had been assassinated by lone fanatics—Robert-François Damiens' attempt against Louis XV was a living memory for many deputies—deposed and imprisoned, even done to death by overmighty subjects. But never before had a king been attacked in order to keep the throne permanently empty. The men of 1792 had to figure out some way of making sure the monarchy was dead. A public trial seemed the only solution. The monarchy had survived assassinations but it could not survive a public judgment. The necessity of some kind of trial followed logi-cally, if agonizingly, from the assumption that Louis must answer to the nation. Once this momentous conclusion was drawn, the deputies had to agree on procedures.

The choice of procedures was fundamental. The Convention could use the traditional forms and procedures of criminal justice established by the Revolution; it could modify these procedures to fit the circumstances of a unique defendant; or it could invent new procedures. Each of these options implied a political choice and quickly became attached to a faction in the Convention. In addition there were men who rejected all three choices, insisting that the king could not be tried at all. For some he remained an anointed king, descended from a long line of anointed kings, and hence could not be judged by men. For some he was immune because of the constitution of 1791. For both groups the question of proce-dures was meaningless. For most, however, a choice had to be made. Those who wanted to try the king, and at the same time maintain some continuity with the laws and procedures of criminal justice as a barrier against the arbitrary justice so often practiced by kings, thought Louis should be tried like any other citizen or magistrate. Those who wanted to try the king yet realized that he was not just another citizen or magistrate wanted the traditional criminal procedures modified. Both these views came to be identi-fied with the Girondins. The Jacobins, on the other hand, insisted that the king had been judged by the highest tribunal in the land, the people in revolution on August 10. The Convention had only to carry out the sentence of death without concerning itself with another trial.

The theoretical and practical issues confronting the deputies were complicated enough, but they were further complicated by the struggle for control of the Convention, the trial of strength between Jacobins and Girondins. The first formal confrontation between the contending factions took place over the issue of the king's trial. The outcome prefigured the political direction the Revolution would take.

The Girondins came to the Convention with a majority among the factions and with a political continuity the Jacobins lacked. From the outset they easily controlled all the offices of the Convention. Pétion was elected the first president. Indeed, a list of the presidents from September 21, 1792, till January 24, 1793, is a virtual catalogue of Girondin leaders. Dominance of the presidency was significant. The president determined the order of speakers and the agenda and ruled on all questions of parliamentary procedure. In addition he appointed the committees. The Jacobins complained bitterly but could do nothing about it. In addition the Girondins controlled the important ministries. Roland was ensconced in the most influential office, the Ministry of the Interior; the other ministries were headed by men either openly beholden to Roland and his friends or at least sympathetic to them. The Girondins clearly had the advantage and set about ostracizing and then destroying their enemies. The strength of the Jacobins was scattered and largely unknown. The most important group of them sat for Paris, which was the Jacobin delegation par excellence. This formidable concentration of radicals was the target of the Girondin attack.

From the opening of the Convention the Girondins showed no interest in bringing the king to trial. They were more interested in discrediting Paris and its deputies. And their decision to hound the Jacobins was not merely a choice of priorities; they genuinely wanted to spare the king. Louis as hostage was more useful to them than Louis dead. He could be used as a barrier against Parisian radicalism, he was a useful pawn in diplomacy, and he might

even be put back on the throne, under Girondin tutelage, at some
future date. In the early weeks of the Convention, then, Louis and
whether or not to bring him to justice was the pretext used by the
Girondins in their bid for power.

Girondin spokesmen put together a plausible if far-fetched thesis: the Convention could not deliberate effectively so long as it was
intimidated by Paris and its deputies; Paris meant social revolution, violence, egalitarianism, the triumph of the vulgar and brutal
—in a word, Paris meant the September Massacres. Paris must be
neutralized, its delegation destroyed. There was probably a good
deal of sympathy for these views, or at least a good deal of anti-
Parisian feeling in the Convention. But, as it turned out, there was
not enough to insure a Girondin victory.

Even before the Convention met, Roland and his friends had
seriously discussed the possibility of moving the Convention out of
Paris. He proposed the lovely town of Tours. When this proved
impossible the Girondins proposed a series of schemes that would
make Parisian influence equal to that of the other eighty-three departments of France. The Girondins wanted to summon a bodyguard from the provinces to protect the Convention from intimidation and violence. They wanted to punish the *septembriseurs* by
purging them from the Convention and bringing them to trial.
They wanted to impeach Marat and Robespierre as leaders of a
conspiracy against the republic and as demagogues who had instigated the September Massacres. They also wanted to impeach
Philippe Egalité, the turncoat cousin of the king who had repudiated his title as prince of the blood to sit with the Paris delegation.
Philippe, the Girondins argued, would be put on the throne as a
Jacobin puppet as soon as Louis XVI went to the guillotine. And
each of these proposals was presented as a contingency: the Convention must be purged, the Paris deputies cowed, the *septembriseurs* punished, an armed provincial guard established, *before* the
Convention could turn its attention to the king.

All these proposals were presented to the Convention, some
more than once, in the name of law and order, civilization versus
barbarism. But these lofty ideals were submerged in the nasty day-
to-day squabbling introduced into the trial and persistently defended. Not only did these Girondin proposals put off the trial of

the king, which was part of their intention, but they also undermined the integrity and authority of the Convention. The Girondins were the first to propose arming one part of the population against the other. They were the first to insist that the antagonisms between the provinces and Paris were irreconcilable, and in fact they encouraged such antagonisms. They were the first to propose seeking support outside the Convention for its actions. They were the first to propose impeaching deputies. Their social philosophy might be more moderate than that of the Jacobins, but their high-handed attempts to manipulate the Convention to achieve dominance at whatever cost were certainly more radical and ultimately destructive. They constantly accused the Jacobins of wanting to destroy the Convention rather than see control pass to those of moderate opinions, yet it is they who acted in this way.

Instead of dealing with the king, seizing the initiative in the trial, they preferred to go after the Jacobins and do everything in their power to delay or abort the trial. They arrogantly disregarded the uncommitted deputies, they drove wavering radicals into the arms of the Mountain, and they failed to convince a majority of deputies to follow Girondin leadership. Each of the proposals mentioned above failed to get a majority in the Convention. Rather than convincing their colleagues that they ought to control the Convention, the Girondins came gradually to be seen as "the Jesuits of the Revolution."

The first formal call for Louis's trial and execution came on October 1, from the Mountain. As might be expected it grew out of a political struggle between the Vigilance Committee of the Commune and the Convention. The Vigilance Committee announced that it had found proof, in the papers seized at the Tuileries, that some of the 194 exdeputies to the Legislative now sitting in the Convention had been in the pay of the court. Merlin de Thionville, a Montagnard and one of the heroes of August 10, seized the occasion to call for Louis's head: "It is time that he fall under the national sword; and that all those who have conspired with him follow him to the scaffold . . . the Convention ought to be, for him, both the jury of accusation and the jury of judgment." Merlin's confused call, confounding procedures with politics and unfortunately insisting that the king and his minions must be judged together, nevertheless had an impact. It began the phase of Louis's trial called the instruction. But first the ponderous inertia of a large and divided political body had to be overcome.

On Barbaroux's motion the Convention began appointing a commission of twenty-four deputies to study the problem. Like everything else in the trial the motion was politically biased. Barbaroux was a Girondin, and since the issue of a trial had been forced on the reluctant Girondins by the Commune and the Jacobins, he tried to guarantee that the trial would be controlled by his friends. All deputies who had sat in either the National Assembly or the Legislative Assembly (a total of 277) or those who represented Paris (another twenty-four, including all the leading Jacobins), were excluded from this commission. Charles-Eléanor Dufriche-Valazé, a retired army officer with scholarly habits and a Girondin, was appointed to head the commission of twenty-four. The sole representative of radical opinion was Drouet, Louis's captor at Varennes. Valazé, an affable and mild-mannered man, was forty-one in 1792. Before the Revolution he had published philosophic and scientific treatises of no special distinction. He was a man of independent means, and his Paris apartment was a frequent gathering place for the Girondins. Valazé was bookish by choice and enjoyed solitude. He was, like Louvet sent to do battle with Robespierre, an unlikely choice.

On October 4 Valazé delivered the commission's preliminary report. Their task had been arduous. Since their appointment the members "have not distinguished days from nights," Valazé reported. There was a mountain of materials: ninety-five cartons, six boxes (one measuring fifty-four cubic feet), twenty large briefcases, thirty-four registers, seven bundles of papers, and several thousand loose sheets packed in flour sacks. The commission had only made a superficial examination. Valazé told the Convention there was "evident and material proof of the conspiracies of the dethroned king." But he could not be specific. The Convention decided, to expedite the commission's work, to move all the materials to the Manège. The commission would break up into teams of two deputies and as soon as they had gone through all the papers they would make a second report. No date was set for this second report.

The sections of Paris, growing impatient, called for the "prompt and severe judgment of Louis the Traitor and Antoinette his accomplice." The Girondins responded with more deliberation. Every legality, they insisted, must be observed, the rule of law must be preserved. Louis's trial must have an unquestioned foundation in legal procedures. Barbaroux called for a careful study of all the available procedures before anything was decided. Manuel called for submitting the decrees which had abolished the monarchy and established the republic to the nation for ratification. Barbaroux's proposal was dismissed as unnecessary; Manuel's as impossible. How could the successful revolution of August 10 be submitted to a vote? But it was clear that something had to be done to pacify Paris and prove to the Convention that the Girondins were serious about a trial. While Valazé's committee continued to go through the captured documents, the Convention's standing committee on legislation was instructed to study the questions, Could Louis be tried? and Who would try him? This committee was headed by Jean-Baptiste Mailhe and came to be known as the Mailhe committee.

The clever and ambitious son of a laborer, Mailhe had studied law at Toulouse and opened a practice there. He quickly acquired the reputation of having a fine legal mind and being a brilliant orator, but his acknowledged gifts were partially mitigated by his secretive and suspicious personality. He inspired little confidence in his contemporaries and often hid his real thoughts in ambiguous declarations. On this occasion, however, Mailhe did his work well. No record of the committee's meetings has survived, but judging from the report itself there had been a careful exploration and discussion of most of the possibilities, which were presented to the Convention in a forthright manner. Alas, the same cannot be said of Valazé's committee, which delivered its second report on November 6, a day before the Mailhe report.

The date is significant. No time had been set for this second report, and coming as it did the day after Robespierre's victory over Louvet it seemed suspiciously rushed to serve as a counterattack.

It was also the day of the victory of French arms at Jemappes, the first time the French had launched a frontal attack against the enemy. The *sans-culottes* in the army rushed the enemy singing "La Marseillaise" and "La Carmagnole." It was a great republican victory, and all of Belgium fell to the revolutionary armies. The news had not yet reached Paris when Valazé appeared before the Convention, but the victory at Jemappes, like that earlier at Valmy, would push the deputies closer to a trial and benefit the radicals.

Valazé's second report was wordy and disorganized, evidence of its hasty preparation. He spoke of flagrant violations of the law but offered only facts long known; and his conclusions were vague. The most Valazé would say is that Louis could not take refuge in his constitutional immunity. Even Valazé's friends found the report hopelessly flabby, and the Girondins were embarrassed by their committee. Barbaroux called for a thorough search for additional evidence against the king and the Convention ordered the report printed and distributed. But the damage had been done: here was yet another example of Girondin ineptitude or reluctance. The Convention had been sitting for more than a month and the king was no closer to trial than he had been in September. Mailhe's report was more satisfactory but it dealt with other matters. The Convention, under Girondin leadership, still had not produced a documented case against the king and seemed in no hurry to do so.

The central question for Mailhe's committee was the question of Louis's inviolability, his constitutional immunity from criminal justice. If the Convention honored the constitution with its inviolability clauses the king could not be tried. Mailhe's committee found a way out of the difficulty that seemed to satisfy most *conventionnels*: Louis's immunity was a privilege granted by the sovereign people, and what had been granted could be taken away. The National Assembly had established the precedent when it suspended the king in 1791, and Louis, Mailhe argued, recognized their right to do so when he accepted the constitution. Thus despite the immunity clauses Louis was responsible for all his actions subsequent to accepting the constitution.

The truly thorny question, however, was not whether Louis was justiciable, but who ought to try him and by what procedures.

Mailhe's committee rejected trial by an ordinary criminal court as unworkable, since Louis could not appear as a defendant until he had been stripped of his constitutional immunity, and only the sovereign people, through their representatives, could do this. In addition, it was probably impossible to find a court in the land that was both disinterested enough to try the king and representative of the nation. The king must either be tried by the Convention itself or first stripped of his immunity and then tried by a special tribunal, appointed by the Convention. He recommended trial by the Convention since it "represents entirely and perfectly the French republic." As to procedures, Mailhe argued that the Convention was bound only by the will of the nation, not by legal precedent—an important conclusion.

Mailhe concluded his report by presenting his committee's recommendations, which would become the basis for the trial: (1) Louis can be judged; (2) he should be judged by the Convention; (3) three commissioners should be appointed by the Convention and charged with collecting all the evidence relative to Louis's crimes; (4) these documents should form the basis of the act of accusation (*acte énonciatif*); (5) the *acte énonciatif* should be communicated to Louis and printed; (6) Louis should be allowed to choose an attorney and see the originals of the evidence against him; (7) after hearing the king's defense, the Convention would reach its verdict by the vote of each deputy. The report was enthusiastically received and ordered printed and distributed. Although Mailhe's report left much unsaid and was unacceptable to the Jacobins, who had their own series of proposals, it provided a workable blueprint for the trial. Mailhe had said virtually nothing about legal procedures or punishment, but the majority of deputies were pleased with his conclusions: the people's quarrel with their king was to be settled in an adversary proceeding conducted by the Convention.

Debate on the Mailhe report opened on Tuesday, November 13, when the president, Hérault de Sechelles, the only Jacobin president during the trial, laconically announced that "the order of the day is the discussion relative to the judgment of the *ci-devant* king." The Girondins immediately proposed a delay. Pétion moved for suspension of the debates until the Convention had examined whether or not the king could be judged. It was an inept request and would have returned the trial to square one. But Pétion's diversionary tactic died from lack of support. The first speaker in the debates was Charles-François-Gabriel Morisson, a lawyer in his forties. In the Legislative Assembly he had earned the reputation of being a royalist by his persistent and deep attachment to the monarchy and the royal family. But in the Convention it was imprudent to advertise one's royalism and Morisson confined his remarks to the constitutional arguments against a trial, prefiguring Louis's own defense. He denied the Convention's right to try a constitutional king who had been made immune from criminal prosecution. In addition, Morisson continued, the constitution specifically said that the only penalty the king could suffer, whatever his crimes, was forced abdication. Louis had paid that penalty on August 10.

Here was a formidable dilemma. The king could not be tried and punished again, and since he had suffered dethronement he was now a free man. The Convention, Morisson argued, is "religiously under the empire of the law"; and the law, the constitution, "made an exception in his [Louis's] favor." Were the Convention to disregard the constitution in order to bring Louis to trial the republic itself would be founded on injustice. "The law is silent," he concluded, "despite the atrocity of his horrible crimes." Morisson's presentation of the constitutional argument, in reasoned and measured tones, exposed the arbitrariness of Mailhe's opinion that the constitution did not mean what it said. And the Mailhe report was in for an even sharper attack from the speaker who followed Morisson to the podium. Louis-Antoine de Saint-Just presented the regicide case in its most extreme and original form.

Saint-Just, one of the most extraordinary men of the Revolution, had just turned 25 in August. He was arrogant, conceited, handsome. His youth, spent in a small Picardy town, had been taken up with sundry love affairs and the pursuit of fame. His first literary work, a philosophic and pornographic poem in twenty cantos, had appeared in 1789. It earned him little fame but did bring him to Paris, where he became possessed by the Revolution. In an age that successfully combined self-dramatization with reserve, sentiment with cynicism, vulgarity with refinement, Saint-Just was a compelling personality. He was willful and fiery, his mind was clear and ruthless. He loved to dress extravagantly, favoring black clothes and an enormous white cravat which he painstakingly knotted while admiring himself in a mirror. His neckpiece, said Camille Desmoulins, Robespierre's school friend and a deputy for Paris, held his head up like the sacred host in a monstrance. To complete his carefully contrived appearance Saint-Just let his dark hair hang to his shoulders and wore a single gold earring. Of moderate height, he had a good physique, a large head, thick hair, and a pallid, almost sickly complexion. He thought himself handsome, as did those who drew his portrait. All his features were large—chin, mouth, nose, eyes—and his eyebrows almost met when he frowned, which was not infrequently. His voice was thought sonorous, and when speaking publicly he had the disturbing habit of making a brutal, chopping gesture with his right hand, which later reminded contemporaries of the blade of the guillotine falling. His personal manners were restrained and even cold, the outward manifestation of his austere republican sentiments. His literary style was laconic and his political principles puritanical. His spectacular political career lasted only twenty-two months, and he was virtually unknown when he delivered his maiden speech on November 13. It caused a sensation, both for its style and its ideas.

The king, said Saint-Just, must be judged by new principles. Louis was neither a citizen nor a defaulting magistrate. He was an enemy alien. "We have not so much to judge him as to fight him," hence the forms of legal procedure have no relevance. If the Convention makes Louis a citizen in order to try him its action will astonish future ages. Tyrants ought to die, not by being elevated to the rank of citizen, but as Caesar died, "with no other formality than twenty-two dagger thrusts." Louis has already been judged by the revolution of August 10. The Convention has only to carry out the death sentence. Up to this point Saint-Just was merely giving words, stirring words to be sure, to the Jacobin thesis: Louis does not deserve a trial and must not be tried. But the most original and radical part of Saint-Just's argument was to cast the king out of the body politic and hence make him an outlaw among his own people. "Louis is a stranger among us." He was never king of the French, he was only "the king of some conspirators." He cannot be tried for treason because treason implies the betrayal of friends or clients or country. Louis had never belonged to the nation hence could not betray it. His crime was tyranny itself, a crime he committed when he first mounted the throne: "a man cannot reign innocently."

Louis the man does not appear in Saint-Just's speech. We see only the political abstraction of the king as tyrant. Louis must die not for what he has done, not for acts of his volition, but for what he is. He must be struck down in his two bodies, his body politic and his real body (an elaborate conceit of generations of royalist apologists), for only in this way will the Revolution declare to all the world that it is free, that it has thrown off the yoke of tyranny.

It was a stunning performance. Saint-Just's youth and obscurity, his brilliance and his logic, all combined to astonish his hearers. The French language, still under the influence of an age of elegance and supreme sophistication, still under the tutelage of classical models, still an instrument for the expression of almost every emotion except political passion, became in Saint-Just's hands something new: a revolutionary idiom. Even deputies who abhorred his principles were impressed by Saint-Just's brilliance. Brissot wrote in his *Patriote français* of the "luminous details" of the speech and "a talent that honors France."

The three major views of what should be done with the king were now on the floor: Mailhe's sophistic interpretation of the constitution; Morisson's strict constitutionalism; and Saint-Just's call for summary execution. The *conventionnels* would adhere to one or another of these theses, but it is Saint-Just's radical statement of the regicide position that moved the debates to the level of a struggle over revolutionary principles. The implication was clear: if the king was innocent the Revolution was guilty. And no revolution could risk a trial of this nature. Throughout the debates the Jacobins reiterated Saint-Just's arguments, both because they believed them and because they feared that a trial in the Girondin-dominated Convention might go badly. The Girondins, with equal tenacity, insisted on a trial in order to counter the Jacobins and did everything they could to abort it.

Roland and his friends were right, the Convention could not deliberate freely in Paris under the watchful and often hungry eyes of
the unruly city. Living under a war economy, with winter coming
on, Paris was again restless. There were food shortages, inflation,
and a steady devaluation of the paper money. It was only a matter
of time before the political agitators at the Commune and in the
sections connected the trial with the very real hardships afflicting
the city. Provisioning Paris had always been a problem, for royalist
as well as revolutionary governments. Parisians knew what it
meant to go short, and the fear of shortages was as potent in
stirring up social unrest as shortages themselves. And it was second nature to blame the government, to see a political reason for
economic distress.

The trial was bogged down and Paris was hungry: there seemed
a causal relationship between these facts. On November 15 the
Convention returned to discussion of the Mailhe report. The Girondins again proposed delays by insisting once more that the declaration of a republic had to be submitted to the voters for ratification before the trial could continue. Danton easily crushed these
proposals under the weight of his prestige and rhetoric. The republic had been sanctioned "by the genius of liberty that rejects all
kings." But the Convention seemed to many to be as far from
bringing the king to trial as it had been nearly two months earlier.
The Commune responded, on November 16, through the mouth of
Anaxagoras Chaumette, who addressed the General Council of the
Commune on shortages and the trial. His thesis was simple: so
long as Louis went unpunished prices would remain high, and
shortages and the profiteering that created them, which Chaumette assumed to be the work of royalists, would go unchecked.

The son of a provincial cobbler and the future *procureur* of the
Commune, Chaumette was fiercely egalitarian and enjoyed telling
the story of how he came to change his name: "I was formerly
called Pierre-Gaspard Chaumette because my god-father believed
in the saints. Since the Revolution I have taken the name of a saint
who was hanged for his republican principles." Chaumette was
twenty-nine in 1792. His political base was his section, his forum
the General Council (composed of elected representatives of all the
forty-eight sections). His language and his actions were equally

ferocious. He had enjoyed supervising the destruction of the stone saints carved on the portal of Notre-Dame cathedral in Paris, convinced that Christianity and counterrevolution were one and the same. Even his radical colleagues on the General Council thought Chaumette excessive. Hébert, himself addicted to frequent calls for more bloodletting, said Chaumette's snout had been designed to dip in blood.

Many people in Paris, Chaumette told the General Council, blamed the food shortages on the consumptions of the army. This was not the real cause. It was Louis XVI himself who was responsible for his people's misery. It was the king who had first stocked the storehouses of Verdun and Longwy and then allowed them to be captured by the enemy. It was the king's extravagance that had created tallow shortages: "Recall the immense and astonishing quantity of tallow that he had burned in his château, in the garden of the Tuileries, along the Champs-Elysées, and by the rich of Paris." And, not troubling to make the connection very clear, Chaumette went on to argue that so long as Louis lived the armies would be hampered. The solution was to punish the king. The revolutionary armies would triumph, thus reopening the trade routes; Paris would be provisioned; and then property could be reorganized on new, republican, principles. The hateful middlemen, the commercial interests who profit from misery, would be destroyed, the "gifts of nature" would become the property of all.

Chaumette was not alone in articulating the impatience of Paris. The city spoke with many voices. The calls for Louis's head multiplied and none was more insistent than Jacques Roux's. Of the many priests who had left the church to join the Revolution none was more articulate and socially aware. Roux's early career as a priest was unexceptional, but in 1790 he was involved in the sacking of some châteaux in his diocese and was defrocked. He came to Paris and threw himself into revolutionary agitation in his adopted section, Gravilliers, one of the poorest in the city. He quickly became an important sectional leader and attracted a group of extreme left-wing popular leaders and agitators, usually called the *enragés*. His speech of December 1, delivered at a sectional meeting, was an impatient call for Louis's head as the first step in alleviating social misery. "The head of the assassin of the French" was to be

the first victory in a war against the profiteers. It is time, he continued, to teach the people of the earth "that nations are no longer
the property of kings . . . and that crime leads to the scaffold." It
is time "that the liberty of the people be consolidated by the legal
shedding of the impure blood of kings." Roux's speech was ordered printed and sent to all the forty-eight sections as well as to
the Convention; and to inculcate patriotism, section Gravilliers
proposed that the speech be read twice a week by the sections, for
a month.

These arguments and accusations were too much for the *conventionnels*, even the Jacobins. The Convention refused to be intimidated by what it chose to consider the intemperance of a few *outré*
agitators. The deputies sought comfort and refuge in puffed-up
language about their dignity and responsibility, their duty to deliberate without outside interference. In December 1792 no one in
the Convention was willing to admit that there was a connection
between high prices, shortages, and the king. And certainly no one
was willing to attack the commercial middle class. But Paris could
not be ignored despite the face-saving posturings of the Convention. Fortunately there was no showdown between Paris and the
Convention because news of a startling discovery of the king's
secret safe in the Tuileries diverted attention from the market to
the Manège.

On November 20 Roland explained, in deliberately mysterious
manner, the conditions under which the safe, with its secret papers, was discovered. Gamain, Louis's locksmith, had led Roland
to the safe, hidden "behind a wood panel, covering a hole in the
wall, and protected by an iron door." The place was so well disguised that "if the only person in Paris who knew about it had not
indicated [the location] it would have been impossible to discover." The minister told the Convention: "I ordered the safe opened
this morning, and I have rapidly looked at these papers." The
drama of the announcement and Roland's smug description—he
insinuated that the newly found papers compromised the Jacobins
—ignited the old Jacobin-Girondin hatreds. Jean-François-Marie
Goupilleau, a Montagnard, shouted out the obvious question: why
was the safe opened by the self-righteous minister with no other
witnesses present besides Gamain? Jean-Lambert Tallien, another

itagnard, asked if an inventory of the contents had been made.
and had no satisfactory answers to these charges, and the Con-
ntion appointed a commission to examine the papers and make a
eport.

Madame Roland, the tireless and clever apologist for her husband, expressed amazement that anyone would dare question
Roland's integrity. Montagnard suspicion that Roland had suppressed papers that might compromise his Girondin friends was a
vile calumny started by Etienne-Nicolas de Calon, a Jacobin deputy
who hated Roland and sought revenge for a social snub. Madame
Roland may have thought her husband's behavior in the affair
"prudent," but from a more impartial point of view, it was certainly stupid. Roland had the deserved reputation of being a zealous
partisan of the Girondins and one of the most vocal opponents of
the Jacobins. He had earlier been denounced at the Jacobin Club,
again by Calon, as having used public funds to have Louvet's
Robespierride printed and distributed throughout France. And he
was on record as despising Paris and its popular leaders. With such
credentials he might have been more careful.

Roland returned to the Convention the next day, November 21,
to defend himself. But to no avail: the Jacobins never forgave him,
he had embarrassed his friends, and Danton's judgment that he
was an opinionated old fool probably won some new adherents.
The discovery of the *armoire de fer*, however, strengthened the case
against the king. Here was the first new evidence in the case since
Valazé had bungled his responsibility. There were 625 separate
items in the safe and the Convention heard a preliminary report on
them on November 23. It was not Jacobin reputations that were
tarnished by the new evidence, but rather the great Mirabeau's
reputation. Here was the evidence of his deal with the court and it
destroyed his heroic reputation.

Otherwise the papers and the existence of a secret safe confirmed what many already believed: Louis was a determined and
devious man bent on destroying the Revolution. The king, the papers revealed, had consistently and tenaciously played a double
game. He had deliberately obstructed the constitution, instructed
his ministers to lie to the Legislative Assembly, sought to bribe

deputies, encouraged the emigration of his friends, and, through Mirabeau, tried to reestablish his authority. The papers also linked Louis to the counterrevolution by exposing his dealings with Lafayette, Talon, and those who had arranged the flight to Varennes. But the most damaging documents were those that proved the king's hatred of the Revolution. There was a letter, written in April 1791 to the Bishop of Clermont, which promised to reestablish the Catholic Church in all its prerevolutionary glory when the king regained power. In another letter, this one to the Baron de Breteuil, he had written: "It is clear to every person who walks on two feet that in my heart I cannot approve the Revolution and the absurd and detestable constitution that makes me less than the king of Poland." These damaging documents, many of them in Louis's own hand or annotated by him, were too useful to be ignored and would be used tellingly in his indictment. The *armoire de fer* papers, while not proving Louis's suspected treasons, certainly compromised the best arguments his champions had. It became increasingly difficult to paint the king as a decent and sincere man who wanted only what was best for his people, a man who had been misled by his advisers into opposing the Revolution. Rather, the *armoire de fer* papers strengthened Jacobin contentions that the king was a stubborn and deceitful enemy bent on destroying the Revolution.

Following the sensational interlude of the *armoire de fer* the debates on the Mailhe report resumed. But the sections, bitterly hostile to Roland, took up where the Convention left off. Section Piques declared that Roland had lost the confidence of the sections and ought to resign; he responded by once again accusing Paris of anarchy and calling for a purge of the Commune. Roland's proposals were carried to the floor of the Convention by the Girondins, who offered a motion to restrict the frequency of sectional meetings. The Convention had no stomach for a confrontation with the Commune and tabled the motion.

Roland had once again played into Jacobin hands. His denunciation of Paris was interpreted as yet another Girondin scheme to abort the trial. The Mountain orators hammered away at their thesis: Louis had been judged on August 10 and must be sent to the guillotine without a trial. At the end of November the trial was hopelessly bogged down in the Jacobin-Girondin struggle. Paris was fed up with the delays. On December 2 the Commune, in a threatening mood, sent a deputation to the Convention. Any delay in Louis's punishment, the Commune told the Convention, was "a political blasphemy." Parisian patience was running out. If the Convention refused to act the Commune would, as it had done on August 10 when faced with a reluctant Assembly. Only two questions were important, said the Commune: "Is Louis, *ci-devant* king of the French, deserving of death? Is it advantageous for the republic to have him die on the scaffold?" The deputation strongly suggested that the Convention spend four afternoons a week answering these questions.

The Commune, with the Jacobins, opposed a trial. The majority of the *conventionnels*, however, seemed determined to give Louis his day in court. On December 3, prodded by the discovery of the *armoire de fer* and the Commune's ultimatum, the Convention moved closer to a judgment. It heard a second report on the secret papers and ordered decrees of accusation against three former ministers of the king. Then Robespierre went to the tribune to prevent, if he could, the movement toward a trial. His speech was a careful reiteration of the themes first announced by Saint-Just on November 13. "Louis is not an accused," said Robespierre, "you are not judges. You are, you can only be, men of state, the representatives of a nation." For the Convention to try the king would violate all accepted legal procedures. Louis's condemnation was not a proper subject for judicial review: it was "a measure of public safety." If the Convention constitutes itself a court it has to accept fundamental principles of French law, which presume a man innocent until proven guilty. If Louis is tried he can, presumably, be found innocent: "But if Louis can be presumed innocent, what becomes of the Revolution?" To try Louis means to try the Revolution itself, an absurdity for Robespierre: "When a king has been annihilated by the people, who has the right to resuscitate him?"

The Convention could not be persuaded. An acerbic debate, punctuated by shouted insults, followed Robespierre's speech.

When the tumult finally subsided Pétion went to the tribune and reversed his earlier views by calling for a trial. His motion—"Louis will be judged by the National Convention"—carried by a huge majority. Having failed to defeat the Jacobins, and under enormous pressure from the deputies and from Paris, the Girondins seemed determined to go through with the trial. They had not, of course, abandoned the political struggle. Pétion's motion bought the faction some time while giving the Girondins more popular support in the Convention than they had previously enjoyed. This support they apparently took as a sign to continue their attack on the Mountain.

On December 4 the Girondins launched another assault on the Mountain. Buzot proposed the death penalty for "anyone who might propose or attempt to reestablish royalty in France." This apparently neutral motion was in fact aimed at the Mountain in the person of Philippe Egalité. The Girondins had long argued that Philippe would be put on the throne as a Jacobin puppet as soon as Louis XVI was dead. Buzot's motion was a clever move. Those who supported it would be accepting the Girondin view of the Jacobins and the Paris delegation. Those who opposed the motion would run the risk of being considered royalists. Marat pleaded with the Convention not to be duped by Buzot, not to lose sight of "the great revolutionary act that we are going to commit," but the Girondins had won a point. The Mountain had to abandon its position on the trial momentarily and defend itself by defending Philippe Egalité, a man few thought worthy of defense.

Philippe Egalité had openly joined the revolutionaries in 1791 when he changed his name, and thus declared war on his cousin the king. He was a man consumed with ambition: he wanted to be king of France. He was, reputedly, the richest man in the country and the man most addicted to intrigue. His vast fortune was freely spent to get political power, and his Paris residence, the Palais Royal, had become a favorite haunt for freelance pamphleteers, journalists, rabble-rousers—in a word, those who had something to sell and knew the former Duke d'Orléans was buying. His taste for political corruption and manipulation and plots was catered to by the brilliant and sinister Choderlos de Laclos, author of the scandalous novel *Les Liaisons dangereuses*, and Philippe's strategist. Many were tainted by Philippe's money or the suspicion of having sought it, but the Girondins never produced any convincing evidence that linked the leading Montagnards to the former duke, or that there was a Jacobin conspiracy to put Philippe on the throne. Philippe was not a popular man, as phenomenally rich men seldom are, and since the Convention was willing to listen to the Girondin charge the Jacobins had to respond.

Several deputies tried to return the discussion to the king's trial but they were ignored or shouted down. Merlin de Thionville, the Montagnard who had first called for a trial in October, bellowed at the disorderly Convention that he regretted not having killed Louis on August 10, which would have spared the country the agony of a trial. Some deputies called for Merlin's censure, which was lost in the general din. Robespierre and Chabot and Camille Desmoulins all rushed to the tribune to defend their comrade. Another Montagnard, Pierre Philippeaux, offered the reasonable proposal that the Convention return to the problem of the king and sit without interruption until Louis had been judged. The Convention ignored the Mountain and in the midst of the tumult Buzot's motion against royalty passed. Robespierre, out of control, demanded the floor. He was shouted down. Over the din he screamed a proposal that would legitimate August 10 and condemn Louis without a trial. The Convention, equally out of control, shouted "To the Abbaye!" (the infamous prison where the September Massacres had begun) and drowned him out. The stormy session ended with the adoption of Pétion's motion that the Convention deal with the king every day, from noon till six. It had been a day of political defeat and frustration for the Mountain. Philippe Egalité was under attack, the Jacobin thesis of no trial had been defeated by unofficial acclamation, and the Girondins were about to proceed with the trial.

By the next day, December 5, the Mountain had regained some of its composure. The Convention heard another report on the contents of the *armoire de fer* and demanded that Mirabeau's remains be dug up from the Panthéon and his statues smashed. Both proposals were sent to committee, but while the committee deliberated Mirabeau's statue in the Manège was vandalized. On December 6 the Mountain made one last attempt to have Louis summarily executed. Bourbotte made the case for the regicides, criticizing the Convention for its lethargy and demanding that Louis be brought before the Convention immediately. Bourbotte's proposal was the first formalization of the Jacobin thesis: Louis would hear the *acte énonciatif* of his crimes and the two commissions, Valazé's and Mailhe's, would put questions to the king. He would not be allowed to make a defense or have a lawyer present. He would then be returned to prison while the Convention pronounced sentence. Marat suggested adding a condition which he hoped would expose the antiregicides in the Convention. He called for a roll-call vote on Louis's punishment and insisted that the vote be published.

The veneer of parliamentary procedure peeled off and the Convention was again thrown into disorder. The secretaries were unable to hear the numerous proposals and motions that were flung at them out of the tumult. Finally the noise died down and the Convention adopted the proposal made by N. M. Quinette, a moderate. A third commission would be selected and charged with preparing the *acte énonciatif* against Louis and fixing the procedures for the trial at the same time. This commission came to be called the Commission of Twenty-one and was composed of men who had not served on either of the earlier commissions. Their accusation would be presented on December 10, accompanied by a dossier of documents that supported each specific charge. On December 11 the same commission would present a list of questions to be put to the prisoner. The Convention passed the necessary decrees, and the president, Bertrand Barère, was charged with taking all the required precautions for Louis's security during his trips to the Convention.

This period of the king's trial, running from October 1 to December 6, is usually called the instruction although it might more accurately be called the decision to try the king. Louis did not appear before the Convention during the entire period. Events and his own fate were out of his hands. It was Paris, the war, the legacy of August 10 as understood by the deputies, and the Jacobin-Girondin struggle for power that would decide what was to be done with "Louis the Last." Paris had spoken and the victory at Jemappes had given the Revolution another breathing space. But the Jacobin-Girondin struggle was far from over. The balance of power in the Convention still lay with the deputies of the Marais, the uncommitted, as it had since the beginning; and they had decided that Louis would have a trial and they would conduct it. On December 9 the deputies went home while the Commission of Twenty-one closeted itself to draw up the *acte énonciatif* against the king.

CHAPTER IV

The Man of the Temple

THE TEMPLE, SEPTEMBER 1792 – JANUARY 1793

 HE KING and his family had spent three uncomfortable days and two uncomfortable nights in makeshift quarters while the Commune and the Legislative Assembly decided whose prisoner Louis would be. The Legislative was reluctant to give up the most important spoil of August 10, but the Commune, armed and flushed with victory, was not to be denied. On August 13, after lunch, Alexandre, the leader of the left-bank troops on August 10, arrived at the Manège to take the royal family to prison. He found Louis in an agitated state. The king was concerned about the staff he would be permitted to have and gave Alexandre a long list of the domestics he required. He refused to leave the Manège until Alexandre promised that he would submit the list to the Commune. Only then, at around 3:30 P.M., the heavily guarded royal prisoners left the Manège, mounted the waiting coach, and began crossing Paris at a funereal pace.

The streets were lined with soldiers and onlookers. An occasional shout "Long live the nation!" broke the silence. For the most part, however, the Parisians confined their insults to symbolism: they refused to remove their hats, just as they had done more than a year ago when the king was returned from Varennes. The king, the queen, and their two children sat in the back of the coach. Madame Elisabeth, the king's sister, Madame de Lamballe, the queen's companion, and Jérôme Pétion, the mayor, sat facing them. Madame de Tourzel and her daughter, Pauline, sat on one side (she was the children's governess), and Louis-Pierre Manuel, the *procureur* of the Commune, with M. Colonge, also representing the Commune, sat on the other side. "All these gentlemen," Madame de Tourzel complained, "had their hats on their heads and treated their majesties in the most revolting manner." Manuel ordered the coach halted in the Place Vendôme so Louis could contemplate the toppled, decapitated statue of Louis XIV, another legacy of August 10. Then the procession continued.

The place chosen by the Commune was the tower of the Temple, a forbidding medieval *donjon* located in one of the radical neighborhoods of Paris. The Temple and its *petite tour* had formerly been the property of the Duke d'Angoulême. He had lent it to the Count d'Artois, Louis XVI's younger brother, for a townhouse. The Count had lavishly furnished the place for his own use but had neglected the tower that lay two hundred yards from the château itself, in the middle of the garden. During the middle ages the place had been the fortress of the powerful Templar knights, hence its name. When that arrogant order was suppressed by Philip the Fair in 1307 the property had been confiscated by the crown. The newspapers were delighted with the Commune's choice. The *Chronique de Paris* gleefully reported that the royal family had to climb 126 steps to reach their apartment in the tower, which had never held "so great a bankrupt." With its narrow slit-windows, deep moat, and thick stone walls the *petite tour* was a grim setting for the drama about to begin.

The king's quarters were on the third floor and consisted of an antechamber with three small rooms radiating off it, each with its own door. The middle of the three served as a bedroom. The other two were, respectively, the king's reading room, which contained a fireplace, and his dining room, which was heated by a large stone stove. What little light there was came from a single large casement window protected by iron bars and shutters. The bars had been built by the Templars, the shutters were added by the Commune. The walls of the tower were nine feet thick.

The square central tower had four round towers at each corner. There was only one stairway in the tower and it led up to the crenellated defenses and down to the garden in the courtyard. Along this stairway the Commune had built seven temporary guard-

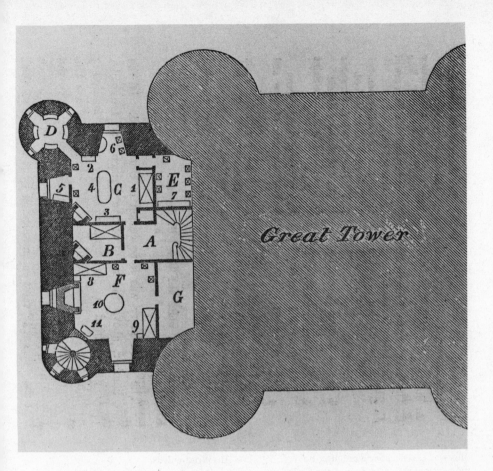

THE "LITTLE TOWER" OF THE TEMPLE

This was Louis's apartment during the first months of his imprisonment before he was moved to the more secure quarters in the Great Tower. This reconstruction of the floor plan—the Tower was razed in 1808—is by A. de Beauchesne.

A. Staircase and landing.
B. Room and beds for the king's servants.
C. The king's room.
  1. The king's bed.
  2. Chest of drawers.
  3. Large canopy of crimson velvet.
  4. Dining table.
  5. Sideboard.
  6. Small table.
     Also: four arm chairs; six straw chairs.
D. The king's study.
E. Dressing room.
  7. Cupboard.
F. An old kitchen, converted into Madame Elisabeth's room.
  8. Madame Elisabeth's bed.
  9. Pauline de Tourzel's bed (daughter of the royal children's governess).
  10. Table.
  11. Chair.
     Also: three additional chairs.
G. Closet or storage area.

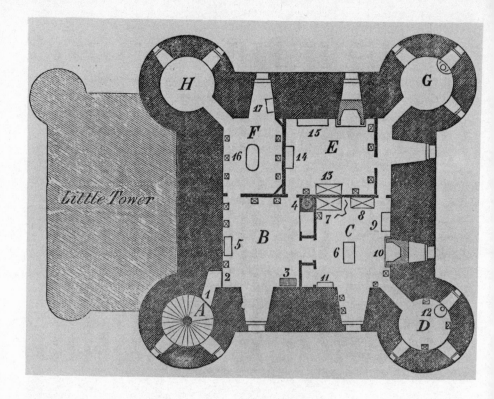

THE "GREAT TOWER" OF THE TEMPLE

This was Louis's apartment after he was moved from the third floor of the Little Tower to the second floor of the Great Tower. It was here that Louis spent his final days.

A. The Staircase.
1. Oak door, studded with nails.
2. Iron door.

B. Antechamber.
3. Card table.
4. Stove.
5. Writing table above which, painted on the wall, is the Declaration of the Rights of Man and Citizen.

C. The king's room.
6. Leather-covered table.
7. The king's bed.
8. The dauphin's trestle-bed.
9. Chest of drawers.
10. Fireplace. On this chimney-piece stood a clock with the name "Chevalier Duterte, of Paris."

11. Writing desk.
Also: two small straw stools; an armchair with cushions; two additional armchairs; a screen, breast high, with six folds.

D. The king's study.
12. Stove.
Also: a cane chair; a straw chair; a stool.

E. Cléry's room.
13. His bed.
14. A chest of drawers.
15. An oak cupboard.
Also: an armchair and four additional chairs.

F. The dining room.
16. The table where the king took his meals.
17. A small table.

G. Wardrobe and storage area.

H. Storage area for wood.

posts. It was impossible to get from floor to floor without passing through these checkpoints, which were constantly manned. Each of the floors of the tower was protected by two doors, one of oak studded with nails, the other of iron. The Commune had made a good choice, for the Templars had been a military order and knew how to protect themselves.

The king's quarters had a false ceiling, and the stone walls had been plastered over. They were covered with some handpainted wallpaper depicting the inside of a prison. Also painted on the wall, in large letters, was the text of the Declaration of the Rights of Man and Citizen, the statement of revolutionary principles published in 1789. The furniture, such as it was, had all been borrowed from the Temple itself. It consisted of a dresser, a small desk, four covered chairs, an armchair, some cane-bottomed chairs, a table, a mirror above the fireplace, and a bed covered in green damask. The guards lived in the tower itself when on duty. The first floor had been converted into a guardroom with some sleeping quarters, but there was no kitchen in the tower so meals were prepared in the Temple and carried across the garden to the tower. The entire château was surrounded by a wall and masons were at work strengthening it. Since ascending the throne Louis had not lived in a place that bore the stamp of his personality. His passions were hunting and locksmithing, not building.

The king's imprisonment falls into two distinct periods which reflect the course of the Revolution after August 10. From the fall of the monarchy to the sitting of the Convention he was relatively comfortable, since some attempt was made to simulate the luxury befitting a French king. The Legislative had approved a generous allowance of 500,000 livres to support the royal family and their servants and companions, who included Madame Elisabeth, who voluntarily accompanied her brother to prison, Madame de Lamballe, Madame de Tourzel and her daughter, the king's valet, a couple of people to help with the housecleaning, and a kitchen staff of thirteen (a chef, an assistant chef, and eleven cooks). In addition, Mayor Pétion was generous in approving the king's requests. During this first phase of his imprisonment the purveyors of luxuries to the court continued to have easy access to their royal patrons.

But even before the sitting of the Convention, at which time the Commune tightened up all regulations, life in the Temple was far from luxurious. The king's bed, little more than a cot, had been the bed of the captain of the guard when the Count d'Artois was in residence, and the prisoners were continually under surveillance. The guards were handpicked patriots from the sections of Paris, and they were instructed to behave toward Louis and his family with the dignity, or insolence, of free men. Section Poissonière complained to the General Council of the Commune, which was in charge of the royal prisoners, about a guard who had "dishonored his character" by doing up a button on Louis's breeches. They called for the dismissal of this man who forgot that he was a citizen and not a lackey.

No man in France sat for his portrait more often than Louis XVI. Relatively few images of the king's mind exist. He was not an intellectual, and hence his written utterances are more expressions of his exalted position than of his personality; but the images of his face, from almost every period of his life, are abundant. Most of these portraits are formal, the work of court artists whose commission was not to depict the man but rather the king, and Louis looks out at us with the arrogance and serene self-confidence of the most powerful monarch in Europe. Madame Campan, who had ample opportunity to see the king at Versailles, said he had fairly noble features which were usually marked by signs of melancholy. But royal melancholy was not thought a fit subject for the painters. Louis appears most often, whether in his robes of state or merely in a simple coat, as the untroubled king of France. He was a large man, heavyset, and gave the impression of being a prisoner of his lethargic body. Men were surprised when he showed bursts of physical energy, walking with a spring in his step or acting impulsively. His features are common to the Bourbons, but in Louis the deep blue eyes of his family lack fire, the large sensuous mouth seems perpetually on the verge of a smirk, the high forehead, sloping backward, like his rather weak chin, gives the face its roundness but no strength. His large nose, usually depicted in three-quarter profile to minimize its size, is his dominant feature. It is a plump face in which the features are homogenized. Even as

THE ROYAL FAMILY IN THE TEMPLE GARDEN, 1792. An engraving by LeBeau, after Desrais. Louis, with one hand extended and the other on his hip, appears to be speaking to his guards. Marie-Antoinette and Madame Elisabeth, along with Madame Royale and the dauphin, are to the right of the scene. The other members of the party are guards. The tower of the Temple, in the foreground, is out of perspective but it is possible to see the large and small towers which made up the old *donjon*. When the royal prisoners were brought to the Temple they lived on the third floor; the king's new apartment, readied soon afterwards, was on the second floor. The château itself, again out of perspective, is in the background. The walls surrounding the entire place cannot be seen here. *Collection Hennin, Bibliothèque nationale*

LOUIS AGONISTES. Pastel of Louis XVI by Joseph Ducreux, done during the last weeks of the king's life. This is the last portrait of Louis. The simplicity of his dress and hair, not to mention the haunting expression captured by Ducreux, are in sharp contrast to earlier portraits, when the king was in his glory. *Carnavalet Museum, Paris*

a young man Louis had a double chin and his ears seem too large. He usually wore his own hair, although it was carefully curled and powdered. It is not a face that sticks in the mind. But in his portraits as in his life adversity created character.

A few days before his execution the king's portrait was done by Ducreux. It is a haunting face, a face filled with sadness. Ducreux's Louis shows us a face that has been lived in. The impression made by the earlier portraits of roundness, smoothness, plumpness is here replaced by the melancholy deliberately avoided by the court painters. His eyes are deepset, accentuated by heavy lids and prominent lines. He looks out directly at the viewer but the focus of his eyes is somewhere in the distance. The sensual mouth is no longer curled at the corners into the slightest hint of a smile. The lips are slightly parted and the lower lip droops a bit. His dimples, obvious in the earlier portraits, are gone, replaced by deeply-etched lines around the mouth. The artist has not sought an angle that will disguise the king's large nose and its prominent hook is evident. He is still double-chinned, but having lost some weight in prison this part of his face appears more articulated. He is wearing his own hair and a simple coat, with none of the elaborate insignia of kingship.

Ironically enough this last, touching portrait of the king is more faithful to the soul of its subject than the portraits done in happier days. For Louis XVI the kingship was not an elaborate theatrical representation. He was a less deliberately dramatic character than Louis XIV, his great-great-great grandfather; less fascinating than the sensual and sometimes brilliant Louis XV, his grandfather. His personality had little variation. He could not adjust the level of monarchical dignity to fit the occasion. In a word, he lacked the instincts of court life, the ability to function easily and gracefully in an artificial world filled with pomp and hypocrisy, a world that revolved, elegantly to be sure, around the person of the king. It is as if Louis were basically uncomfortable as king, yet he did have the gift of making himself liked through his seriousness and simplicity, and his personal habits won respect even from the most seasoned and cynical courtiers.

While clearly a man of his age, many of the tastes and inclinations of the French aristocracy in its heyday of extravagance, self-

indulgence, and elegance, had little hold on Louis. He was chaste
and even a bit prudish, devoted to his family and children. Refinement and the sophisticated cultivation of decadence were no
part of his character. The walls of his quarters in the Temple were
decorated with a curious blend of revolutionary symbols side by
side with the *ancien régime*'s banal and titillating versions of the
Greek myths. When Hué, one of his valets, first saw the wall decorations he remarked to his master on their indecency. Louis was
indifferent to such refined sensuality, but told Hué: "I wouldn't
want my daughter to see such things."

The hundreds of anecdotes about Louis reveal a man with unexpected qualities for a French king. Théodore de Lameth, for example, reports a story about Louis as king. Lameth was never an
intimate of the king but he saw him often. One day, after a hunt,
Lameth was invited to dine. After dinner Louis invited his guest to
join him in a game of billiards. Lameth accepted. As they were
walking to the billiard room Louis said: "We won't play for high
stakes. I don't play for more than an *ecu*." "Your Majesty," said
Lameth with the irony of an experienced courtier, "doesn't want
to ruin himself." Louis missed the wit and replied with feeling:
"When you gamble it is with your own money. I risk everyone's
money." The episode caused Lameth to reflect, as it caused many
another man to reflect, on Louis's character: he did not have the
familiar vices associated with a Bourbon king of France. The court,
and later the revolutionaries, were continually surprised by Louis.
To the former he seemed not a proper king. His virtues were palpable but somehow misplaced in a king. To the latter his admirable
personal qualities were a bit of an embarrassment. Jacques Necker,
the finance minister at the outbreak of the Revolution and never a
favorite of the king, wrote, with a sense of wonder and admiration,

> that I have never seen, that I have never discovered in this monarch, so
> cruelly treated, a single spontaneous movement, a single thought de-
> riving from him alone without outside influence, springing immediately
> from his soul, which would not manifest to careful observers his desire
> for good, his compassion for the people and his naturally soft and
> moderate character.

Lazare Carnot, a Montagnard deputy and the organizational genius who conceived and executed France's military recovery dur-

ing the Revolution, summed up Louis with an aphorism: "The best
has paid for the worst. Bad causes have their martyrs just like good
ones." Barbaroux, who had fought Louis at the Tuileries on August 10, thought it a piece of luck for the revolutionaries that they
had to deal with an unwarlike king, a characteristic that perplexed
the men of the nineteenth century. As Sainte-Beuve, the great critic, wrote, all the disasters of Louis's reign might have been avoided
had he only remembered "that he was the last king of a military
race."

Louis was an avid reader, perhaps the best-read of all French
kings, and his months of imprisonment only confirmed Necker's
testimony: "It is always the great works of history, of moral philosophy and of politics, written in French or in English, that I have
seen the king occupy himself with, with taste and diligence." The
minds a man chooses to understand often tell us more about him
than the objects with which he surrounds himself. Louis was fond
of the classics, as were all educated men of his age, and he seems
to have known the works of Cicero and Horace, and the Roman
historians, with some intimacy. Among French authors he had a
particular affection for Racine and Corneille, the great tragedians
of the seventeenth century, and Montesquieu, the eloquent creator
of an aristocratic ideology. He had much less affection for the more
liberal *philosophes*. Neither Voltaire's wavering skepticism nor
Rousseau's radical effusions interested Louis, nor for that matter
did the encyclopedists. One day, according to Hué, the royal prisoner pointed to a bookcase stuffed with the works of Voltaire and
Rousseau: "These two men have destroyed France." The king
shared the views of the Church on much contemporary French
literature. The only other French *philosophe* Louis enjoyed reading
was Buffon, the author of a *Natural History* in many volumes. For
the rest he preferred the Latin authors, sacred and profane, ancient
and modern. In prison he spent four hours a day reading in Latin.
Thomas à Kempis' *Imitation of Christ*, a classic of religious literature, was a constant companion. He also liked travel literature and
books on geography.

On November 21, as he was recovering from illness, Louis sent
the General Council a list of books he wanted. There were thirty-
three titles, most of them in Latin, and he wanted specific editions.

The list included most of the Roman historians, plus Virgil, Terence, and Ovid. He also requested La Fontaine's *Fables*, a Latin
grammar, a French grammar, Bishop Bossuet's *Maxims*, a Latin
version of Phaedrus' *Fables*, Messang's *Lives of the Saints*, and a
French translation of Virgil annotated by Burrett. The cost of the
books would be a little more than 180 livres, a royal sum indeed.
The General Council considered the list. Some members wanted
the books immediately bought and sent to the Temple, the titles
were harmless enough, they argued, and would relieve boredom.
The more cynical members of the Council argued that Louis "had
hardly two weeks of existence" left (an exaggeration) and the requested books were enough to occupy a man for years. The rest of
the discussion focussed on the nature of the books themselves. If
they were destined for the education of the dauphin, some said,
censorship should be exercised: the Latin books would be unintel-
ligible to the boy, while Ovid taught a morality antithetical to republican virtue. Martin, a Council member, wanted to substitute
books with a radical bias, books that would inculcate revolutionary
principles. This patriotic proposal was rejected by the Council and
the books were sent to the Temple.

Louis's taste in literature was conventional although he conspicuously avoided many works thought essential by the men of his
generation. He asked for no Bayle, no Diderot, no Voltaire, no
Rousseau. He asked for no Mably and no novels or romances. He
asked for no Helvétius, no Turgot. In a word, he asked for none
of the works of the critics of the *ancien régime*. He had some interest in scholarship; but again only that scholarship, such as the
notes to a classical text, which implied no criticism of the world he
had grown up in and continued to revere. His taste ran to the
moralists, whether in French, English, Italian, or Latin, for he read
these languages with relative ease. During his imprisonment, for
example, he was reading David Hume's *History of England*—not
unexpectedly, the volume on the early Stuart kings—in English,
and Tasso in Italian. With the single exception of Ovid, whose
unabashed sensualism was always a problem for the Church as
beneficiary of the classical heritage, Louis avoided the poets of
sexual love as he avoided the republican moralists. He had a taste
for epic poetry, but except for his intense interest in Thomas à

Kempis he totally neglected the literature of the Middle Ages, once again conforming to the accepted tastes of his day. History, foreign languages and their structure, and geography dominated Louis's intellectual makeup: the three disciplines in which memory and diligent application are most important, the three disciplines held in contempt by the social critics of the Enlightenment as exercising the least refined and elevated capacities of the mind. Louis's mind had been formed not by the social and cultural critics, the *philosophes*, but by the Jesuits, his teachers. Here again he was separated from his subjects, from those men who would try him, many if not most of whom had rejected this conservative and religious tradition.

Louis's piety and devotional readings were regular and took up a fixed part of his day. Throughout his imprisonment he was forbidden to have a priest in the Temple and no mass was said there during his captivity: a frightful deprivation for a devout Catholic. Louis looked after the needs of his soul as best he could. Each morning he read the office of the Chevaliers of the Holy Spirit, and he had ordered his valet, Cléry, to get him a copy of the breviary used in the Paris diocese. Deprived of the ritualistic comforts of his religion, Louis diligently observed all the special days in the liturgical calendar. On December 21, for example, he refused breakfast because it was the Quatre-Temps, one of the four periods of the liturgical year, at the beginning of each season, marked by three days of fasting and prayer. He began and ended each day with prayer and conscientiously supervised the prayers of his children. Louis made a point of listening to his son's prayers almost every night. He himself had written the prayer which he had the boy memorize:

> God all powerful, who created and redeemed me, I adore you. Conserve the days of the king my father and of those of my family. Protect us against our enemies. Give Madame de Tourzel the strength necessary to endure the evil she suffers because of us.

To those closest to him, like Cléry, Louis's devotions were evidence of his "pure and enlightened" religion. For those less devoted to the king his prayers were dismissed as "jesuitical principles" that reenforced his narrow views. But Jesuit-inspired or not, Louis's piety was sincere and profound. He had never cultivated the sentimental devotions so dear to his sister, who was anxious to surround herself with priests noted for their piety coupled with good manners. Louis disliked priestly courtiers as much as he disliked their secular counterparts. His religion needed no public dimension, no certification of authenticity. He was punctilious in his devotions and attention to ritualistic detail but he never called attention to his worship. He loved, in a direct and uncomplicated way, the familiar observations of his faith. He was not particularly superstitious, as are so many who might share his need for regular observances. No priest of his kingdom could have said of Louis what Bishop Bossuet had said of Louis XIV: that his was the Christianity of a charcoal-burner (thought to be the most ignorant Christians in the kingdom). Yet Louis often had difficulty in separating the sacred and profane words. Despite two generations of attack by the *philosophes* Louis continued to believe that God's Providence was palpable in the world, that he, Louis, had been chosen as the vessel of a divine scheme, and that the world was shot through with God's presence. In his last months Louis regularly nourished his faith, caring for his soul with the same concern he showed in nourishing his mind.

Louis believed himself king by the grace of God. His mission in life resembled a ministry and he believed the care of twenty million French souls had been entrusted to him by God. The language of religion was familiar and comforting, and when he wanted to express a state of mind or a feeling of particular importance he instinctively resorted to biblical language and references. His was a mind that made little sense to his contemporaries who tended to dismiss his piety as mere posturing or sophistry. Principles, for the revolutionaries, could not exist in Christianity, which they considered the historical repository of superstition. Yet Louis's politics were derived from his religious beliefs. Basically the king despised politics, now a fatal taste in a monarch. At the beginning of the Revolution he had refused to follow the advice of Mirabeau, whom he thought devious and perhaps un-Christian. His own political ideas were few, by his own lights straightforward, and stubbornly held. Raised in the traditions of French absolutism, Louis never questioned the basic assumptions he lived by. He did not so much despise the revolutionaries—an emotion he reserved for men of his own class who had deserted their traditions—as find them incomprehensible. That they thought him a tyrant, for example, was beyond his ability to understand. "Me a tyrant," he indignantly told Malesherbes, "a tyrant does everything for himself. Have I not constantly done everything for my people? Who among them has ever hated tyranny more than me? They call me tyrant and they know as well as you what I am." Louis considered himself motived by decency, by devotion to his subjects, by the humility incumbent on a Christian. He had read Tacitus—he was reading the Roman historian during the trial—and he knew he did not fit Tacitus' classical description of a tyrant. He had learned, from his Jesuit tutors, that wicked deeds could only spring from wicked intentions, that even apparent wickedness was often no more than misdirected goodness of intention. Besides, even the wicked could be saved by God's grace if they recognized the way of their errors. Louis was willing to admit he had made errors of judgment as king, but to his mind he had done so only out of love for his people. He had done nothing that might be construed as done for personal gain; egomania was no part of his personality. His resistance to the Revolution sprang, he believed, from his devotion to his divinely ordained magistracy, a heavy obligation that compelled him to stand stubbornly for what he believed in while most of the men around him succumbed to personal ambition or expediency. It was God's will that he had been chosen to sit on the throne. It was God's will that France be a monarchy. And justice, like vengeance, must be God's alone.

Louis wrote his will on December 25, the same day he completed his defense. It is difficult to know which of the two he considered more important. His last testament is a profoundly Christian document, a declaration of faith, a summing up of his moral life. Louis asked God's forgiveness for whatever personal sins he may have committed, he asked forgiveness for any mistakes he may have made as king. Royalist ideology was so far decayed in 1792 that only the shell of what had once been a vital organism remained. Still, the king was at least as concerned with commending his soul to God as he was with defending himself before his subjects in rebellion. The testament carefully details the sincerity of his faith and his constant attachment to the Church, even at the risk of personal inconvenience or even danger. He reaffirms his acceptance of the Church's authority and hierarchy and asks forgiveness for anything he may have done to compromise the Church. He prays God to receive his confession "and above all, the profound repentance that I had to put my name . . . to acts that could be contrary to the discipline and the belief of the Catholic Church to which I have always remained sincerely attached at heart." There is no self-pity in the testament: "I pardon with all my heart those who have made themselves my enemies, although I have given them no reason to be, and I pray God to pardon them, just as those who through a false zeal or a mistaken zeal have done me a great deal of harm." He then goes on to pray for his family:

> I recommend to my son, if he has the unhappy fate of becoming king, to think that he owes himself completely to the happiness of his fellow citizens; that he must forget all hatred or resentment, and especially everything that has to do with the misfortunes and afflictions that I have suffered.

This touching bit of advice (it is interesting that the king wrote "citizens" rather than "subjects") was then modified in the will by an assertion of the need for royal authority. The happiness of the people, the king writes, could only be assured by a monarch "reigning according to the laws," and a government in which the king is made powerless renders the king "more harmful than useful."

In the spirit of noblesse oblige Louis goes on to make what provisions he can for his friends and servants. He begs the authorities not to punish those who have served him faithfully. He specifies some personal effects to be given to Cléry, and he even forgives the guards at the Temple for "the harsh treatment and insults which they believed it their duty to use towards us." He thanks his lawyers for their services and concludes his testament with a declaration of innocence: "I close by declaring before God, before whom I am about to appear, that I do not reproach myself for any of the crimes alleged against me."

There was little self-delusion in Louis and little arrogance. His ambitions reached no higher than his capacities, which were limited. He had never pursued glory in war, nor had he erected lavish monuments to himself in peace. He was weak and wielded absolute power with the pusillanimity of an indecisive man, but he was not driven by the usual demons who seem to pursue absolute kings. Louis did love the people more than he loved the crown: this was his political and personal tragedy. He was a good man, a loving husband, a devoted father, a sincere Christian, a conscientious king, a loyal patron, and an incompetent prince.

Louis's days in the Temple were regular and simple. All his life he had been a prisoner of habit: confinement did not disrupt his orderly life. Freed of the numerous distractions and duties of the court the king, who had never much liked being a part of a public and contrived monarchy, fell gratefully into the routines forced on him by imprisonment. He awoke at 6:00 A.M., shaved himself—an idiosyncrasy that surprised his servants—and had Jean-Baptiste Cléry, his valet in prison, dress his hair. He then retired to the corner tower that served as his study to read and pray. The door connecting the study with the bedroom was kept open by order of the Commune so that Louis would be always in the sight of a guard. Kneeling on a small cushion the captive king began his day with several minutes of prayer. Then he read until 9:00. During this reading period Cléry made up the bed, set the table for breakfast, and descended to the second floor where the rest of the royal family was confined. Marie-Antoinette would open her door to no one but Cléry, and her undisguised contempt for the guards offended several of her keepers. The haughtiness that had alienated many of her subjects continued to isolate the queen. When Cléry arrived he would bathe the dauphin, do the queen's hair, and assist Madame Elisabeth and Madame Royale with their coiffure. Promptly at 9:00 the family mounted to Louis's apartment for breakfast, which Cléry served. While the royal family ate, Cléry, assisted by a certain Tison and his wife, would descend to the queen's apartment and make up the beds.

Breakfast was ample, consisting of coffee, chocolate, fruits, and dairy products. The talk around the table was "affectionate" and the first meal of the day always began with the domestic ritual of the entire family embracing and kissing the king. When breakfast was finished around 10:00, the family assembled in the queen's apartment, where they spent the day. Louis occupied himself with the dauphin's education. In preparation for these lessons Louis brushed up on his Latin by translating the *Odes* of Horace, parsing some Cicero, and rereading Corneille and Racine, his favorite poets. The boy was made to recite passages from Corneille and Racine which Louis thought particularly appropriate or particularly impressive. This was followed by the dauphin's geography lesson. The king, on the testimony of his enemies, was "the best geographer of his kingdom." This was perhaps an exaggeration, but since the death of Bourguignon d'Anville, the greatest French geographer of the century, Louis may well have been the most learned amateur of the subject in France. Louis used a map of revolutionary France, with its political divisions of eighty-three departments and with many of the traditional names of places altered in an attempt to obliterate the Catholic and royalist past. Covering parts of the map with a piece of paper, he drilled his son on the names of the new departments, the districts, the cities, the courses of rivers, and the physical and political geography of the kingdom. He thought such knowledge important to a king and seems to have deliberately given the boy an education that would serve him well when he came to sit on the throne. He may have been putting on a bold front, but he refused to accept that the monarchy was in mortal danger.

While Louis gave geography lessons Marie-Antoinette instructed her daughter in the domestic arts. In keeping with the customs of the day the royal couple neglected their daughter's intellectual training. The royal school lasted until 11:00 A.M. The rest of the morning was passed in sewing, knitting, or needlepointing while the king read or chatted with his family. At noon the three women retired to Madame Elisabeth's room to change; they were not accompanied by a guard. At 1:00, if the weather was good, the family was permitted to walk in the garden. Accompanied by guards they descended the stairs, passing successively through the seven checkpoints. The guards ostentatiously presented arms to their colleagues and just as ostentatiously reversed arms when the king and queen passed. Madame Elisabeth, Marie-Antoinette, and the faithful Cléry were offended by this deliberate snub. The king showed no signs that he was upset.

During their promenade the royal prisoners were accompanied

by four municipal officers regularly stationed at the Temple, and an officer of the National Guard. Sometimes Cléry was allowed to join the walks and he would play with the children, rolling a hoop with Madame Royale, tossing a ball with the dauphin. At 2:00 the prisoners were returned to the tower for lunch, again served by Cléry. The food was consistently ample and carefully prepared, if the testimony of the guards is reliable, since they tasted each dish, each wine, before Cléry was permitted to carry it to the king. Louis's taste ran to rich food and, except for a dessert carafe of Madeira, light wines. A typical prison lunch was a brioche, a pâté, and a half bottle of modest, unsparkling wine from the Champagne district, followed by Louis's customary carafe of Madeira. Hardly a frugal meal and not especially healthy, but certainly more modest than the meals the king had indulged in while at Versailles, and nothing like the trencherman prodigies reported of Louis XIV. The king, who had acquired the not undeserved reputation of overindulgence, seemed content with the simple meals prepared for him in prison. He always ate heartily, his appetite unimpaired by his circumstances or surroundings. He also slept soundly, almost like a child passing through life thoroughly enjoying the animal pleasures.

While the prisoners were lunching, Santerre, commander of the Paris National Guard, visited each of the rooms in the tower on his official inspection tour. Sometimes the king spoke to him. Marie-Antoinette refused to say a word to the former brewer. After lunch the prisoners again went to the queen's apartment, where Louis often played cards with his wife. At 4:00 Louis took his afternoon nap, with his family around him. When he woke up he usually initiated conversation and frequently invited Cléry to sit next to him. While Louis looked on Cléry instructed the dauphin in penmanship. Cléry would copy out passages selected by the king from "the works of Montesquieu and other famous writers" as models of elegant French, which the boy would copy in a notebook, learning style and script at once. After his lesson Cléry took the boy into Madame Elisabeth's room, where they played with a ball or a shuttlecock.

In the afternoon and early evening the royal prisoners sat around a table in the queen's apartment while Marie-Antoinette read aloud, usually some work of history chosen by Louis, but sometimes a work "designed to instruct and amuse the children" while encouraging melancholy reflections on their present circumstances. The entire family would join in these sad reflections, often shedding tears over their fate. When Madame Elisabeth did the reading she chose devotional works. Reading aloud lasted until 8:00 P.M., when Cléry served the dauphin's dinner as the family looked on and kept the boy company. Afterward Louis played briefly with his two children, posing riddles to them from a book he had found in the tower's library. Then Cléry undressed the boy, and Louis or Marie-Antoinette, and sometimes both, listened to his prayers. Then Cléry put the boy to bed, and when he returned he passed on to the king whatever news of the outside world he had gleaned from the guards or the public crier.

The king dined at 9:00 while the queen and Madame Elisabeth took turns sitting with the dauphin. This was the only time during the day that Cléry was able to talk to his master without witnesses. After dinner Louis went briefly to his wife's apartment to bid her goodnight, then returned to his own apartment and read until midnight. Once Louis had returned to his quarters the prisoners were forbidden to visit each other. Cléry fetched the king's cot out of the storage room and set it up for the night. Louis, who disliked the slightest change in his routine, would not go to bed before the guard was changed at midnight. If he did not know his guard by sight he sent Cléry to find out his name and some personal details.

By almost any standards other than those of royalty, the king's imprisonment was not harsh. Every day in Paris thousands of prisoners suffered more discomfort and harsh treatment than the king was forced to endure. But if the king was not subjected to physical deprivations, his imprisonment was punctuated by a series of petty insults and annoyances coupled to a policy of icy politeness. The guards at the Temple served forty-eight hours at a time, half on duty and half off, but during this period they were not permitted to leave the Temple. They were specifically instructed not to let the prisoners out of their sight, always to wear a hat in the king's presence, to sit down whenever they wanted to, to speak to the prisoners only when directly questioned, to tell them nothing of what was happening outside the Temple, and to address them only as "Monsieur" and "Madame," neither republican nor royalist. These regulations, all designed to remind the captives that they were no longer the rulers of France, troubled Marie-Antoinette more than the king. Most of the guards were considerate, but it was easy for a zealous republican to consider bad manners and insults a form of patriotism, and a few such men enjoyed showing their contempt for the royal family. An officer named James once followed Louis into his reading alcove, sat down next to the king, and refused to leave. Louis was forced to give up his reading for the day. Le Clerc, another guard, one day interrupted the dauphin's writing lesson by launching into a diatribe on how the boy should be given a revolutionary education. Simon, another guard, delighted in being rude and insolent to the king. Madame Royale, the only one of the royal prisoners to survive the Revolution, later complained bitterly in her memoirs of prison life about the guards who had "little respect for the king." Some of their behavior was downright silly but nevertheless offensive. The guards stopped the arithmetic lessons Madame Elisabeth gave the dauphin, insisting he was being taught a numerical code. The queen's needlepoint was not allowed out of the Temple for fear that she had embroidered messages in the work. In general, however, largely due to the king's efforts, the relationships forced on everyone at the Temple were polite. Many of the guards found the royal family "affable, simple and even gay," and the king went out of his way to learn the names, the state in society, the manners, even the places of residence of his guards. Louis, through years of practice, had learned the art of being gracious to his servants.

There were, of course, serious problems and even dangerous moments during the months of Louis's captivity which made petty acts of incivility trifling annoyances. On September 3, the second day of the September Massacres, the royal prisoners had a nightmarish few hours. They came very close to being butchered themselves. There were too few guards at the Temple to protect them from the bloodthirsty crowds roaming the streets. The best they could do was to string a tricolor ribbon across the entrance to the château and hope the crowds would respect it. The royal family was playing cards in Marie-Antoinette's apartment when a head stuck on the end of a pike was thrust at the casement window.

The head was that of the queen's friend and confidante Madame de Lamballe, and her blonde curls floated in the air grotesquely as the pike was waved. The queen fainted. The king, once again courageous in the face of personal danger, had her carried to another room and he alone faced the frenzied soldier who burst into the apartment, sword in hand. Louis berated him, then dismissed him. The ingrained habits of command and obedience probably saved Louis and his family.

The Commune, concerned about security at the Temple and groping its way toward rules and regulations, was disturbed at the crowds that gathered nightly outside the walls of the Temple. The imprisoned king had become one of the sights to see in revolutionary Paris. During the day Parisians lingered at the gates hoping to catch a glimpse of Louis and his family walking in the garden. At night the gatherings were more numerous and potentially dangerous. Sometimes as many as four hundred people were reported at the gates. Some played airs on the flute, some gave what the guards took to be signals, and cries of *Vive le roi!* were heard. The *Annales patriotiques* reported, a bit prematurely, that "the family imprisoned in the Temple has fallen into so profound a scorn that it inspires not even the interest of curiosity." Still the crowds continued to gather; the Commune tightened security.

On September 26 the General Council forbade Louis to wear his medals and decorations and discussed curtailing his walks in the garden. Three days later they decided to move him to more secure quarters in the tower. The new apartment was not yet finished. It still reeked of paint, which made it almost uninhabitable, and the new quarters were more austere and cramped than his original apartment. There was no room for Cléry to set up his cot and he was ordered to sleep in another part of the tower. Only with the greatest difficulty, and it must have been humiliating even to ask, did Louis persuade his captors to let Cléry stay with him at night. The General Council was not content merely to curtail Louis's freedom of movement; it became obsessed with the idea that Louis would cheat the guillotine by taking his own life. With the usual insensitivity of authority the Council disregarded the king's deep attachment to his religion, which made suicide impossible. The Council confiscated all weapons, even the king's ceremonial sword, along with all pens, ink, and paper. The prisoner, addicted to daily reading, had to borrow a knife from his guards to cut the pages of his books. Even Marie-Antoinette's sewing scissors were confiscated. And the king was forbidden to shave himself.

Louis responded to these orders with his usual combination of dignity, courage, and stubbornness. When he was deprived of razors he went on strike, letting his beard grow. He refused to be shaved by anyone else. By the last weeks of December the exasperated guards decided to forward the king's repeated requests for razors to the General Council. The next day the Council gave in. Louis would be allowed to shave himself, but only in the presence of four guards. The razors were delivered each morning by four guards and immediately taken away when Louis was finished with them. The king's morning shave had taken on the ritualistic dimensions of Louis XIV's *levée*, when select members of the court had been permitted to gather in the royal bedroom and assist the Sun King in his ablutions.

The question of razors was minor compared to the other harassments of the General Council. On November 27 the Temple guards reported that the dauphin was being heavily influenced by his mother and ought to be taken out of her care: "This child is of the age that he ought to be in the company of men." The Council agreed and the next day, when the discussion of the dauphin was on the agenda, the question of his upbringing and the supposed extravagances at the Temple were lumped together. Coulombeau, a Council member, insisted that all the servants be dismissed except for Cléry and a single cook. The Council decided to reduce the staff drastically, but also decided that the boy could, for the moment, remain with his mother. On December 11 the Council again considered the question of the dauphin, a question they never resolved until the boy died in prison, probably as a result of the general neglect of his captors. For now, they decided that the king would be separated from his family. The Convention thought this measure unnecessarily strict and suggested a compromise: Louis could see his children, but they in turn could not see their mother until after December 26 when the king was scheduled to appear before the Convention. Throughout Louis's imprisonment the Convention proved itself milder than the General Council, but the

Convention did not make the rules governing the prisoners. Louis again went on strike and refused to cooperate:

> Whatever pleasure I might have had in seeing my children and enjoying the option given to me by the present decree, it is impossible for me to accept it. The business that takes up my whole day [he was preparing his defense] would not permit me to spend time with my son; and as for my daughter, she should not leave her mother.

About to be deprived of his only comfort and pleasure in prison, the company of his family, Louis threw himself passionately into more reading and prayers while he worked on his defense. He refused to walk in the garden, his only form of exercise in prison: "I cannot bring myself to walk alone." Increasingly he sought solace in religion.

Gradually imprisonment undermined the king's health, both emotional and physical. On November 15 he fell ill. From the reported symptoms—a high fever, sweating, loss of appetite (a serious matter with Louis), a running nose, and a sore throat—it seems to have been some kind of flu. As rumors of the king's illness trickled out of the Temple there was talk in Paris that the king was dead or dying, that he would, in fact, cheat the guillotine. To dispel these rumors the Commune ordered daily health bulletins sent to the General Council and many of them published in the press. Before the Revolution the king's health had been a matter of national concern. The prayers of a nation were devoted to its king at Versailles, and the announcement that the royal patient had recovered was greeted with joy and the ringing of church bells. Once again the king had become the subject of a national vigil; but the prayers for his recovery were either private, clandestine, or sprang from macabre hopes that he would live to be executed. On November 23 Louis's private doctor, LeMonnier, summoned out of semiretirement, reported his patient much improved. The king would live to be judged.

In the course of his imprisonment we get a glimpse of the man Louis might have been had fate not made him king; we get a glimpse, in addition, of his considerable capacities for personal popularity. In many ways Mirabeau's dream of a patriot king deriving his power from the love of his subjects, was not so far-

fetched. In adversity Louis proved himself an attractive, even admirable character. In many ways these months in prison reveal a
man who might have been, under other circumstances, a bourgeois king, who might have been what King Louis Philippe aspired
to be in the next century. In prison Louis was a model of bourgeois
rectitude: a pious man, a devoted husband and father, a decent
man. And the newspapers of the day were full of the mundane
details of his life, broadcasting to the nation a more favorable picture of the king than any it had seen when he was at Versailles.
These stories and anecdotes endeared Louis to many of his former
subjects. For the first time in his reign he was interesting not only
because he was king. The Commune and the Convention wanted
to demystify the monarchy and the monarch. They were successful, but only partly successful. In stripping Louis of his powers, his
court, even his sword and medals, they revealed not that the king
had no clothes, but that his natural dignity did not need elaborate
costumes, a proper theatrical setting, and hundreds of fawning
courtiers to be impressive.

Adversity rendered Louis not so much a popular figure, it was
too late for that, but at least a sympathetic character. While the deputies in the Convention contemptuously spoke of him as Louis the
Last or Louis the Traitor, while they sought to present a bloodless
abstraction of deceit and arrogance, superstition and irresponsibility, the people were hearing stories of Louis *en famille*, of his love
for his children, his concern for his wife and sister, his personal
devotions. The regicides were fairly successful in keeping Louis
the man out of the trial. They were less successful in controlling
public opinion. The touching tragedy of a fallen king, the very stuff
of classical and neoclassical tragic drama, was now more than a
literary convention, more than a fiction. The spectacle of a king
laid low still had the power to move men's hearts. The General
Council was sufficiently concerned to ask the newspapers, in December, to stop reporting details that might win sympathy for the
prisoners. But the Revolution had a free press, and editors gave
their readers what they thought they wanted to hear.

The more radical newspapers tried to neutralize the growing
concern for the king by preaching the virtues of harsh justice. "Citizens," wrote Prudhomme, "the place for Louis-Nero and Medici-

Antoinette is not in the tower of the Temple. The very evening of August 10 their heads should have fallen under the guillotine." And just to drive the point home, such newspapers regularly reminded readers of the inherent evils of monarchy and just as regularly described the luxury of the royal table and the size of the king's staff while Paris was forced to live on short supplies.

Louis himself resolutely refused to exploit his situation, just as he had, years earlier, rejected Mirabeau's advice. His subjects might bring him to justice since they had the power to do so, but he believed his fate lay in God's hands. He was determined to live out the role of king as he saw it or, as he himself put it, resorting to the language of religion: "I shall drink the cup to its dregs."

THE KING'S FIRST INTERROGATION, DECEM-
BER 11, 1792. An anonymous engraving that first appeared in the *Révolutions de Paris* for December 8–15, 1792.
Louis is accompanied by the mayor, the *procureur* of the
Commune, and, probably, Santerre. The oversized king,
drawn out of perspective to catch the eye, is receiving the
individual pieces of evidence against him from Valazé,
who refused to face the king when performing this task.
The president, on the high dais, is Barère. There are a
number of curiosities in the engraving: Louis is standing
at the secretaries' table, not at the Convention's bar; the
ceiling, which was slightly vaulted, is here depicted as
flat; the windows are not evident. The moment captured by the artist is after Louis has heard the accusation
and responded; he is now being asked to identify the
pieces of evidence. *Collection de Vinck, Bibliothèque
nationale*

CHAPTER V

The Accusation

THE MANÈGE, DECEMBER 10–11, 1792

ESPITE THE weeks and weeks of debate on legal procedures, despite the recommendations of the Mailhe and Valazé committees, the Convention had not decided on exactly how it would try the king. Without precedents, with every issue in the trial hopelessly enmeshed in the factional struggles of Jacobins and Girondins, surrounded by a restless urban population and almost daily bombarded in the press and in petitions with calls for the king's head, the Convention improvised as best it could. And these improvisations took the form of finding some compromise solution that all the deputies could live with. The constitutional argument had been rejected in order to bring Louis to trial, and there were a number of deputies who were distressed by the Convention's willingness to accept Mailhe's clever suggestion that constitutional inviolability was a gift of the people as sovereign and could be taken away. But the constitutional issue proved less bothersome than the questions of procedure. Long before the trial several influential deputies had spoken publicly against royal inviolability, among them Pétion, Buzot, Robespierre, Collot d'Herbois, Condorcet, and Grégoire. It seems that the factional leaders were not troubled on this point. But in an assembly where every other man was a lawyer or familiar with the law it was difficult to find new procedures that were familiar. The Criminal Code of 1791, one of the important pieces of revolutionary reform, was very specific. The Code was drawn up in reaction to the arbitrary justice meted

out by French kings. It was designed to prevent such abuses of procedure, and hence justice, in the future.

The Code said that an accused could be prosecuted for a crime only after indictment by a jury of accusation impaneled for that purpose. In the English-speaking world the jury of accusation is equivalent to a grand jury. This jury of accusation would examine the evidence, and there were strict regulations about how that evidence was collected, call witnesses if necessary, and decide whether or not there was a case for a trial. Then the accused would appear before a criminal tribunal whose personnel was different than the jury of accusation. Before an indictment was delivered by the jury of accusation the defendant was entitled to have one or two lawyers; and once the indictment was brought in the accused had to be given adequate time to prepare a defense, had to be given access to the evidence to be used against him, and had to have the opportunity to call witnesses; and the entire trial had to be conducted in public. Every one of these procedures, save the last, was violated in Louis's trial, and each violation was exhaustively debated in the Convention. The majority of deputies thought Louis ought to be tried, ought to be punished for acts that would have sent any other Frenchman to the guillotine, but they also wanted his trial to be impeccably correct. This proved to be impossible.

The commission appointed by the Convention to function as the jury of accusation and draw up the *acte énonciatif* did its work well and quickly. In terms of the Criminal Code of 1791 it also did its work illegally. The men who served as the jury of accusation were all drawn from the Convention, and all subsequently participated in the trial itself and decided on Louis's punishment. All the written evidence, whether confiscated at the Tuileries or found in the *armoire de fer*, was used in the *acte énonciatif* without regard for the rules governing such evidence. The king was not given a lawyer at this time, no witnesses were called, and Louis did not know what was in the accusation against him until he appeared before the bar of the Convention on December 11 to be interrogated.

The task of writing the *acte énonciatif* fell to Jean-Baptiste-Robert Lindet, a hard-working Norman, passionately devoted to the Revolution. Lindet's prerevolutionary career, as with so many of his colleagues in the Convention, is obscure. The Revolution thrust hundreds of talented and ambitious provincials into prominence, made national figures of men whose reputations had reached no farther than their town or district before 1789. At forty-six Lindet was older than many *conventionnels*. He had been a successful lawyer in his native Bernay, where his wealth and prestige were sufficient to get him elected mayor of the town and then deputy to the Legislative and Convention assemblies. In the Legislative Lindet had consistently voted with the Left. In the Convention he sat with the Mountain and staunchly defended it. He later served on the famous Committee of Public Safety yet managed to remain independent of Robespierre's group. Lindet had great personal courage and considerable humanity. On August 10, when the slaughter of the Swiss was going on at the Tuileries, he hid a Swiss colonel who had managed to get away and then arranged for his escape to Switzerland.

Lindet did most of the work on the *acte énonciatif*, and he exhausted himself in the process. Going without sleep and working incessantly at the document, he was forced to take to his bed with fatigue on December 10. Barbaroux, another member of the Commission of Twenty-one selected on December 6, read Lindet's report to the Convention. It is worth noting that the Commission of Twenty-one was the first such appointed committee in the trial that was not completely dominated by Girondins, and Lindet's *acte énonciatif* is closer to the Mountain's view of the trial than to that of the Girondins. Initiative in the trial was passing to the radicals.

Lindet's accusation is in the form of a history of the Revolution, from May 1789 till August 10, 1792, and successfully cuts through all the distracting proposals and assumptions that had emerged during the debates. It is a chilling accusation of treason against the king. Lindet begins his accusation on the eve of the calling of the Estates-General. Having bankrupted the nation, he argues, the king was forced to summon the Estates for the first time in 175 years. Louis's intentions were to use the representatives of the nation to raise money for the crown and then send them home with a few token reforms. The king first tried to intimidate the deputies and then called out the troops to coerce them. Thwarted by the unexpected courage of his subjects, led by the commons, the king had to change his tactics: he resorted to force. He stalled, refusing to sanction the decrees of the National Assembly, while he massed troops at Versailles. Paris responded by seizing the Bastille and a few months later marching on Versailles and bringing the king to Paris.

Still, Lindet continues, Louis plotted against the Revolution; he bribed parliamentary leaders, entered into secret correspondence with exiled royalists, and, when these schemes failed, fled the country: "Louis left France as a fugitive in order to return as a conqueror." Captured at Varennes he submitted to the National Assembly and hypocritically accepted a constitution he despised. Despite his oath to the constitution Louis encouraged the Prussians to invade and at the same time refused to cooperate with the Legislative Assembly, vetoing its decrees. The papers discovered in the *armoire de fer* prove that the king was duplicitous. By the summer of 1792 Louis realized that his designs for undermining the Revolution were ruined: he decided to attack. He massed troops at the Tuileries and thus provoked the insurrection of August 10. When he saw he would be defeated he left the château to take refuge in the Manège without surrendering. The Swiss were left to betray the insurgents and suffer death for their loyalty to an undeserving king.

Louis's crimes would be treasonous regardless of who committed them. But even more important for Lindet is the pattern of betrayal and duplicity. The king had opposed and fought against the Revolution from its outset. He wanted either "to reestablish his throne or to bury himself under its debris. . . . Louis is guilty of all these outrages of which he had formed the design from the beginning of the Revolution, and which he several times tried to put into execution."

Lindet's *acte énonciatif* simply ignores all the procedural and constitutional questions. He accepts the Mountain view that Louis's major crime is the kingship itself, and that Louis must answer to the people for what he has done. A number of the "crimes" singled out by Lindet and the Commission of Twenty-one are not criminal actions as such but rather the assumed motives of the king in calling the troops to Versailles, or summoning the Estates-General—in other words, not the kinds of accusations that would normally be permitted in a criminal procedure. But the Convention had no significant objections to the *acte énonciatif* and decreed that Louis be brought to the Convention the next day to hear the accusation and answer it.

There was a good deal of trepidation about Louis's appearance before the Convention. The *conventionnels* themselves had no authority in the matter since the king was the Commune's prisoner. Yet they had little to worry about. There had been no attempts made on Louis's life, nor for that matter any attempts at rescuing him from prison, but royalist sympathies were widespread and much feared, and this would be Louis's first excursion since he was locked up in the Temple in August. The precautions taken by the Commune were elaborate. The General Council met on December 9 and decreed that the commandant general, Santerre, and the *procureur*, Chaumette, would be charged with the general security of the city. All the sections were alerted and ordered to remain in permanent session "on all the days that Louis Capet will leave the Temple." The entire city was to be involved in the solemn transfer of the king. And the careful, even excessive, military preparations reflect more than general nervousness about the king's safety. Louis's appearance at the bar of the Convention was designed to make a political and symbolic point: Louis was to be seen as the prisoner of the nation, ordered to answer publicly for his actions. Everything was arranged to insure this effect.

The coach carrying the king—apparently the mayor's coach— would be accompanied by an escort that was a small army. A troop of *gendarmerie* would lead the procession, with three cannon and an ammunition wagon. Then would come a double row of infantry, each three men deep, in the middle of which would roll the coach carrying the king. The rear guard would be composed of a detachment of cavalry of the line, with three additional pieces of artillery. Every man under arms on December 11 had to carry a special card, issued by the Commune, identifying him, his section, and his right to be there. Each of the handpicked escort would be supplied with sixteen cartridges. The route to the Convention was cleared of all traffic, and it was a route that ran through the heart of Paris. All the Parisians were thus encouraged to contemplate their former king about to confront his accusers. Anyone found on the night of December 10 or the following day without proper identification in the form of a citizen's card issued by his section was arrested on the spot. Those who wanted a place in the galleries of the Manège began lining up on the night of December 10, many of them sleeping on the ground outside. They far outnumbered the available places. By 6:00 A.M. on December 11 all the passages leading to the galleries were mobbed. There was not a space to be found in or around the Manège by 9:30, when the Convention began its session.

The route leading from the Temple to the Manège was similarly mobbed and by early morning all the choice spots were occupied and troops held the crowd back. Specially picked guards were sent to patrol all the public buildings in the city, to foil any escape or assassination attempts, and to prevent looting. The famous Marseillais, the heroes of August 10, were sent to guard the Abbaye prison, to assure the terrified prisoners that they would be protected from the crowds. The Jacobins and Cordeliers, along with the municipality of Paris, had placarded the city during the night, calling for calm and dignified restraint. Almost all the citizens the journalist Prudhomme saw on the streets were armed. Indeed, anyone found without arms was sent back to his section. Just as the Parisians were to be impressed by the republican solemnity of the occasion, so too were they to be impressed by their own remarkable display of strength. And this revolutionary population in arms would also serve as a warning to the crowned heads of Europe who were anxiously watching the trial. Symbolism and security marched hand in hand on December 11.

Louis himself had made no special preparations for his appearance before the Convention, although he was obviously nervous. Unable to give his son his customary geography lesson, he was playing Chinese checkers with the boy when one of the guards announced that the mayor of Paris, Nicolas Chambon, accompanied by representatives of the Commune, had come to fetch him to the Convention. Louis hastily embraced his son, told him to hug his mother, and sent him out of the room. The king then asked one of the guards, Albertier, if the mayor, whom he had never met, was a small or a large man, young or old, fat or thin. Albertier answered that he knew the mayor only vaguely, but thought him of average age, average bulk, a bit thin, and on the tall side. This hopelessly vague description was fairly accurate: Chambon was a nondescript man, physically and politically. He was forty-four years old and before his election as mayor, as a Girondin sympathizer but also as a compromise candidate, he had been a distinguished Paris doctor. He served only two months as mayor before resigning, and then disappeared completely from political life, presumably returning to his practice.

Accompanied by a secretary who was charged with making an official record of the transfer of the king, Chambon entered Louis's apartment. The representatives of the Commune found the king pale from months of imprisonment and he had lost some weight during his November illness, but otherwise Louis appeared in good health. Coulombeau, the secretary, read the decree of December 6 ordering the king to the bar of the Convention. Chambon then invited the king, whom he called "Louis Capet," to descend to the waiting coach. Louis hesitated for a moment and then turned abruptly to his escort: "I am not called Louis Capet. My ancestors had that name but I have never been called that. As for the rest, it is the consequence of treatment I have experienced by force during four months." Louis talked on, complaining that their arrival had deprived him of his daily visit with his son. Chambon and Coulombeau ignored the king's lamentations. Louis paused again as if thinking, decided he had no more to say, and started down the stairs. He saw no familiar faces at the guard posts; special troops manned the checkpoints, and the new faces were disquieting. In the courtyard of the Temple Louis turned around to look back at the tower he had just left and reportedly shed a few tears. Then he mounted the coach.

The king was seated next to the mayor and the windows were left open so that the Parisians could, as the report put it, "contemplate Louis Capet at their ease." Louis himself was curious about everything and he gave no indication "either of sadness or bad humor." When the coach passed the triumphal arches of Saint-Martin and Saint-Denis, built by Louis XIV to celebrate his military triumphs, the king asked which of the two the Commune proposed to tear down. Moëlle, one of the guards, tells the story of

Louis asking Chambon about the latter's wife. The king, says Moëlle, noticed how difficult the mayor's position was and wanted to put him at ease. When the coach rolled up to the Manège Louis was turned over to an armed guard commanded by Santerre. The Commandant General put his hand on Louis's arm and led the king to the bar of the Convention.

Louis was simply dressed in a plain olive-colored silk coat, wore his own hair, seemed quite composed, and looked remarkably well despite his prison pallor. A wooden chair had been provided for the king just behind the railing of the Convention's bar.

"I announce to the Assembly," said the president, Bertrand Barère, "that Louis is at the door. Representatives of the people," he continued, "you are about to exercise the right of national justice," and "the dignity of your session ought to correspond to the majesty of the French people. It is about to give, through you, a great lesson to kings, and a useful example for the emancipation of nations." The former butcher, Louis Legendre, who sat with the Mountain, admonished his colleagues: "It is necessary that the silence of a tomb terrify the guilty man." Then Barère gave a signal and Louis was led in. For a moment he stood uncomfortably at the bar, surrounded by Generals Santerre and Wittinghof, the mayor, and two municipal officers. Louis, who had spent most of his life sitting or standing in public, as he pleased, while the rest of the world conformed to his will in these matters, had to wait for Barère to give him permission: "Louis, the French nation accuses you. The National Assembly decreed, on December 3, that you would be judged by it. On December 6 it decreed that you would be brought before the bar. We are going to read to you the *acte énonciatif* of the crimes imputed to you. You may sit down."

The Convention had decided that the president would first read through the entire *acte énonciatif*, then reread the accusation, clause by clause, so that Louis could respond to each charge with a "yes" or "no." Valazé, during this second reading, would show Louis the evidence supporting each charge. The king was not permitted to have a lawyer. Perfectly composed, Louis listened attentively to the first reading. Then Barère began the interrogation.

Barère: Louis, the French people accuse you of having committed

a multitude of crimes in order to establish your tyranny b
stroying its liberty. You suspended the meetings of the Es
General, dictated laws to the nation at the royal *séance*, and po
armed guards: What do you have to say?

Louis: There did not exist any laws concerning these things.

Barère: You ordered troops to march on Paris and in the days before the fall of the Bastille you spoke as a tyrant.

Louis: I was then the master of whether or not the troops
marched; but I have never had the intention of shedding blood.

Barère: You persisted in projects against national liberty by delaying the decrees abolishing personal servitude and delaying recognition of the Declaration of the Rights of Man and Citizen, at the
same time doubling your bodyguard and summoning the Flanders
regiment to Versailles. You encouraged these troops to insult the
national cockade and the nation.

Louis: I made the observations on the first two projects you mentioned that I believed to be just. As to the cockade, that is false; that
scene was not enacted before me.

Barère: You violated your oath and attempted to corrupt Talon
and Mirabeau [on July 14, 1790].

Louis: I don't recall what happened at that time; but all of it is before my acceptance of the constitution.

Barère: You spent public money for the purposes of corruption.

Louis: I had no greater pleasure than to give money to those who
needed it.

Barère: You first tried to flee the kingdom by going to Saint-
Cloud [April 1791].

Louis: That accusation is absurd.

The flight to Varennes Louis dismissed as a "trip" and said he
had already explained his motives to the National Assembly. The
massacres in the Champ-de-Mars he said could "in no way be attributed to me." He denied that he worked to overthrow the constitution: that "is the responsibility of my ministers." Throughout
the interrogation Louis pleaded innocence and blamed his ministers: "I executed all the orders proposed to me by the ministers."
As soon as he learned, he said, that sending money abroad to his
bodyguard in exile was illegal he "forbade them to touch any payment." To all the charges that he encouraged his brothers to raise

money and troops in his name the king responded: "I have dis-
avowed all the actions of my brothers as soon as the constitution
proscribed them to me, as soon as I had knowledge of them." All
matters dealing with foreign affairs—his responsibility for the war,
his encouragement of the enemy, his neglect of French military
preparations—were the responsibility of his ministers: "All the
correspondence passed through the ministers," and "I gave all the
orders to the ministry." When specific decrees were not provided
by the Legislative Louis continued to behave as he always had: "I
did not believe it my duty to change."

Barère: On January 29, 1792, the Legislative Assembly issued a
decree against factious priests, which you suspended.

Louis: The constitution left me the right of sanctioning decrees.

Barère: You used money from the civil lists to encourage counterrevolutionary activity.

Louis: I had no knowledge of the projects they were engaged in.
Never did the idea of counterrevolution enter my head.

Barère: Who are those to whom you promised or gave money in
the National and Legislative Assemblies?

Louis: None.

Barère: You reviewed the troops on the morning of August 10 and
extracted from them a personal oath of obedience. This was a prelude to your proposed attack on Paris.

Louis: I reviewed all the troops who were assembled at the Tuileries that day. The constituted authorities accompanied me, the
department, the mayor, and the municipality. I even asked for a
delegation from the National Assembly, and I finally went, with
my family, to the Assembly.

Barère: Why did you gather troops at the Tuileries?

Louis: All the constituted authorities saw them, the château was
menaced, and since I was a constituted authority, I had to defend
myself.

Barère: Why was the mayor called to the Tuileries on the night of
August 9, 1792?

Louis: Because of the trouble that was brewing.

Barère: You are responsible for shedding French blood.

Louis: No, Monsieur, it was not I.

When the interrogation was over, after three hours, Barère asked Louis if he had anything to add.

Louis: I ask to see the accusations and the pieces of evidence that accompany them, and the right to choose a counsel to defend me.

Valazé, who refused to stand in the king's presence and refused to face Louis, pulled a chair up to the bar of the Convention and disdainfully passed the documents, one by one, over his shoulder to the king. "The king," says Moëlle, "responded to all of them with precision . . . and without the least hesitation." And his responses were always the same: "I don't recognize it," or "I don't know about it," or "I don't recognize it any more than the others."

Valazé: Do you recognize this as your own handwriting?

Louis: No.

Barère: Did you build a secret safe in the Tuileries?

Louis: I have no knowledge of it.

The king similarly refused to recognize his signature on many of the documents and explained to Barère that the presence of the Seal of France on a document did not mean that the king had affixed it.

Barère: I invite you to retire to the conference room, the Assembly is going to deliberate.

Louis again requested a lawyer but he was ignored. Santerre escorted the king out of the main hall. It was 5:00 P.M. Louis sat in the conference room waiting for the order to be returned to the Temple. Chaumette, the *procureur*, was hungry and took a piece of bread and a bottle of brandy from one of the guards and started eating. Louis had eaten nothing since breakfast: "Alas, my dear Monsieur Chaumette, I have eaten no more than you. Give me a bit of bread as a favor." When the order to return to the Temple arrived Louis was still clutching his piece of bread. He had eaten only the crust. The escort led him to the mayor's coach. After he had remounted Coulombeau took the morsel from the king and threw it out the window. "Ah," sighed Louis, "it is not good to throw away bread, especially when it is so scarce." Some banal conversation continued in the coach for a bit, then everyone was silent. The streets were still lined with armed Parisians and the coach rolled slowly through the silent crowd. Louis reached the

Temple at 6:30. And as the mayor was about to depart, Louis reminded him to tell the Convention he wanted a lawyer.

The king's appearance at the bar, the humiliation of enduring an interrogation, profoundly impressed contemporaries. It was not just the uniqueness of the event but the king's behavior, minutely observed by everyone who could find a place in the Manège, that struck them. Louis had shown emotion only when charged with shedding blood, and witnesses reported they saw "a few tears appear to fall." Otherwise the king's voice was firm, his manner assured, his comportment dignified. "I was moved almost to tears by his touching words," wrote Durand de Maillanne, who "admired the clarity and precision of his responses, pronounced in a sonorous and firm voice." Colonel Monro, the spy of Lord Grenville, the British foreign secretary, sent his master some newspaper clippings for December 11, along with a covering note:

> I assure you this conduct [of the king] has made a considerable revolution in the minds of people here, and those that were perhaps indifferent to what had passed before begin now to regret the approaching and most probable loss of a sovereign, whose life they considered as sacred: papers are publicly hawked about saying in his praise what would have cost a man his head, had he dared to utter so much some weeks ago.

Like all spies Monro exaggerated, telling Grenville what he wanted to hear. But there is some truth here. The trial had ceased to be a distant prospect, the occasion for abstract debates on procedures and the meaning of justice: it had become a painful confrontation between king and Convention. This was Louis's first intervention in his own trial, and his ability to move his accusers made many uneasy. Indeed, Louis's personality, his sense of dignity, his courage and composure were the best arguments that could be made in his behalf. But it was not only his presence that was disquieting. He had raised basic questions about the entire trial and he had laid down, in his responses to the interrogation, the foundations of his defense.

Louis had not seen the accusation prior to his appearance in the Convention, he had no lawyer to advise him, and many of the charges were so complex that they defied a simple "yes" or "no" response. Louis accepted the offer of a legal duel and fought to save his life. He insisted that he could not be held responsible for any actions prior to his acceptance of the constitution, for, he maintained, he was not answerable to the nation before he became its constitutional monarch. Even as constitutional monarch, Louis said, he could not be prosecuted for vetoing decrees. The constitution gave him the veto and he could, and did, use it as he saw fit. If there were violations of the constitution the blame lay with the king's ministers, for Louis adhered strictly to the old medieval notion that the king could do no wrong although he was often misled by bad advice. Louis assumed the pose of a scrupulous magistrate who confined his activities to those given him by the constitution: he was simply the executive power in the state and could not be charged for exercising his office as he saw fit, so long as he did not break any laws. And his answers demonstrate that he did not believe he had broken the law. When he refused to recognize his signature or documents in his own hand, which infuriated the deputies, he was adhering to the legal guarantees of due process set out in the Criminal Code of 1791. His papers had been illegally seized and it was up to his accusers to prove that they were the king's papers, written in the king's hand. Having decided to try him, Louis reasoned, the Convention was bound to see that he got a fair trial. Louis was doing no more than honoring their commitment to a trial and protecting himself by insisting on a strict reading of the Criminal Code.

Louis had made an important political decision on December 11. He knew, as well as did the many royalists who offered him advice from the safety of exile, that he had essentially three choices: he could refuse to recognize the competence of his subjects to try him, as did Charles I of England a century earlier; he could throw himself on the mercy of the court and hope for the best; and he could take seriously the offer of a trial and defend himself, thus recognizing the right of his subjects to try him. He knew that whatever he did his subjects were determined to bring him to justice. They had the power and the will to do so. Disdaining his judges or asking for their mercy offered no hope at all; that way led directly to the guillotine. Whatever else the king may have been he was no one's dupe. He made his own decisions, many of which were inept, but the stubborn king was not easily manipulated, as dozens

and dozens of his courtiers and advisers had discovered, nor was
he easily intimidated, as the rioters of June 20, 1792 had discovered, nor was he a pathetic weakling, as Lafayette had discovered.
True, he had little political sense, he was indolent, and he could be
persuaded into unwise decisions, especially by his foolish wife
(whose advice was uniformly disastrous). But when he did make
up his own mind he would follow his chosen path with unwaver-
ing determination.

So it was with his trial. His choice was noble, perhaps even cun-
ning. He sincerely believed he was innocent, just as he sincerely
believed he was not answerable to his subjects. As king he had
honored his coronation oath and tried to rule as a Christian prince.
He felt no obligations to the Revolution or his subjects in revolution. He always thought of the Revolution as a rebellion of a minority of his subjects, men whose passions and ambitions had been
ignited by impossible metaphysical schemes for remaking the
world. He would be judged by his subjects not because might
made right, but because might made necessity. And since he was
forced to answer for his actions he would do so in the only way
that offered any hope of success. By accepting the offer of a trial
Louis sought to force his accusers to prove him guilty, which he
believed they could not do without violating the legal procedures
and guarantees created by the Revolution itself. If his subjects
condemned him they could do so only by exposing themselves
as arbitrary, only by resorting to illegal measures.

Louis understood that this was a political trial, that he was being
brought to the Convention's bar as an enemy of the Revolution,
and that the Revolution and the monarchy could not live side by
side. He knew he would probably be killed, but he hoped at least
to win a moral victory. By insisting on a fair trial he would compel
his accusers to live up to their supposed admiration for the law.
Let them give me a fair trial, he thought, and he would be exonerated. Unlike Mary, queen of Scots, unlike Charles I, Louis thought
this moral victory worth fighting for, and he certainly had no interest in the glories of martyrdom. He would appear in court protected only by the law. He would neither beg for his life nor try to
overawe his judges. He would appear before the Convention as a
man unjustly charged, as a man who had not violated the laws of

men or God. He was neither a criminal nor a tyrant. He dared his
accusers to *prove* him guilty.

Louis's stance pleased no one. Théodore de Lameth, a hero of
the American Revolution, an important spokesman for the Right in
the Legislative Assembly, and an intelligent conservative, argues
in his *Mémoires* that Louis "should have made a declaration in
which he would have said that his innocence could not be questioned. That, moreover, inviolable because of the sanction of centuries, still so by the freely expressed will, legally proclaimed, of all
the French, no jurisdiction could be exercised against him. He
could be killed, but not judged." For Lameth, as for all the royalists, the throne itself and the principles of legitimacy were at stake.
He knew the king could die, but only if the king refused to accept
the trial could the monarchy itself be saved. Louis had, alas, put
the crown as well as himself into the prisoner's dock. Even the revolutionaries realized what Louis had done. J. B. Givey, who did
much of the writing for Brissot's *Patriote français*, compared Louis
to Charles I: "be it weakness, be it reason, be it the hope of making
his cause better" Louis had decided to render homage "to the national sovereignty."

The deputies were equally annoyed. As soon as Louis left the
Manège a violent debate broke out. Marat ran to the tribune from
his aerie atop the Mountain: "This is not a question of an ordinary
trial. We don't have to concern ourselves with the chicaneries of
courts." Marat was the voice of radicalism and regicide in the Convention, but Louis had forced the deputies to rethink their offer of
a trial. It was the old, unresolved question of procedures: could
Louis be convicted using familiar legal procedures, and if not—
since almost all the deputies thought him guilty—could they modify or disregard these procedures? The Convention had already decided to disregard the constitution of 1791, would it now have to
disregard the Criminal Code as well? Pétion, hoping to save the
Convention from the tedious debates such a dilemma would create
and hoping at the same time to inflict a blow against the Jacobins,
proposed that Louis be given a counselor to help him prepare his
defense. The Mountain was furious. It had consistently opposed
the need for a trial and now maintained that Louis's appearance at
the bar made it clear that the king was duplicitous. He would de-

mand protection of the laws he himself had consistently violated while on the throne. Some Montagnards insisted that Pétion's motion be decided by roll-call vote "so that the republic know the royalists." Most deputies did not construe giving Louis a lawyer as an act of royalism, and the session collapsed into a shouting match. Finally, the president had to suspend the meeting by putting his hat on his head. Once order was restored—and this was usually only a matter of time, an interlude of insults before the deputies returned to their seats and were willing to get on with parliamentary business—the Convention voted, by voice, that Louis should have a lawyer of his choice. This was the first formal test of Jacobin strength in the Convention, and it lost to a more moderate, if ambiguous, position. Louis would have his day in court. The Convention was more willing to ignore the Criminal Code than it was to accept the Jacobin thesis of summary execution.

CHAPTER VI

A Lawyer for the King

THE MANÈGE, DECEMBER 12–25, 1792

ouis's request for a lawyer, ignored on December 11 during his interrogation, was the first piece of business the next day. It was proposed that a commission be sent to the Temple to get from the prisoner the names of those he wished to defend him. The commission, with Alexis Thuriot, a Montagnard, at its head, was immediately appointed and set out for the Temple. When they returned to the Convention they reported that Louis had chosen Guy-Jean Target and, if he declined, François-Denis Tronchet. The Convention decreed that the two men would be immediately informed and the Commune would be asked to give Louis's counsels free access to their client and provide the prisoner with pens, paper, and ink.

Target, then fifty-nine, was a man of the *ancien régime*. He was a member of the French Academy and had defended Cardinal de Rohan in the infamous Diamond Necklace scandal in 1785. He had sat in the Estates-General and was one of the authors of the constitution of 1791. He had the reputation of combining great legal learning with a fine oratorical talent. But Target was a prudent man, bewildered by the course of the Revolution, and he declined the offer to defend his former master whom he would gladly have served in past years. His health, Target said, was not good. His letter of refusal also rambled on about the duties of a republican to defend even a tyrant, and then apologized for refusing the responsibility. A year later, however, he would find no difficulty in serving as secretary to the Revolutionary Committee in his section during the Terror. Target's caution earned him the scorn of royalists and revolutionaries alike.

Tronchet, however, accepted the appointment, signing himself "the republican Tronchet" in his letter of acceptance. Another renowned lawyer of the *ancien régime*, Tronchet was sixty-six when he became Louis's counsel. A fine-looking man, with well-defined features, he too had sat in the Estates-General, where he threw his energies and abilities into questions of legal reform and served with distinction on the important Judicial Committee, ironically enough one of the committees responsible for the Criminal Code of 1791. When the Estates-General declared itself the National Assembly, Tronchet retired to the suburbs of Paris: he was no radical. His self-imposed retirement was a not unusual response of moderate men who could not bring themselves to join either the Revolution or the counterrevolution in exile. After the king's trial Tronchet slipped quietly back into retirement and lived out the Terror. He emerged (and once again entered politics) with the fall of Robespierre (July 1794), and as a member of the senate under the Directory he welcomed Napoléon's bid for power. He died (in 1806) peacefully at the age of eighty, and was buried in the Panthéon.

In addition to Tronchet several of Louis's former subjects volunteered to defend him, an act that involved potential risk and certain opprobrium. Lamoignon de Malesherbes, friend and protector of many of the *philosophes* during the years of royal censorship, this reforming minister of the *ancien régime*, offered his services. Malesherbes was the incarnation of the finest qualities of the service nobility, the *noblesse de la robe*. He was tough-minded yet compassionate, and at the age of seventy-two could easily have lived out his days in peace; but on December 11 he wrote the Convention a letter that does honor to an illustrious career and a courageous man. "I want Louis XVI to know that if he chooses me for this function I am ready to devote myself to it." Before the Revolution he had been "called to be counsel of he who was my master during the time that this function was sought after by everyone. I owe him the same service now that so many men find it dangerous." Malesherbes's sense of duty would eventually cost him his head, the victim of one of the many and unnecessary examples of petty revenge that disgrace the Revolution. The habits of a lifetime of royal service and his own deep conservatism led Malesherbes, even in front of the Convention, to refer to Louis as "Sire." The recently created archaism, thought a deliberate insult to the equality of the Revolution, provoked a deputy to ask the old man what made him so bold: "Contempt for life," Malesherbes answered. Even Marat admired Malesherbes, celebrating his courage while disparaging the pusillanimity of Target, who dared call himself a republican while refusing to defend the king at whose feet he had groveled for so long.

There were other volunteers: "Sourdat, citizen of Troyes" offered his services on December 12; Olympe de Gouges, the sometimes actress and playwright and full-time eccentric, volunteered on December 15, assuring the Convention that "heroism and generosity are also possessed by women." The Convention sent these letters along to Louis, with Tronchet's letter of acceptance, in which he complained of being "dragged" from retirement, but concluded "as a man I cannot refuse my aid to another man above whose head the blade of the law is suspended." Louis gratefully accepted the services of Tronchet and Malesherbes. The Commune, however, was reluctant to give the lawyers free access to the prisoner. The General Council yielded to the appeals of the Convention at last, but insisted on a thorough search of the visitors, "including the most secret places." These distinguished men were forced to disrobe and put on new clothes before the guards would conduct them to the king's apartment. The Convention complained to the Commune of these "vexatious and excessive" measures, but to no avail. And Robespierre, who had no tolerance for the discomforts and no interest in the tribulations of the former rulers of France, supported the Commune on the floor of the Convention. He excoriated those who showed so much concern for Louis or his lawyers and so little for "the people [they] oppressed." Louis was nothing but a criminal, and Robespierre peevishly demanded that "measures be taken so that we do not have to hear, each time someone prejudges the destiny of an accused, these insults of cannibals." Robespierre was splendid in his role of ideologue to the Mountain, but he could not let pass an occasion, no matter how in-

significant, to remind the Convention of the mistake it was making
in granting Louis a trial.

The session of December 15 began with procedural matters. The
Convention heard first from the Commission of Twenty-one, who
had drawn up the *acte énonciatif*, that copies of all the documentary
evidence used in their accusation would shortly be finished and
given to the king. The Committee then asked for instructions on
how the originals were to be made available to Louis and his lawyers. According to the Criminal Code the accused had to have access to the original documents as well as copies for their own use.
This request led, naturally, to the question of verification. Since
Louis had, at his interrogation, refused to recognize his signature
or any of the documents, they could not be used in the trial until
they had been verified by a handwriting expert. This verification
was a regular procedure in a criminal trial and every defendant had
a right to ask for it. A few deputies called for a handwriting expert.
Others argued that Louis's signature was familiar to everyone; calling in an expert was only a tiresome scruple. The Convention simply disregarded the Criminal Code. It had accepted the documents
as authentic and announced to Louis and Europe that it had no
intention of letting the king off on a legal technicality. Louis had no
choice in the matter. His strategy for discrediting the documentary
evidence against him had failed. He had won a point (he would
have a lawyer) and lost a point (the evidence was declared authentic). The question of how the evidence was collected did not even
come up at this time.

Having swept aside the question of authenticity, the Convention,
after an acerbic discussion, decided that Louis would be heard in
his own defense on Wednesday, December 26. The session ended
with a long discussion of whether or not he would be allowed to
see his family during the trial. The General Council of the Commune, whose reasons are obscure on this matter, had ordered
Louis separated from his family. The Convention thought this
overly harsh. The Convention could discuss and decree, but Louis
was the Commune's prisoner: the Convention proposed, the Commune disposed. Louis had to answer to two authorities, a fact that
frustrated him, angered the Convention, and introduced into the
trial itself an additional set of antagonisms. Before the trial began

it was not very important who determined the king's schedule in prison, who fed him, who guarded him. But once the Convention had decreed that it would try Louis these conflicting jurisdictions became significant. The Commune used its control of him as a way of forcing the Convention to get on with the trial, or, as in the case of giving Louis's lawyers access to their client, as a means of expressing its criticism of the Convention's procedures. As usual the Commune won, insisting that Louis be separated from his family and his lawyers submit to a search. Only reluctantly did the Commune agree to allow Louis and his lawyers to meet alone, without a guard present.

Since the first week in December the Convention had devoted itself to the king's trial, but the Jacobin-Girondin struggle had not been forgotten. Indeed, it informed all the business done by the assembly. The brief hiatus between Louis's interrogation and his scheduled defense was taken up with a new Girondin assault on the Mountain. This attack centered on Philippe Egalité. In the summer of 1791, after Louis had been captured at Varennes and suspended from the monarchy, when France had no king, there had been talk of putting Philippe on the throne. At the time it seemed a good tactic for the Left. They had little power in the National Assembly, the conservatives were determined to find a way of reinstating Louis, and Philippe was favorable to the Revolution. Were he to sit on the throne the old court party would be destroyed, the conservatives in the National Assembly would be undermined, and the duke's friends and cronies, many of them isolated from power, would rule France. The tactic would also preserve the letter of the constitution since the monarchy would remain in the Bourbon family, and all those who supported Philippe hoped the fabulously wealthy and ambitious duke would remember his debt to his friends.

On December 16 Buzot and the Girondins again attacked the duke. Let him go elsewhere, Buzot said, to carry a name "which the ear of a free man can no longer hear without being wounded." Louvet continued the attack, this time donning the toga of the first Brutus, who had called for the expulsion of the Tarquins, the kings of ancient Rome. Lanjuinais, another Girondin leader, supported the proposal. The attack was clever. It forced the Mountain to defend a man it despised. It had either to join in the attack on the duke or defend him and in so doing give at least the appearance of being allied with his disreputable character and scandalous past. Camille Desmoulins, the most brilliant journalist of the Mountain, immediately saw the thrust of the attack and explained it to the Jacobin Club:

> They said to themselves [the Girondins]: the patriots will not want to abandon Egalité, and will make the Mountain seem like a faction . . . We were very embarrassed . . . It was the height of art to make us appear royalists, and it forced us to defend Egalité.

Even Marat, who hated the duke, came to his defense. Philippe was, for Marat, an "unworthy favorite of fortune, without virtue, without a soul, without guts, having for merit nothing but the jargon of the alley." But he was also a representative of the nation and must be defended as such. The Jacobins had to walk a tightrope by insisting they were defending not the man but the principle that deputies could be removed only by their constituents. Colonel Monro, the English spy, who had access only to public sources of information, saw clearly what was going on, and he easily made the connection between the attack on Philippe Egalité and the king's trial. "Rolland's [sic] and Brissot's party," he wrote Lord Grenville on December 17, "are certainly struggling to save the king in order to humble Robespierre's party, and I myself from everything I can learn have not the smallest doubt but they will succeed."

The Convention postponed discussion on the expulsion of the Duke d'Orléans from December 16 to 18. The Mountain, sufficiently recovered from its initial shock, launched a counterattack. Robespierre denounced all those who demanded the duke's exile as creators of discord, a familiar charge used by both factions. Robespierre's speech, with its familiar blend of highminded theory and arrogant contempt for those less virtuous than himself, set off a shouting match. It was Jean-François Rewbell, a moderate, who restored the discussion to reason. Rewbell tried to separate the attack on the duke from the king's trial, asking for a postponement of Buzot's inflammatory motion until after the judgment of the king. Paris, he reminded the deputies, was restless and impatient; the expulsion of the duke would be an unnecessary provocation.

But the Girondins were unwilling to give in. The attack on the duke was proving a useful tactic while at the same time delaying the trial which had long been a Girondin goal.

This time both Jacobins and Girondins had misjudged the temper of the Convention itself and Paris. The backbenchers were growing impatient with the endless factional bickering and wished to get on with other business. The Commune was equally impatient and expressed its impatience by peevishly making Louis's imprisonment more of a burden than it needed to be. The Paris press too had had its fill of the factions and their vendettas and wanted to get on with the trial. The Girondins, realizing they had lost the attention of the majority, reluctantly yielded; Pétion asked that the question of the duke be postponed.

This Girondin retreat was not an expression of goodwill or even of good sense. They had been forced to retreat. Louvet, who habitually resorted to a conspiratorial explanation for everything that went wrong for the Girondins, was for once correct: the retreat was the result of "a revolt of the Jacobins, the Cordeliers and of the Commune." Throughout the trial the two factions had been locked in bitter strife. The king had become either an embarrassment or a useful object for throwing at each other. This self-serving use of the king was familiar to the deputies of the Marais, who were still in the majority. But by December these men were losing interest in the struggle. Both Jacobins and Girondins seemed determined to delay the trial, although for radically different reasons. It was clear to virtually everyone, inside and outside the Convention, that the Jacobin-Girondin struggle could not be separated from the trial, and it was equally clear that the outcome of the trial would have an enormous, perhaps decisive, impact on the factions. But it was the trial itself that obsessed contemporaries more than the Jacobin-Girondin struggle. It was time to get on with the business at hand. Both factions momentarily bowed to this pressure.

Still, the damage had been done. The breach between Jacobins and Girondins widened and Paris was further alienated. The sections, never quiet for long during the trial, pressured the Convention once more, demanding an end to the trial and "death for assassins." On December 23, section Faubourg-Montmartre pointedly accused those who urged any further delay of propagating "fanatical maxims" designed to create sympathy "for the fate of this guilty man." It was time for France to rid herself of "the last of our kings." Such threats might be disturbing, but they could not be ignored. On December 17, before the attack on the Duke d'Orléans had completely collapsed through lack of support, the Convention returned to the details of the trial. The Commission of Twenty-one reported that the documents used in the accusation against Louis had been delivered to the prisoner and his lawyers. Once again the Commission had asked the king if he recognized his own handwriting and signature, and once again he had disowned most of the pieces of evidence. This report was followed by a letter from Louis's lawyers lamenting that the date set for the king's defense did not give them enough time to prepare. They pleaded for more time, and for another attorney, informing the Convention that Louis had chosen Raymond DeSèze. On December 18 the Convention voted to accept DeSèze but refused to delay the king's appearance at the bar.

Here was yet another procedural violation. The Criminal Code specifically said an accused could have one or two lawyers, but no more. The addition of DeSèze thus violated the Code that Louis was about to stake his life on. But if this violation of procedures benefited the king, the Convention's refusal to delay his defense was a serious blow to Louis's cause. Again the Code was specific: the accused had to be given adequate time to prepare his defense. The fortnight granted by the Convention might have been sufficient in a less important or complicated case. In Louis's case it was an impossibly short time. Almost the entire two weeks was taken up with merely reading through the materials, and the Convention was slow in getting copies to the king and also inept; Louis's lawyers wrote frequent letters asking for this or that document which they had not received. Indeed, it is not clear that by the time the defense was written Louis and his lawyers had seen everything they were entitled to see. Once again Louis had won a procedural point and lost one; and the loss was more significant than the victory, although DeSèze was an important addition to his defenders.

DeSèze was a brilliant lawyer from Bordeaux who had come to national prominence in 1789 when he successfully defended the Baron de Besenval against a charge of high treason. He was forty-four when he agreed to come out of semiretirement, at the personal request of Tronchet and Malesherbes and Louis himself, and defend the king. A remarkably good orator whose perorations were celebrated for their passion and their ability to move men's hearts, DeSèze was, in addition, considered a fine legal thinker and strategist. He was one of the more distinguished representatives of the most respected legal tradition in France, that of Bordeaux and its famous law faculty. He was sympathetic to the monarchy and resolutely refused to accept any appointment from the Directory or from Napoléon, both of which governments he considered illegitimate. He preferred retirement to betrayal of his convictions, and suffered imprisonment during the Terror for his rectitude. Upon his release from prison, in 1794, he immediately disappeared from public life. He emerged from retirement only when summoned by Louis XVIII, the restored brother of Louis XVI, to assume a judgeship and accept election to the French Academy. He died at the age of eighty, having been venerated and covered with honors by a grateful Bourbon family, and was eulogized by Chateaubriand, a fitting memorial for a loyal and honorable man.

The Convention now had little to do but wait for Louis's defense. Neither the Girondins nor the Jacobins had much stomach for another fight. It was best to wait and see what the king would say and how the deputies would react. For the moment the Jacobins appeared to have the stronger position. They had lost some minor points—giving Louis a lawyer, for example—but had won an equal number of such points. The Convention had refused to impeach Philippe Egalité and the Girondins had been forced to retreat. The accusation against the king expressed, in general, the views of the Mountain, and even though Louis would come to trial the Montagnards had little fear that he would be found guilty. They had not been victorious, but they had held their own. It would be politically unwise, at this point, to jeopardize their slight advantage. And both factions, like everyone else in France, were anxious to hear the king's defense.

THE KING'S INTERROGATION, DECEMBER 26, 1792. Detail of an engraving by Le Beau, after Desrais. The entire engraving, entitled *Conquêtes de la République française*, contains eight roundels of scenes from the Revolution, which surround the detail reproduced here: Louis, sitting at the bar, being shown some additional pieces of evidence at the time of his defense. This is a more accurate rendering of the Manège than the one depicting Louis at the bar on December 11, although it too contains inaccuracies. *Collection de Vinck, Bibliothèque nationale*

CHAPTER VII

The King's Defense

THE MANÈGE, DECEMBER 26, 1792

 RISES AFFECT men differently, unpredictably. Louis, as ruler of France, was inept. He wielded his enormous power, when he was roused from his usual lethargy, without design. The traditional rulers of France, the Church and the nobility, at first thought the king a dubious ally and eventually considered him and the monarchy he embodied as the enemy of their pretensions. One of the most curious "causes" of the French Revolution is the brief but crucial alliance between aristocrats and bourgeoisie on the eve of the Revolution. The *cahiers de doléance*, solicited by the crown from each of the three estates and intended as the basis for reforms, are almost unanimous in their insistence that too much power is concentrated in the hands of the king and must be distributed to other interests in the kingdom. The kingship, in a word, brought out the worst in Louis, and his pusillanimity, coupled to his fits of stubbornness about his prerogatives, alienated his nobility and drove them to seek support outside the court, without, at the same time, replacing noble support with popular support. But imprisonment and a trial revealed in Louis qualities he had scarcely manifested at Versailles. Stripped of his advisers, his ministers, his courtiers, forced to make his own decisions, bereft of the power to do good or evil, he emerges as a man of character and dignity. He behaves more like a king during his months of anguish than he ever did on the throne. In the last weeks of his life Louis literally comes alive. The strange passivity of August 10 is replaced by decisiveness.

The king had decided on his defense at the time of his interrogation, and it was his decision and his alone. He would defend himself not as an anointed king, but as a constitutional monarch who had fulfilled his oath of office. He was determined to fight for his life by proving his innocence in an adversary proceeding. He had no illusions about the outcome of the trial, as he told Malesherbes at their first interview:

I am sure they will make me perish; they have the power and the will to do so. That does not matter. Let us concern ourselves with my trial as if I could win; and I will win, in effect, since the memory that I will leave will be without stain.

Louis threw himself energetically into preparing his defense. He welcomed the opportunity to escape the stultifying routine of prison life, to do something more emotionally and intellectually stimulating than give his son geography lessons while his wife and sister and daughter needlepointed. The few feverish days of preparation were, ironically, among Louis's happiest in prison. His mind was momentarily distracted from the small miseries of prison life. He was able to talk with men of the world, men of quick intelligence who were deeply devoted to him. The king was once more living in the world of men and events.

Louis had first talked with Malesherbes on December 12, the day after his interrogation. Tronchet arrived in Paris two days later, and DeSèze joined his colleagues on December 17. From December 14 until December 26 Louis saw his counsels every day between 5:00 and 9:00 P.M. Every morning Malesherbes came alone to the Temple, bringing with him the latest published opinions of the deputies and often a copy of the *Moniteur* so Louis could read the previous day's debates. The two men, closeted in the king's apartment, without a guard present, would then plan strategy and decide what would be worked on in the evening when Tronchet and DeSèze arrived. And Louis was not the passive receiver of advice. Quite the contrary. He insisted that his defense follow the contours established at the interrogation. Malesherbes, in fact, thought Louis ought to challenge the competence of the Convention to try him; Louis said no. He knew, as well as his accusers, that legal procedures were no barrier against injustice, but he insisted his lawyers defend him as the hapless victim of unprecedented procedures, that they accept the offer of a trial as he did.

Through the closed door of the king's apartment the guards could hear, nightly, the lively conversation between Louis and his lawyers but could not make out what was being said. We are luckier than the guards. From the anecdotes of Malesherbes and Cléry, from the text of Louis's defense, his *plaidoyer*, we can piece together if not the conversations that took place at least the general nature of these strategy sessions. Every piece of evidence was read by Louis himself and he participated in every aspect of his defense. The task of writing the *plaidoyer* was entrusted to DeSèze, the youngest and most brilliant of the three lawyers, but the arguments were worked out in common and in conformity with the king's wishes. Louis insisted he had not broken the law once he accepted the constitution, that he was not answerable to the nation for any acts prior to his acceptance of the constitution, that there were important procedural violations in the trial, that the documentary evidence against him had been illegally seized, that he had never wanted to shed blood, and that even though he was immune from prosecution he could, and would, defend each of his actions as morally correct and faithful to the letter of the law. His lawyers had only to find the legal arguments necessary to make his case convincing.

When DeSèze drew up the *plaidoyer* he went without sleep for four nights running. When it was finished he read it to Louis, Malesherbes, and Tronchet. "I have never heard anything as moving as his peroration. Tronchet and I were touched almost to tears," said Malesherbes. Louis too was moved, but he insisted that DeSèze's original peroration be suppressed (no copy of this first effort has survived): "I do not want to play on their feelings." Louis was willing to argue for his life, but not beg for it. This stubbornness, completely in keeping with his responses to the *acte énonciatif*, may have weakened his defense. A number of *conventionnels* and journalists pointed out that the *plaidoyer*, with its revised peroration, was able but cold, lacking the passion men had come to expect from DeSèze.

On the morning of December 26 the mayor, Nicolas Chambon, again came to the Temple to take Louis to the Convention. The same elaborate security measures were in effect as on December 11. Louis once more made the trip in the mayor's coach and, again, remarked on the unfamiliar formation of his escort. During the journey across Paris Louis maintained his customary dignity and tranquillity. The secretary of the Commune, who rode in the coach, was surprised that he could be so calm, "with so many subjects to fear." But Louis was never fearful in the midst of his subjects. He had the instincts to be a popular monarch, but exercised them usually at the wrong time (as during his flight to Varennes, when he insisted on dismounting and talking to the men changing horses for the fugitives, which delayed the royal family and exposed their incognito) or for the wrong reason (as during the invasion of the Tuileries on June 20, when he charmed the invaders only to refuse their demands). He enjoyed and took seriously the role of father of his people, and even in captivity welcomed a chance to see them, talk to them.

The small talk in the coach turned on Latin authors. Louis expressed his opinions "with a great deal of exactness" and showed familiarity with the classics. One of the passengers said he disliked reading Seneca because the stoic's love of riches contrasted so sharply with his convictions and he had dared mitigate Nero's crimes before the Roman senate. The remark troubled Louis, about to have his own actions explained to the representatives of the nation, but he kept silent.

The Convention had begun its session at 9:00 A.M., but long before that hour the Manège was mobbed by spectators. Yves-Marie Audrein announced, on behalf of the Commission of Twelve (Valazé's committee), that they had discovered a bunch of keys in the possession of Louis's former valet, Thierry, and that one of the keys opened the infamous *armoire de fer*. The tag identifying the key, written in Thierry's hand, read "key given to me August 12 by the king, in the court of the Feuillants." Louis had, of course, denied any knowledge of the secret safe at his interrogation. The Convention decreed that the key would be shown to Louis for identification at the end of his defense. The Assembly then did some miscellaneous business before the president, Defermon, announced: "Louis and his defenders are ready to appear at the bar. I forbid the members or spectators to make any noise or show any kind of approval." The Convention was obviously as nervous as Louis and his defenders, worried that his appearance and his defense, the work of one of the most respected lawyers of the age, might impress the deputies and the people. Accompanied by his three lawyers, Chambon the mayor, and Santerre the commandant general, Louis walked slowly to the bar. "Louis," said the president, "the Convention has decreed that you would be heard definitively today." "My counsel," said Louis gesturing toward DeSèze, "will read you my defense."

DeSèze was on the verge of exhaustion. He had gone for days without sleep to prepare the *plaidoyer*. Now he had to call on all his reserves of energy, all his endurance, for the most significant performance of his professional life. Legal pleading, during the Revolution as during the *ancien régime*, was flamboyant, dramatic, passionate. The age, perhaps from Rousseau's influence, adored self-dramatization as much as it adored oratory. DeSèze had a sonorous and ample voice capable of considerable tonal variation. His gestures, although grand, were thought dignified, and with his large head, thick eyebrows, and erect bearing he made an impressive figure. He delivered the *plaidoyer* standing with his text in hand while Louis sat behind the bar, attentive and composed. The renowned Bordeaux school of lawyers were famous for their broad humanity, their lapidary style, and their presence; DeSèze was a brilliant representative of this tradition.

Obedient to his master's wishes DeSèze presented two principles as central to his defense: the question of Louis's constitutional inviolability, and the question of the nature of the trial itself. "Citizen representatives of the nation," he began, "the moment has come when Louis, accused in the name of the French people, can make himself listened to in the midst of the people themselves." Inviolability, he argued, was fundamental to any monarchical government. No monarchy that denied its king legal immunity could survive and function. The constitution-makers of 1791 had recognized this truism. The chapter "Royalty" in the constitution said, quite simply, "the person of the king is inviolable and sacred." No conditions were placed on this clear statement of principle, no exceptions were made, no nuances weakened it. The constitution did, however, specify three hypothetical situations in which the king would lose his inviolability by being forced to abdicate. Article V said that if the king refused to swear an oath to the constitution, or having sworn an oath reneged, "he will be considered to have abdicated the throne." Article VI said that if the king led an invading army against his country, or failed to oppose an invasion, "he will be considered to have abdicated the throne." Article VII said that if the king fled the kingdom and refused to return "he will be considered to have abdicated the throne." Article VIII said that once forced from the throne the king "will be in the class of citizens, and can only be accused and judged like them for acts posterior to his abdication."

None of these articles apply to Louis's situation, and even if they did Louis had already paid the prescribed penalty of forced abdication and could not again be tried for anything he may have done as king. There is no positive law that could be used against Louis, since the only laws in existence at the time of his supposed crimes made a clear and specific exception in the king's case. Under the constitution Louis as king was a class of one. In the absence of positive law could an appeal be made to natural law? "Citizens," said DeSèze, "here is my response. I read in Rousseau these words: 'In the case where I see neither the law which it is necessary to follow, nor the judge who should pronounce, I cannot rely on the general will. The will, being general, cannot pronounce on a man or on a fact.'" The authority of Rousseau was not exactly apposite, but the king could quote him as readily as could his accusers. But if statute law made the king immune and natural law did not apply to an individual, what then was the basis for the trial? Force, DeSèze answered: "There is not today a power equal to yours," he told the Convention, "but there is a power you do not have: it is that of not being just."

Having thus made the constitutional argument for Louis's innocence because of his immunity, DeSèze turned his attention to the question of legal procedure. "Citizens, I will speak to you here with the frankness of a free man. I search among you for judges, and I see only accusers." Then, in a series of staccato paradoxes, he drove the point home:

> You want to pronounce on Louis's fate, and it is you yourselves who accuse him!

You want to pronounce on Louis's fate, and you have already declared your views!

You want to pronounce on Louis's fate, and your opinions are dis-
seminated throughout Europe!

Louis has become the only Frenchman for whom there exists "no
law and no procedures!" He has "neither the rights of a citizen nor
the prerogatives of a king!" He has the benefits "neither of his
former state nor of his new state!" He is, in fact, what Saint-Just
had so brilliantly made him on November 13, an enemy alien
among the French, a man without a country, without rights; an
outlaw merely because he had inherited the throne. For Saint-Just,
of course, Louis's alienation from his country, and hence from its
legal protection, was a theoretical "fact" that logically called for
summary execution. For DeSèze this alienation had been forced on
Louis by men bent on killing him and willing to violate all procedures, all laws, to do so.

DeSèze knew that such arguments were not likely to save his
master. He was not trying to persuade the radicals, an impossible
task, but rather to win the support of the moderates in the Convention. There was no point in alienating men who might be persuaded to spare the king. Louis's accusers were, he knew, attached
to traditional legal forms and procedures. He now appealed to
their attachment:

> But I do not insist on these reflections. I leave them to your consciences.
> I do not want to defend Louis only with principles. I want to oppose the
> prejudices that have been articulated concerning his motives and char-
> acter. I want to destroy them.

It would be best to let the deputies contemplate the numerous ille-
galities of the trial while he moved on to consider the *acte énonciatif*,
point by point. Lindet's accusation was cast in the form of a republican history of the Revolution; DeSèze countered with a royalist
history.

Men have forgotten, he began, that it was Louis himself who began the Revolution with the calling of the Estates-General. They
have forgotten that in 1789 the people had proclaimed the king
"the restorer of French liberty." They have forgotten that Louis
was the first of his house to relinquish voluntarily some of his
power for the happiness of his people. In purely legal terms none

of Louis's actions before September 1791 can be included in the accusation. His acceptance of the constitution in that year was an act of oblivion for everyone in France. The Convention's retroactive revenge on the king is unworthy of a great and generous nation. DeSèze concentrates his attention on the postconstitutional accusations, dividing them into two classes: those legitimately directed against the king; and those more correctly directed against his ministers. Under the constitution Louis's powers were limited by law. He was incapable of being the all-powerful tyrant accused in the *acte énonciatif*. His accusers have tried to hold Louis responsible for all the upheavals that revolutions cause. But the king, after 1791, hadn't the power to do either great good or great evil. Louis did indeed veto many pieces of legislation, but he was given his veto power by the constitution. He cannot now be judged for his use of his constitutional authority. And if he did veto legislation desired by the representatives of the nation, for example many of the decrees having to do with the Church, he did so because he feared "that he would betray himself in sanctioning them." DeSèze's Louis certainly made mistakes, certainly showed bad judgment on occasion, but he conformed to the law of the land and acted out of the best intentions.

Much if not all the evidence supporting the *acte énonciatif*, DeSèze then reminded the deputies, was illegally gathered. In the "tumult of the invasion [of the Tuileries]" important documents may have been lost or destroyed. Louis had a legal right not to recognize these documents and his repudiation of the evidence does not make him guilty. Here again DeSèze had little chance of success. The Convention had declared the evidence valid and would not reverse itself. As with the constitutional arguments DeSèze decided to let his remarks percolate through the minds of the *conventionnels*. So he descended from these legal arguments to deal with the contents of the evidence itself. All the accusations in the *acte énonciatif* were contrived to reveal a pattern of counterrevolution instigated by the king and carried out by his court. The same accusations, DeSèze demonstrates, can reveal another pattern, one more flattering to his master. Louis's use of public funds, for example, proves that he was a generous benefactor, that the spirit of noblesse oblige was deeply imbedded in his character. "Thus all these liberalities that he has been reproached for do honor to his heart, and not a single one can be used to cast suspicion on his principles."

The law, as DeSèze understood it, deals with actions and not motives. A man can be tried for violating the law, but not for disliking the law. But in a political trial, a trial where the courts and procedures are used for political ends—questions of public safety, as Robespierre put it—men are less interested in procedures (which they tend to see as so many unnecessary delays to justice), more interested in securing the required verdict. DeSèze was, consequently, in a difficult, if not impossible situation. Louis had decided not to challenge the competence of the Convention, and the Convention was sovereign in France; it could make and unmake laws, observe or ignore precedents. DeSèze had to find a way of questioning the trial itself and the conduct of the trial without, at the same time, attacking the Convention. The problem becomes acute when he reaches the accusations dealing with August 10. The king's lawyer had to admit the legitimacy of August 10 and yet defend his master against preparing an assault that might be construed as occasioning the insurrection. The Convention, of course, would not tolerate any interpretation of August 10 that even suggested the king was innocent and the revolution guilty. The Girondins had already come to grief on this very issue. If Louis had been preparing an attack in the summer of 1792 then he was guilty of treason as charged. But if he was only attempting to defend himself, his family, and the monarchy from attack, then the charge would fall to the ground.

DeSèze's version of what happened on August 10 is the same as the king's: isolated by local and national authorities, he decided to defend the château against another attack. Where, asked DeSèze, is there any evidence of treason? Before Louis left the Tuileries there had been no bloodshed. After he left he had no responsibility for what happened; he was the prisoner of the Legislative Assembly. His motives are not in question, but his actions are. And since what the king may have thought is irrelevant in a trial, for DeSèze at least, and since it is impossible to know what Louis was thinking at the time, only his actions matter. Louis is not *legally* responsible for the killings at the Tuileries.

DeSèze had been speaking for more than an hour. The Manège had become fetid, packed as it was to the ceiling with bodies and heated by the single stove that gave off more fumes than heat. DeSèze was soaked with perspiration. He had delivered about half his defense and he knew his listeners wanted a long, dramatic *plaidoyer*, faithful to classical models. He knew the deputies were savoring his phrases, mentally noting the strong and weak points of the argument, his mastery of paradox, his celebrated style. He knew too that they were patiently awaiting the peroration, the high point of any *plaidoyer*. The king remained calm and collected as DeSèze launched into his peroration.

"Citizens," he began, referring to August 10, "if at this very moment one were to say to you that an excited and armed crowd was marching toward you, that without respect for your sacred character as legislators it wanted to tear you from this sanctuary, what would you do?" Probably something similar to what Louis did, Louis who has an abhorrence of shedding blood:

> You accuse him of shedding blood? . . . Ah! he bemoans as much as you the fatal catastrophe . . . it is the most profound wound inflicted on him, it is his most frightful despair. He knows very well that he is not the author of bloodshed, but that he has perhaps been the unhappy cause of it. He will never forgive himself for this.

The Revolution has coarsened men, weakened "the sentiment of humanity." But Louis is not to blame. He deserves compassion rather than an accusation of high treason. Here is the famous conclusion to DeSèze's defense, apparently less passionate and moving than his first draft which it replaces:

> Louis ascended the throne at the age of twenty, and at the age of twenty he gave to the throne the example of character. He brought to the throne no wicked weaknesses, no corrupting passions. He was economical, just, severe. He showed himself always the constant friend of the people. The people wanted the abolition of servitude. He began by abolishing it on his own lands. The people asked for reforms in the criminal law . . . he carried out these reforms. *The people wanted liberty: he gave it to them.* The people themselves came before him in his sacrifices. Nevertheless, it is in the name of these very people that one today demands . . . Citizens, I cannot finish . . . I stop myself before History. Think how it will judge your judgment, and that the judgment of him [the king] will be judged by the centuries.

The phrase *"the people wanted liberty: he gave it to them,"* which is italicized in the printed speech, caused a sensation in the Convention. DeSèze had wanted it struck from the published *plaidoyer*. The Convention, on a motion by Barère, refused to allow so useful an indiscretion to be suppressed; but it did allow DeSèze to add an explanatory note:

> One of us had struck this phrase from the manuscript, out of respect for the Convention, and because it had excited murmurs in the tribunes. But this abridging having become the subject of a decree [of the Convention], we believed ourselves obliged to say that by the word *donna* [he gave], we had no other intention than that of recalling that Louis had prepared the liberty of France by ordering the convocation of the Estates-General, and the decree of the nation, of August 4, 1789, which had proclaimed Louis *restorer of French liberty*, had inspired in us this phrase.

When the Convention certified the *plaidoyer* for publication it added an additional note on the celebrated phrase: "We certify that the phrase *the people wanted liberty: he gave it to them*, which was pronounced exactly as it appears in the manuscript, and which had later been crossed out by one of Louis's defenders, has been restored by us." Doubtless Louis and his defenders would have preferred to see such scrupulousness exercised on the evidence rather than the *plaidoyer*.

DeSèze had spoken for more than two hours. He was exhausted. Louis asked for a fresh shirt for his counsel and the president sent someone to fetch one. Then the king addressed his accusers:

> You have heard my defense. I will not reiterate it. In speaking to you, perhaps for the last time, I declare to you that my conscience reproaches me for nothing, and that my defenders have spoken only the truth.
>
> I never believed that my conduct might be publicly examined; but my heart is torn to find in the accusation the charge of having wanted to shed the blood of the people, and above all that the unhappiness of August 10 could be attributed to me.
>
> I confess that the multiple proofs that I have given at all times of my love for the people, and the manner in which I have always conducted myself, appeared to me to prove that I had no fear in exposing myself [to danger] in order to spare its blood and to remove forever such an imputation.

The extraordinary confrontation between Louis and the Convention ended with a brief interrogation. The king was shown the keys taken from Thierry and asked if he recognized the key to the *armoire de fer*. He remained consistent, saying he remembered giving some keys to Thierry but did not remember what the keys were for. "Do you have anything more to add to your defense?" president Defermon asked. Louis answered "No" and was invited to leave.

On the ride back to the Temple Louis chatted with his captors about hospitals, remarking that it would be useful to have one in each section of the city, to care for the poor. He may have noticed, as the coach reached the Temple, an additional patrol outside the tower, eighty-seven new men assigned to the prison, along with masonry crews reenforcing the walls. Still, any outing, even one that led to the bar of the Convention, was a welcome diversion for the king.

As with all Louis's public utterances after his fall from power his closing remarks to the Convention have a note of pathos that springs from his inability to accept that the people he sincerely loved would deliberately take his life. Kings might do wrong, but that was not for men to determine; legally the king could do no wrong. Louis believed himself innocent, which is doubtless why he accepted the offer of a legal duel. Like so many men of his generation he had faith in laws. Had he not himself instituted a number of legal reforms on the eve of the Revolution, before his subjects rose in rebellion against him? He certainly seems to have understood what his former subjects wanted: power, office, his life, and a republic. The ambitions of men were a familiar spectacle to a man who had spent his life at court. And he even accepted these desires, not as right but as comprehensible. All the more reason, as he saw it, to have a king who was above such ambitions and the passions that drove them. His failure to defend the nobility and the Church, he may now have realized, had exposed the monarchy directly to attack by the have-nots. He profoundly believed they were wrong, for he profoundly believed in the monarchy. Kings had been instituted by God to hold men's passions in check, to prevent the ruinous excesses of ambition, to be a flail for the wicked and a model of benevolence for the good. Had he been hauled before an ecclesiastical court, or even before a court of his magnates, he could have acknowledged what was happening. Both the Church and the nobility shared his values, saw the world as he did. But these revolutionaries, these commoners, these men who desperately needed a king's love and strength, lived in another world, a world they themselves had made through revolution.

The kingship and its prerogatives were not fit subjects for the profane inquiries of a court of law, let alone a court of law composed of men of the Third Estate, Louis believed. A king's subjects might petition, but they could not judge. Louis was willing to die for his beliefs, although he had little choice in the matter, but the central injustice of the entire trial for him was that he was the victim of men whose passions were familiar while their pretensions were unacceptable. His defense was a faithful reflection of these convictions. DeSèze's *plaidoyer*, written in haste and under the most unfavorable conditions—he had only eight days for preparation—was the best defense Louis could have expected. DeSèze's most telling points are those aimed at the procedures of the trial. He argued, articulating Louis's beliefs, that the king was the victim of political expediency; and if traditional procedures were used Louis could not be convicted. DeSèze and his master could take little comfort in the outcome of the trial. It was clear that virtually all the deputies thought the king guilty of treason. But they could take some comfort in their symbolic victory; Louis could be convicted only by abridging or disregarding traditional criminal procedures. Interestingly enough Louis made no attempt to argue for his life by invoking royalist ideology. He had abandoned this tactic when he decided to face the Convention sitting as a court of law.

Contemporaries thought the *plaidoyer* elegant but cold, conscientious but not very convincing. Most applauded DeSèze's attempt to find a balance between the moribund kingship and the revolutionary Convention. "The very defenders of Louis XVI," Choudieu says in his *Mémoires*, "did not contest the right of the Convention to pronounce the end of monarchy if the king's guilt were to be proved." But Louis and his accusers understood proof differently. For the revolutionaries Louis was guilty because he was not himself a revolutionary. For the royalists, most of whom

prudently addressed their countrymen from exile, Louis was innocent because he was king. As an anonymous royalist pamphleteer
wrote, everything about DeSèze's *plaidoyer* was admirable except
the admission that Louis could be judged: "If ever something was
patently absurd it is, without doubt, the joining together of these
two words, *Sovereign Nation.*" Here was Louis's dilemma: he could
not argue, under the circumstances and in 1792, that he was above
the law, king by the grace of God, any more than he could accept
the revolutionary formula that no king can reign innocently. In
seeking a middle ground between these two extremes he offended
the royalists without pleasing the revolutionaries. The entire failure or success of his defense rested on the Convention's willingness to observe all the guarantees of the Criminal Code of 1791.
They refused to do so, and Louis was lost.

DeSèze did the best he could and he impressed a number of
Louis's judges. Gorsas thought the defense had been presented
with "method and logic" and pronounced with authority "by a
man convinced of Louis's innocence." Brissot, in the *Patriote français*, wrote that DeSèze responded "to the grandeur of the cause
and the renown of his talents" but his performance only succeeded
in winning sympathy for his client without proving his innocence.
Marat, too, was favorably impressed:

> DeSèze read a long speech made with a great deal of art. He began by
> trying to win pity for the fate of the tyrant, in painting a picture of the
> human vicissitudes and the blows of fortune which suddenly plunged
> those who had for so long been masters of the world into the obscure
> crowd.

The Commune also praised a great effort in a hopeless cause. The
plaidoyer was "very adroit" but the peroration "lacked passion."
DeSèze did succeed in deflecting some of the accusations against
Louis onto his ministers, but this was not enough to save the king.
For Robespierre the defense was "simple and weak." DeSèze had
failed to exploit fully the pathos of the situation and similarly failed
to delay the trial. Robespierre believed Louis had more capable
defenders in the Convention itself, obviously referring to several of
the Girondin chiefs.

The *plaidoyer* changed few minds. More important than the arguments, more important than DeSèze's considerable skill as a trial

attorney, was Louis himself. His composure and dignity, the inevitable symbolism of a great man brought low, made more of an impression on contemporaries than did arid legal arguments. An English visitor wrote:

> The king's appearance in the Convention, the dignified resignation of his manner, the admirable promptness and candour of his answers, made such an evident impression on some of the audience in the galleries, that a determined enemy of Royalty, who had his eye upon them, declared that he was afraid of hearing the cry *Vive le roi!* issue from the tribunes.

The spy Monro said much the same thing in his dispatch to Lord Grenville.

As soon as Louis was ordered back to the Temple and left the Manège the debates resumed. The session lasted for another four hours and was frequently out of control. The Mountain called for an immediate vote; the Girondins called for delay. The deputy Hardy wanted a postponement of three days and quoted Rousseau: "The people commit an act of tyranny when it judges a man." The Montagnard, Turreau de Linières, countered by shouting, "It commits an act of justice when it assassinates a tyrant." Calls for delay and haste alternated like a seesaw. Parliamentary order collapsed. Once again the trial was stalled, thanks largely to the Girondins. But even deputies who stood aside from factional strife were reluctant to take the last fatal step from which there could be no return. It was easier to debate on procedures than to vote on the king's fate. As Louis was whisked off the stage to return to prison, the *conventionnels* prepared themselves for a renewal of the Jacobin-Girondin struggle. Neither of the factions was powerful enough to sway the Convention at will, but both could and did control the direction and the nature of the debates. For a brief moment Louis had intervened on his own behalf. Now his fate was returned to the Convention, to the factions, to Paris, to the Commune—to the revolutionaries.

CHAPTER VIII

The King and Desperate Men

DECEMBER 27, 1792 – JANUARY 13, 1793

 HATEVER the newspapers might say or the deputies deny, the king's defense made a profound impact on contemporaries and changed the course of the trial. For the second time in a month Louis had appeared in public to confront his accusers; and both times he had affected them significantly. It was not Louis's answers to his interrogation or even DeSèze's eloquence that caused men to pause and think about the trial. The king's dignity and composure accomplished what words could not. The king's character and presence proved the best arguments in his defense. Not only was Louis not a figure of universal scorn for his former subjects, he was a sympathetic figure. His months of imprisonment had made him appear the victim of the Revolution, almost a tragic figure. His two appearances at the bar of the Convention reinforced this impression and gave his defenders courage to act. Plans long contemplated for saving the king, plans that seemed to have no chance for success a week before his appearances at the bar, were now set in motion. They came from several quarters, indicating that many men for many reasons thought there was a possibility of saving the king and that now was the time. The king's defense bought his friends time, and in a Revolution time is perhaps the most precious commodity.

However dissimilar the various schemes were, however elaborate or inept, they all sprang from the same source, the unexpected and widespread sympathy for Louis that his defense had created or reignited. And all depended for success on an elaborate parliamentary maneuver introduced into the trial by the Girondins, which came to be known as the appeal to the people. Saint-Just was the first speaker of the day on December 27 and he was well aware that Louis had impressed the deputies and made them receptive at least to a delay in the trial. He tried to keep the momentum going by attacking DeSèze's *plaidoyer*, by insisting, as he had on November 13, that the Convention had only to judge a hateful abstraction, an absolutist king who was an alien among the French and had betrayed those he illegitimately ruled, and to remind the Convention that "the Revolution begins when the tyrant is done for." And, because the appeal to the people calls into question the competence of the Convention to judge Louis, he had to remind the deputies that they were the elected representatives of the nation and consequently had the authority and the duty to settle the nation's quarrel with its king.

It was no easy task. The *plaidoyer* and Louis's appearances at the bar had interjected the king's personality into the trial: his real body as well as his body politic were now in the prisoner's dock. Saint-Just's abstract tyrant, a monster he had created for the Mountain, was overshadowed by Louis the man, and Louis the man was a touching if not popular character. DeSèze's Louis—decent, honorable, dedicated, conscientious, law-abiding, sincere—was, for Saint-Just, a conjurer's trick. There was no evidence of Louis's supposed virtues in his confiscated papers, not a single project for the reformation of France. The king had made no attempt to detach himself from the views of his predecessors, no effort to cleanse his court, let alone cooperate with the Revolution. He had done nothing to mitigate the inherent tyranny of his office, and in Saint-Just's harsh psychology a man who refused to change his wicked ways must pay the price for his consistency. The price was death: "Have the courage to say the truth, the truth [that] burns in every heart like a lamp in a tomb."

But Saint-Just argued and pleaded in vain. The Mountain's thesis of summary execution, never widely popular in the Convention, could not, in December, even get a hearing. The initiative had passed to the Girondins. Jean-Baptiste Salles was the next speaker. He was a doctor who had sat with the Right in the National Assembly and made no attempt to hide his royalist sympathies. At one point he had said that he would rather die than see the executive power taken from the king. It is Salles the royalist, so discreetly silent until now, who first proposed the appeal to the people to the Convention. The appeal to the people, although subject to various interpretations in the course of the debates, was a simple proposition: Louis's judgment must be submitted to the 44,000 primary assemblies of revolutionary France for ratification. The political overtones of the proposition were farreaching. The appeal to the people rested on two assumptions: Paris, with its unruly and radical population, was exercising a disproportionate influence on the trial; and, a necessary corollary to this assumption, the true expression of the nation's will and republicanism could come only from citizens not embroiled in the political struggles of the capital. An obscure deputy, S. J. Coren-Fustier, succinctly stated the issue in two sentences: "My opinion consists of this simple proposition: the sections of Paris have tried to influence the Convention by petitions. To avoid being reproached for this influence it is necessary that the entire nation be consulted."

The question of the appeal to the people was, during the trial, the most significant and sustained confrontation between Jacobins and Girondins. It was the issue around which the Girondins decided to fight for supremacy, the issue they thought would have the broadest appeal to the Marais deputies. The Girondins calculated that support for saving the king was widespread in the Convention and that the appeal to the people would draw the scattered supporters of the king into a coherent group, led by the Girondins. The trial would be delayed, the king saved, Paris thwarted, and the Mountain defeated. Both factions sent their best speakers to the tribune: Salles and Joseph Serre for the Girondins on the 27th; Buzot and Jean-Paul Rabaut-Saint-Etienne on December 28; the intemperate Biroteau the next day; Vergniaud on December 31; Brissot on January 1; Armand Gensonné on the following day; and Pétion on January 3. The Jacobins sent Saint-Just to the tribune on December 27; Robespierre on December 28, along with Joseph-Marie Lequinio; and Jeanbon Saint-André on January 1. The dra-

matic and ideological high point of the debates was the confrontation between Robespierre, the acknowledged leader of the
Mountain, and Vergniaud, the greatest speaker of the Gironde.
And it became increasingly clear that to support the appeal to the
people meant supporting the Girondins, and supporting the Girondins meant sparing the king.

The idea of an appeal to the people was not new in December.
Barbaroux says that he had first discussed the tactic with a few
friends, all of them Girondins, as early as August 12, 1792. It was
the growing sympathy for Louis that encouraged the Girondins to
resurrect the scheme. The appeal to the people had not been
worked out in any great detail since much of its attraction as a tactic lay in its plasticity. The appeal was easily molded to accommodate different political views, and if the plan attracted some curious, even dubious allies, the Girondins thought they could deal
with such inconsistencies or contradictions when the time came to
do so. For the moment they had to convince the *conventionnels* of
the virtues of the appeal to the people, which they saw as several.
Salles presented the appeal as a political Pascalian gamble: if the
Convention found Louis guilty and the primary assemblies agreed,
the decision would have been a true expression of the nation's
will; if the Convention found Louis guilty and the primary assemblies disagreed, the deputies would have been saved from violating the nation's will.

Joseph Serre, a former corporal of marines and a royalist who,
like many with similar politics, felt closest to the Girondins, argued
that the appeal to the people would assure the king of an impartial
judgment, which was impossible in Paris. Rabaut-Saint-Etienne,
the oldest son of a Protestant minister and himself a minister, delivered a rambling speech, full of homily, commonplaces, and political anger. He presented the appeal as a check on the disastrous
course the trial was taking. He had consistently argued that the
Convention alone was not competent to try the king, and the appeal could save the Revolution from the charge of injustice result-
ing from illegal procedures. Buzot, the next Girondin speaker, was
more dramatic. The appeal, he argued, would constitute the primary assemblies as a kind of supreme court to judge the actions of
the Convention. "Should I be the first victim of assassins," Buzot

told the Convention, "it will not stop me from speaking the truth." Unless the king's judgment were sent to the primary assemblies Paris and the radicals would triumph. The Duke d'Orléans would seat himself "on the smoking ruins of . . . [the] throne."

Even obscure deputies who had taken almost no part in the trial, and who would take little part in the subsequent history of the Convention, saw the appeal as an attractive alternative to the Jacobin thesis. Jacques Engerran, a lawyer whose most singular accomplishment seems to have been living to the age of ninety-two, is typical of such support from the Marais. He wanted the Convention to vote for death and then have the primary assemblies "condemn him to a punishment more worthy of its grandeur and clemency; that of banishment." All those who spoke for the appeal, either implicitly or explicitly, saw it as a means of saving the king from the guillotine while at the same time avoiding the dreadful responsibility thrust on them by the Revolution. The most convincing case for the appeal to the people was made by Vergniaud, a complex yet appealing character, enormously gifted yet driven by contradictory urges. He was a great speaker (some said the greatest of the Revolution) who was reluctant to exercise his gift. Because of his oratorical genius he was the natural leader of the Girondins, but he despised the brutality of political infighting and left such dirty work to others who had less ability. He had a keen analytical mind but was more interested in art and imagination than in analysis. When he was inspired and stood before the Convention he was magnificent, but he lacked the singleness of purpose so essential to a political leader and seemed happiest when he was absorbed in contemplating the fantasies of his own imagination. He had little interest in money, or power, or even political glory. He liked good conversation, good friends, and lots of leisure for the cultivation of his very sophisticated and subtle mind. Vergniaud was a remarkable man who might have done anything supremely well except be a revolutionary leader.

Brilliant, supple, humane, eloquent, possessed of a sonorous voice, an imposing presence, and calm gestures that were thought "noble and grand" by his contemporaries, Vergniaud (along with DeSèze) was the most distinguished representative of the Bordeaux school of lawyers. His speech of December 31 put the debates on the appeal to the people on a theoretical level while endowing the scheme with his own amiability and compassion. Sovereignty, he argued, belongs to the people. The elected deputies were but an imperfect expression of this sovereignty and thus the appeal to the people must be made, for only the entire body of the sovereign people could judge a king. Besides, there were numerous legal improprieties in the trial. The Convention had assumed to itself the functions "of grand jury, of jury, of legislators determining the form of judgment, and of judge." This concentration of power in the Convention was a step toward despotism which only the primary assemblies could reverse. In the provinces, he continued, was the true home of republicanism. There the Paris radicals "have been repulsed with scorn." The Parisians and their delegation "threaten with death those citizens who do not have the misfortune to think as they do." Proper procedures and a solemn respect for the nation's sovereignty enbodied in the primary assemblies are the only guarantees of justice, the only barriers against terror. Following his eloquent oration, much admired by his hearers and delivered without a text, as was his custom, Vergniaud sat down and seemed to fall into a dreamy lethargy. The task of completing the case for the appeal to the people fell to more aggressive men.

Brissot developed the theme of the impact of the trial on foreign affairs. The allies, he argued, wanted Louis dead. If the king were kept alive the enemies of France would be forced to deal with the new republic on its own terms. They would see, after the appeal to the people, that the Convention and the Revolution were "not directed by any particular movement, but . . . bound only by the principles of grandeur." The Jacobins, whom he called "ambitious imbeciles," despised the appeal because they despised the people. Gensonné, the thirty-four-year-old son of an army doctor and the only Girondin leader who came from humble origins, carried on the struggle. He was thought the best intellect of the Girondins, with the exception of the great Condorcet. Gensonné had a speech impediment and was called the "duck of the Gironde," but through a great effort of will he had learned to stand before an audience and depend on his intellectual powers to overcome his defect. He concentrated on the Jacobins, accusing them of desiring class warfare, of encouraging "permanent insurrection." The appeal to the people would "expose this faction to the entire nation."

The last of the important Girondin speakers on the appeal was Pétion, the former mayor of Paris. A native of Chartres, like Brissot, Pétion had practiced law in his native town before being elected to the Estates-General. There he attached himself to the extreme Left and was inseparable from Robespierre, whom he described as the man he most loved and esteemed. When the self-denying ordinance made both men ineligible for the Legislative Assembly they gradually drifted apart. Pétion thirsted after popularity. When he was elected mayor of Paris he took the distinction as evidence that he was the most important and popular and influential man in France. Madame Roland cultivated Pétion's friendship assiduously and cleverly, introducing him into the scintillating circles that regularly gathered at Roland's home. He fell easily and became a passionate adherent to the faction. When the Paris voters rejected him as a deputy to the Convention Pétion swallowed his pride and secured a seat for his natal department: "I am one of the most striking examples of the fickleness of popular opinion." Pétion argued that the appeal to the people was necessary simply because Louis was not an ordinary defendant, he was, as king, "a being apart."

By the time the Girondin speakers had finished explaining the appeal to the people there was not one but several appeals. The Mountain attacked these inconsistencies. Lequinio called the appeal a "strange abuse of reason" since the Convention was thought competent to declare the republic yet incompetent to judge the king. Sending Louis's judgment to the primary assemblies would hopelessly undermine the Convention's authority. But it was Jeanbon Saint-André and Robespierre who delivered the most telling blows against the appeal.

Saint-André's major accomplishments lay in the future, but he had already lived a remarkable and romantic life as ship's captain, student of the Jesuits, merchant, and Protestant minister. He was forty-three at the time and his strengths were practicality, clarity of expression, considerable knowledge of the world, and a passionate attachment to the Mountain. Saint-André argued that the several versions of the appeal to the people represented the usual hypoc-

risy of the Girondins. They were not interested in the principles of
popular sovereignty, but only in saving the king. In fact the appeal
would only complicate procedures and delay the trial indefinitely.
Robespierre's speech on the appeal to the people was an attempt to
put the entire question into a general revolutionary perspective, as
he had done in November when he responded to Louvet's accusation. Vergniaud had demanded the appeal to assure a fair trial for
Louis. Robespierre responded that the trial was fair, if a bit unorthodox. The king himself had told the Convention, on December
26, that he had nothing more to add to his defense. Any other
criminal "with evidence a thousand times less convincing, would
have been condemned in 24 hours." What more did the Girondins
want? Did they want to see more documentary evidence? Did they
want to hear witnesses? Did they think Louis's crimes were un-
proved? No. The appeal then was politically motivated, yet another attack on Paris and the Mountain.

The appeal was a "willful, absurd and dangerous supposition."
The Girondin picture of a peaceful and idyllic countryside, peopled
by staunch and independent republicans gathered in their primary
assemblies, was a dangerous Girondin conceit. Attendance at the
primary assemblies had been consistently poor and local men of
standing often dominated the meetings, intimidating the people.
Calling the primary assemblies to judge Louis would be an invitation to royalists and conservatives to reassert themselves and
undermine the Convention and hence the Revolution. It would, in
addition, take months for the thousands of primary assemblies to
reach a decision, and during this time the Convention could do
nothing significant, lest its decision be reversed. Delay would put
the Revolution in jeopardy. The Girondins were "cruel sophists"
who argued that "the means of destroying tyranny is to keep the
tyrant alive." If the appeal to the people was proposed as a check
on the procedures used in the trial, the primary assemblies were
incompetent to decide legal procedures. If the primary assemblies
were to be used to curb Parisian radicalism the Girondins were
sacrificing the Revolution to the royalists and conservatives, for the
assemblies were politically unreliable. If the assemblies were to
scrutinize the Convention's judgment they would have to see all
the evidence, and it was virtually impossible to put the evidence

into the hands of 44,000 primary assemblies. And if the primary assemblies were to be permitted only to ratify the Convention's decision this would be putting a limit on the people's sovereignty, a logical and political impossibility.

Vergniaud's eloquence and Robespierre's challenge had paralyzed the Convention. The contending factions had once again succeeded in tying Louis's fate to their own. Louis himself had vanished into the background. It was the intervention of Bertrand Barère, on January 4, that returned the trial to the question of the king rather than the factions. So important was the speech of Barère that it was commemorated in a portrait, attributed by many to Jacques-Louis David, the greatest painter of the age and a deputy who sat with the Mountain. Sporting a red waistcoat that catches the eye and focuses it on him, Barère looks out at us with studied arrogance. He appears a self-consciously proud orator, aware of his powers, in full manhood, handsome and flamboyant. He is standing at the tribune, his famous speech a pile of holograph sheets before him, left hand on hip, eyes ablaze, long hair slightly ruffled, his waistcoat an ostentatious challenge to the monochrome taste of the day, a symbol of his penchant for self-dramatization.

Barère was the son of a minor court functionary in his native Bigorre and had inherited enough land so that he could legitimately call himself Barère de Vieuzac, unlike many of his contemporaries who had foolishly grafted a bogus patent of nobility onto their bourgeois names. At twenty he was already registered as a lawyer in the *parlement* of Toulouse. He was elected to the Estates-General where he leaned toward the Left and wrote a respected newspaper, *Le Point du Jour*. He came to the Convention an admirer of the Girondins and he frequently dined with Vergniaud. But Barère was a trimmer by nature. Brilliant, supple, even devious, clever, remarkably gifted as an orator, and possessed of a keen political intelligence, he was a compromiser and later "a reluctant terrorist." He had the gift of attaching himself to the opinions of others without becoming completely identified with them. He was neither a sycophant nor a cipher; his personality was too strong. Rather he was a charming and gregarious opportunist who had the talent of putting other men's ideas together in a coherent and convincing way. His sense of order and logic imposed more coherence

JACQUES-PIERRE BRISSOT
(1754–1793). An engraving by N. F.
Maviez, after a painting by F. Bonneville. The engraving was made before the sitting of the Convention.
Brissot is wearing his own hair and
this, along with his open collar, proclaim the informality cultivated by
the republicans. Such engravings
were popular at the time and could
be purchased at virtually any book-
seller. They were relatively inex-
pensive and could thus be easily
replaced if one wanted to be au
courant with revolutionary politics
and the changing leadership.
Bibliothèque nationale

JEAN-BAPTISTE LOUVET
(1760–1797). An engraving done by
Bonneville after the fall of the
Jacobins in 1794, when Louvet returned from exile in Switzerland
to reenter politics as a deputy to
the Council of Five Hundred for
the department of Haute Vienne.
During the Thermidorian reaction that followed Robespierre's
fall, and the Directory government, dress became more formal,
although wigs were a thing of the
past. *Bibliothèque nationale*

FRANÇOIS-NICOLAS-
LÉONARD BUZOT (1760–1794).
An engraving by L. F. Mariage, after
an earlier portrait by Bonneville. Another of the many popular series of
important deputies done during the
Revolution, this one in 1792. Buzot
is dressed in the prerevolutionary
style, with elaborate cravat and wig.
Bibliothèque nationale

MARGUERITE-ELIE GUADET
(1755–1794). An engraving celebrating Guadet as the president of the
Legislative Assembly, January 22,
1792. Again he is formally dressed
and wears a wig. *Bibliothèque
nationale*

MADAME MANON-JEANNE
PHILIPON ROLAND (1754–1793). An
informal portrait attempting to suggest the
simplicity of republican Rome, but at the
same time with a touch of the emerging romantic sensibility, which Mme. Roland herself seems to personify, both in her life and
her imagination. *Bibliothèque nationale*

MARAT BY BOZE. An oil painting, which now hangs in the Carnavalet Museum, in Pa and is thought to be Boze's fir work. It is ironic that the form court painter, compromised in the Boze Affair, should have be most inspired by Marat. The painting is informal and migh even be thought Romantic at fi glance. Marat seems about to speak, and Boze has made him more attractive and heroic tha he was thought by most of his contemporaries. *Carnavalet Museum, Paris*

GEORGES-JACQUES DANTON (1759–1794). A lithograph by Delpech, after the oil portrait (artist unknown) that hangs in the Carnavalet Museum in Paris. Some of the detail in the painting has been lost in the reproduction, for example, the scarred lip Danton received as a youth when he was gored by a bull's horn. But his impressive physical stature (verging on corpulence) and his vitality come through. *Bibliothèque nationale*

LOUIS-ANTOINE DE SAINT-JUST
Reproduction of a drawing by Guérin. Perhaps more than the full-face portraits, this drawing captures the flamboyance of Saint-Just, complete with gold earring, carefully tied neckcloth, and hair worn long, to his shoulders. The original is in the Carnavalet Museum, Paris. *Bibliothèque nationale*

GABRIEL HONORÉ RIQUETTI, COMTE DE MIRABEAU (1749–1791). Oil on canvas, artist unknown. Mirabeau has been captured in a relatively quiet moment, yet his characteristic arrogance, intelligence, and energy are apparent. He appears impatient to be off and doing something. *Carnavalet Museum, Paris*

JEAN-MARIE ROLAND (de la Platière) (1734–1793). This engraving, by Nicolas Colibert, captures Roland's own vision of himself. He effected simple and somber clothes, reminiscent of the Quakers (whom he admired), and an austere republicanism. The engraving was done when he was minister of the interior. *Bibliothèque nationale*

PIERRE-VICTURNIEN VERGNIAUD (1753–1793). A lithograph by Maurin after an engraving by Delpech, which seems to catch some of the melancholy of the great orator. *Bibliothèque nationale*

ROBESPIERRE AT THE TRIBUNE. An anonymous sketch which captures the fastidiousness, stiffness, and rectitude of the man. His holograph speech is on the tribune before him, for in an age of flamboyant and often extemporaneous oratory, Robespierre wrote his speeches out with great care, and read them to his hearers. He always dressed in the style of the *ancien régime*, even at the height of *sans-culottisme*. The eyeglasses he usually wore, or pushed up on his forehead, are absent here. *Bibliothèque nationale*

BERTRAND BARÈRE (1755–1841). An engraving by Mariage, after Bonneville, done during the sitting of the Convention. The formality of the portrait misses the flamboyance and charm of this connoisseur of so much in life. *Bibliothèque nationale*

on the appeal to the people than any of its supporters had been able to create, although he ultimately ended up supporting the Mountain against the Girondin.

Louis, Barère argued, had received a fair trial, albeit an unorthodox one. Everything in the trial had been done openly and judgment would be reached by the solemn ritual of a roll-call vote. This very publicity guaranteed justice for the king in a way that no traditional procedures could. The appeal to the people, then, was, as Robespierre had argued, politically motivated. And the reason the appeal seemed so popular was partly because it was so plastic and partly because it had been blessed by Vergniaud's genius, which appealed to all the most generous springs of the human heart, which was filled with compassion and dignity. But republicans, Barère warned, must resist such human temptations in favor of the severity of the laws, "the terrible necessity of destroying the tyrant in order to remove all hope of tyranny." With the Jacobins Barère believed the king must be killed in his two bodies, his own and his body politic, so that the monarchy itself would be dead. And if the trial was to be a truly revolutionary act, then, if necessary, all the tyrant's laws must be broken to send the king to the guillotine, a slight modification of Saint-Just's original argument. The deputies could not shirk their dreadful responsibility, nor shy away from the implications of judging the king. He concluded his extraordinary speech, which lasted several hours, with an eloquent plea for an end to party passion:

> In the midst of passions of every kind that have agitated and given offense in this great cause, a single passion has the right to be heard, that of liberty. Let us unite ourselves to some opinion and save the republic. You are going to pronounce before the statue of Brutus [which occupied an honored place in the Manège], before your country, before the entire world; and it is with the judgment of the last king of the French that the National Convention will enter into posterity.

Barère's intervention changed the course of the debates. In one stroke he had swept aside all the rhetorical embellishments, all the factional and personal hatreds, and exposed to the Convention not only the essence of the appeal to the people, but the need for unified action. And because he was not attached to either the Jacobins or the Girondins he appeared the voice of reason. On January 7, when the debates resumed once more, Guadet, for the Girondins, called for an end of debate. The Convention unanimously supported the motion, decreeing that all unheard opinions would be published at government expense. Barère had saved the Convention from itself. "It is impossible," Fabre d'Eglantine told the Jacobin Club on the night of January 4, "to find anything finer."

On January 3, the day before Barère's speech, the Mountain made a serious attempt to discredit the appeal to the people by discrediting the Girondins. They had no way of knowing Barère would join their cause and the appeal seemed to have general sympathy in the Convention, so the Mountain sent Thomas-Augustin Gasparin to the tribune to reveal a scandal involving several leading Girondins. The scandal, which came to be called the Boze affair, may have been known about for some time. At any rate, January 3 seemed a good time to use it in the struggle against the Girondins. The Girondin speakers, and especially Vergniaud, had insisted on the appeal to the people as a necessary counterpoise to Jacobin and Parisian intrigue and intimidation, and by implication insisted that the Girondins were the true republicans, untainted by the ambitions that drove the Mountain to betray the Revolution for their own ends. The revelations in the Boze affair were designed to implicate the Girondin leaders in a plot with the king on the eve of the revolution of August 10.

Gasparin, a former regimental captain from Picardy, told the Convention that he had lived, during the turbulent summer of 1792, in the same house with Joseph Boze, a compatriot from Picardy and the former court painter to Louis XVI, whose best work, ironically, is his portrait of Marat. "We often saw each other in the morning," said Gasparin, "and we would talk about the Revolution like true *sans-culottes.*" Around the middle of July—just about the time the sections and the federals were contemplating and planning the dethronement of the king—Boze told Gasparin that negotiations were being conducted between the king and "several members of the [Legislative] Assembly." Boze himself was involved as a go-between. The painter told his friend Gasparin that the king had requested a report which he, Boze, had delivered. It was signed by Vergniaud, Guadet, Gensonné, and perhaps Brissot. The report contained "several articles, one of which concerned changing the ministry." Gasparin made some notes on the general contents of the report before being posted out of Paris in the fall of 1792. He had shown his notes to two Jacobin friends, Jean-Pierre Lacombe Saint-Michel, and Lazare Carnot. Nothing was done at the time, but when the *armoire de fer* was discovered in November the three Jacobins who knew about the report were astonished that it was not found in the safe. They suspected Roland had suppressed the report to avoid compromising his political friends.

Now, some months later, Gasparin turned his notes over to the Convention and demanded that Boze be called to explain. The charge was serious. If Gasparin's accusation were true then the Girondin leaders had tried to prevent the insurrection of August 10 by making a secret deal with the king. And if they were capable of making a secret deal with the king to save his throne in the summer of 1792, surely they were still capable of making a deal to save the king, this time by using the appeal to the people. Boze was immediately sent for, and while the Convention waited for him to appear Guadet and Vergniaud explained their versions of the story and Roland appeared to defend once more his handling of the *armoire de fer* incident. When Boze arrived he nervously told the Convention that he could not remember the incident of the report clearly enough to give a detailed account, but he admitted passing the report to the king and believed that its gist was advising Louis "to sanction several decrees that he had refused to sanction" and pleading with him to recall the recently dismissed Girondin ministers.

The Boze revelations proved to be less damaging than the Mountain had hoped but they did cast some doubt on the motives of the Girondins in calling for the appeal to the people. Many *conventionnels*, and not just those who sat with the Mountain, were skeptical about Girondin tactics, which often seemed self-serving and irresponsible. Even without definitive proof of complicity with the court, the Boze affair was yet another piece of evidence in the growing dossier of Girondin duplicity. In the Jacobin-Girondin struggle neither faction had yet won a decisive victory. This would not happen until the appeal to the people came to a vote. In the

meantime it was a good tactic to sow doubt, to build up a convincing case against the Girondins by exploiting every scrap of evidence, every error of judgment the Mountain could lay hands on.

The response of Paris to the king's successful defense of himself was predictable. The city was angry and frustrated by the sympathy Louis received. And with the proposal of the appeal to the
people the Parisian radicals saw a new round of delays and the
possibility of exoneration for the king. Paris, as always, could not
be ignored and Mayor Chambon was summoned to report on
the state of the city. On January 5 he told the Convention that
the streets and cafés of the capital were filled with talk about the
king's punishment and "it is not easy to say what will be the outcome of this fermentation." The mayor's disquieting report implied that Paris would not tolerate the appeal to the people, whatever its outcome. For the Girondins, of course, the mayor's report
was useful ammunition; it reinforced what they had long been
saying, Paris was dangerous and both too powerful and too influential. Yet further evidence of the need for the appeal. And
immediately after the mayor's report the Convention heard an
equally disturbing address from the department of Haute-Loire.
Haute-Loire offered to send volunteers to Paris to protect the Convention from the Commune. The session exploded into Jacobin-
Girondin recriminations and threats. The Jacobins shouted that the
address from Haute-Loire proved that the provinces were counterrevolutionary. The Girondins countered by insisting it proved that
Paris did not represent the nation. Here was the problem Mirabeau
had long ago warned against, had long ago advised the king to exploit: Paris and the provinces were antagonistic and this antago-
nism could lead to civil war. Both factions accused each other of
desiring civil war, either by supporting or not supporting the
appeal to the people.

Indeed the provinces had become as restless as Paris itself. The
king's defense encouraged all those favorable to the king, whether
in the Convention, Paris, or the countryside, to try to save him.
The debates on the appeal to the people only further prodded the
king's friends, and the long delays in the trial, now extended,
made provincial restlessness more and more probable. The debates

on the appeal to the people touched off a near insurrection in Rouen, the most important city in agriculturally prosperous Normandy. And it was royalist-inspired and led. Here were more of the dubious allies attracted by the Girondin appeal to the people. A certain Aumont, a local lawyer in Rouen, drew up a protest against the judgment of the king, published it, and invited all those interested in signing it to gather at his house. The petition-signing turned into a riot, and Aumont and some of his royalist friends, emerging for the first time in months from a prudent retirement from public life, shouted slogans long unheard in a major French city: "Long live the king!" and "To hell with the republic!" The Rouen authorities put down the riot, not without difficulty, but not before a number of symbolic insults had been inflicted on the republic—tearing up the tricolor cockade, burning a tree of liberty which they uprooted, hoisting the white Bourbon flag.

While attention was fixed on Rouen Paris itself became the scene of some enthusiasm for the king's cause. On January 2 a feeble play, *The Friend of the Laws* (*L'Ami des lois*) was presented at the Theater of the Nation. The theaters had remained open in Paris throughout most of the Revolution, and the bourgeoisie continued to frequent them. But since August 10 no play critical of the Mountain had been on the boards. The topical interest of *The Friend of the Laws* was unmistakable, its attack on the Mountain overt, its time of presentation favorable to the king. The Jacobins were the villains of the piece. *Duricrane* (Marat) was depicted as a madman, "denouncing in the morning what he dreamed the night before." *Nomophage* (Robespierre) was depicted as a cruel fanatic, while *Plaude* (representing popular Parisian democracy) ran about the stage calling for the immediate destruction of private property. The hero, *Deversac*, was a former gentleman with liberal ideas, perhaps intended to represent the Girondins. He did not regret the loss of his privileges under the Revolution, but he believed that "a king, a nobility, are necessary for a great empire."

The Convention was too embroiled in debate on the appeal to the people to react, but the sections were outraged. Section Réunion demanded that the Convention close the offensive play; section Cité appealed to the Commune to see that nothing "contrary to the principles of true patriotism and good morals" be presented on the stage. On January 11 the Commune temporarily closed down *The Friend of the Laws*. The following day Mayor Chambon asked the Convention to support his action. The deputies rambled on about their reluctance to interfere in an issue involving freedom of the press and then moved on to other business without reaching a decision. The Commune then made its closure permanent, describing the play as "an apple of discord thrown among the citizens of Paris to stir up the fury of parties."

Sympathy for the king was apparently widespread, and if the appeal to the people had a chance of passing the Convention, delay would be assured and the king's sympathizers encouraged. "Spring will come," moaned the *Annales patriotiques*, "to find us still occupied with his trial or his judgment." The radical press took up the lament, blaming social unrest on delay and delay on the Girondin appeal to the people. Marat's *Journal de la république*, in December and January, was filled with a series of violent attacks against "Roland and his faction" who were accused of wanting to "prevent the judgment of Louis Capet." And Marat's journalism was equaled in verbal violence by René Hébert's *Père Duchesne*, the favorite newspaper of the *sans-culottes*.

While the radical press tried to forge the scattered pieces of evidence of social unrest into a conspiratorial theory implicating the Girondins and the appeal to the people, others took the opportunity to do what they could to save the king. The appeal to the people was crucial for all these plots and schemes. If the appeal carried, the king would probably be saved by the primary assemblies, or if not saved at least the delay in the judgment would provide a breathing space, time for men to concoct plots, time for the deputies to reconsider their opinions, time for corruption and manipulation. If the appeal failed so too would all the plots to save Louis. Little was known at the time about the details of the several plots that were afoot, but suspicion was widespread, certainly on the Mountain. The Jacobins feared the worst and their fears were not farfetched. Charles-François Dumouriez, the revolutionary general who was the victor at Valmy and a close friend to the Girondins, had returned from the front and was using his personal

influence to win support for the appeal to the people. When Dumouriez was denounced, in June 1793 (he deserted his post and
France in April 1793) by the Montagnard René Levasseur, he was
accused of approaching Drouet, the hero of Varennes responsible
for capturing Louis, and trying to persuade him to use his influence to support the appeal to the people.

Dumouriez' scheme collapsed, but there were others desperate
to have the appeal to the people carry. Spain was willing to buy
votes at the national and local levels to save the king, but first the
appeal to the people had to pass the Convention. On January 3 the
Spanish *chargé d'affaires*, Chevalier d'Ocariz, wrote his master, the
Duke of Alcudia, that "the most favorable decision that one can
expect from the National Convention on Louis XVI is that which
will send it to the primary assemblies." If the appeal carried then
the Spanish government would need agents to go "even into the
smallest districts" of France to deliver bribes. And to assure pas-
sage of the appeal an important (unnamed) deputy, or deputies,
would have to be bought off. The whole scheme, d'Ocariz estimated, would cost Charles IV of Spain about "three millions."
Charles was willing to spend the money to keep his cousin from
the guillotine and about two-and-a-half million was delivered to
d'Ocariz.

A couple of Montagnards, Choudieu and Azéma, knew something was going on but they had no specific evidence. "Considerable sums of money" had been offered to several deputies but
Choudieu said he had "no material proof of corruption." The
rumors persisted that there was a market for those interested in
selling their support for the appeal to the people, and some Spanish gold may have passed into French pockets. But this plot too
came to naught.

There were at least two additional schemes for saving Louis, and
they both were devised by famous deputies, Danton and Tom
Paine. The former was an opportunist and was anxious to save the
king because Louis would be an indispensable chess piece in the
elaborate end game Danton was playing in foreign affairs. The
latter was motivated by his genuine abhorrence of bloodshed and
his equally genuine belief that the removal of the king from the

throne was all that was necessary for the success of the Revolution.

Danton's actions are the more questionable. During the weeks just before and after August 10 Danton had been the incarnation of the militant Revolution, engineering the coup d'état at the Hôtel de Ville, calling the nation to resist the foreign invasion, and serving as the minister of justice in the interim government that ran France after the king was dethroned and before the Convention met. His revolutionary credentials were unquestioned, so too was his passionate devotion to the republic. But Danton was personally corrupt. He took bribes and, much like Mirabeau before him, had little patience with the tedious pace of a parliamentary body. Danton preferred to do his own negotiating with foreign courts, and his dynamic personality made it very hard for him to work in concert with other men. He was an audacious and brilliant man but he was also an egomaniac, which proved his downfall. Danton was absent from Paris from November 30 till January 11, on mission with the armies. He did not participate in the debates on the king or the appeal to the people, but his friends in Paris kept him well informed about what was going on. On December 18 Danton sent the abbé Noël to London to see W. A. Miles, Prime Minister Pitt's confidant. "He declared himself a friend to humanity and although a Republican he was perfectly persuaded that the death of the king would not be of any service to the new government in France," Miles wrote in a memo to Pitt. There was in London, Noël told Miles, a man "who commanded the means" to save the king, but direct negotiations were impossible. Miles refused to get involved, explaining that Pitt's policy was to remain neutral. As soon as Danton learned Pitt had rejected his scheme he threw himself, unequivocally, into the regicide cause.

Tom Paine's scheme did not involve bribery. He planned to attract supporters through his enormous prestige as a professional revolutionary, the hero of the American Revolution who had been elected by several French constituencies as their representative to the Convention. The American ambassador in Paris, Gouverneur Morris, says Paine told him in confidence "that he was going to support the appeal to the people and couple this support with a proposal to send him [the king] and his family to America." Paine did support the appeal to the people and made his proposal for exiling the king in America, a proposal no other deputy could be persuaded to support.

The appeal to the people was the most serious threat mounted against the regicides. The several plots to save Louis that exploited the appeal for their own ends served to discredit both the appeal and its Girondin supporters. The Girondins themselves were not royalists and it is doubtful that they wanted to restore the monarchy. Why then did they throw all their energies into the appeal to the people, why did they, either inadvertently or deliberately, provide the counterrevolution with so useful a proposal? The Girondins had consistently delayed the trial and a couple of times had tried to abort it. Only the concerted pressure of Paris with its sections and Commune, the Parisian press, and the Mountain forced them to get on with the trial, and they did so only reluctantly. But if the Girondins wanted to save the king, said Napoléon, "They had only to vote for deportation, exile or adjournment." Instead they called for the appeal to the people, which was "the height of inconsistency and was impolitic." The appeal, for Napoléon as for the Jacobins, was an invitation to civil war. Napoléon's political opinions are not to be despised, and they are shared by a number of revolutionaries. Dubois-Crancé, a former colleague of Robespierre's and a future Thermidorian reactionary, thought the appeal a "strange contradiction." The Girondins did everything they could to save Louis from being judged, and then they voted for his death. Vergniaud himself later called the appeal "a political error" forced on the Girondins by their enemies who wanted the king dead yet refused to banish the Duke d'Orléans.

In general this is the pattern of Girondin explanations of the appeal to the people. It was necessary to stop the Mountain and thus save the Revolution from excessive radicalism. Gorsas wrote that "more than 600 members of the Convention had shown, either at the tribune or in their writings, their support for the appeal to the people." But the day before the vote on the appeal Gorsas says he saw "menacing people, I don't dare call them citizens, publicly brandishing their sabres and announcing the horrors of carnage" if the appeal carried. Gorsas's count of the supporters for the appeal is grossly exaggerated, and he is the only deputy who apparently saw "menacing people," although the theme of Parisian intimidation runs through the writings of the Girondins like a catch in a rhyme. Brissot too insisted that a Jacobin conspiracy coupled with Parisian intimidation had defeated the appeal. The "cannibals" of Paris, the men who had massacred the prisoners in September and who were the shocktroops of the Mountain, "wanted to suck his [Louis's] blood, drop by drop. They wanted to tear him to pieces and to savor his sufferings with pleasure." Such hyperbolic apologies for failure do not throw much light on the problem.

The greatest mistake the Girondins made was associating the death sentence of the king not with Louis's guilt, but with Paris radicalism and the Mountain. Here they were absolutely consistent, from the opening days of the Convention to the time of their deaths. This conviction took many forms during the trial and led the Girondins to pursue an irresponsible course in the Convention. This is most clearly seen in the appeal to the people. It is one thing to be ambitious for power, to believe only you can save the Revolution from disaster; it is quite another to be willing to do almost anything to achieve power. With the appeal the Girondins were willing to ally themselves with royalists, pit provincial France against Paris, purge the Convention, and undermine the authority of the only governmental institution in the country, the National Assembly. Almost all the Girondin tactics in the trial were devious. Dumouriez, who admittedly had an axe to grind, thought them the Jesuits of the Revolution. They seemed to hold the majority of the deputies in contempt. The Marais deputies did not have to be seduced or flattered, they had to be hoodwinked, so thought the Girondin strategists. And all the Girondin proposals were contingent; Paris must be curbed, the *septembriseurs* punished, the Jacobins impeached, the appeal sent to the primary assemblies *before* Louis could be judged. They offended the Commune and then accused it of being hostile. They threatened the Mountain and then accused it of desiring the destruction of the Girondin. They insisted the king have a procedurally correct trial and then proposed a series of procedural novelties. They insisted the Duke d'Orléans must be expelled from France and then did everything they could to save his royal cousin.

It is not difficult to see why men who were royalist at heart were attracted to the Girondin cause. Whatever the motives of the Girondin speakers in December and January they certainly encouraged royalist agitation. The royalists saw that the only group in the Convention interested in saving the king was the Girondins, and consistently throughout the trial the Girondins found themselves encumbered with royalist support. If they did not seek this support they were either politically naive—a fatal flaw in a revolution—or convinced they could manipulate such dubious support to their own ends—an equally fatal conceit. Either, they argued, the Convention must judge Louis and suffer criticism for its decision, or the judgment must be submitted to the primary assemblies for a long delay with unpredictable results. Suppose, it was asked then and can be asked now, the primary assemblies, after months of deliberation, declared the king innocent or declared the death penalty excessive or reached no clearcut decision, what then? The Convention would have been paralyzed, there would have been risk of civil war, the royalists would have been given time to mobilize, the crowned heads of Europe might well have decided to act in concert against France, Paris might well have resorted to insurrection once again, and the counterrevolution would have had, in Louis, a rallying point for its activities.

The appeal to the people offered the Convention a choice between Girondin leadership and Jacobin leadership. And Girondin leadership meant saving the king. The *conventionnels* were not happy with the choice, for the majority had no particular love for the Mountain or Paris and the Commune. But the majority did believe that Louis was guilty, guilty of acts that for any other man deserved death. They rejected the appeal to the people, not to show support for the Mountain, but rather because they believed Louis must die for the Revolution to live. And this was the view of the Mountain throughout the trial. The appeal to the people offered the Convention a choice between Louis and the Revolution. Reluctantly, hesitatingly, painfully, the deputies chose the Revolution.

CHAPTER IX

The First Two Votes

THE MANÈGE, JANUARY 14–15, 1793

HE SESSION of January 14, which lasted twelve hours, concentrated the struggle between regicides and antiregicides. The dreaded moment had arrived when theoretical speeches on justice and elaborate parliamentary maneuvers were no longer tolerable: the deputies would have to vote. But before voting they would have to fix the order and the wording of the questions.

The three questions to be voted on—Louis's guilt, his punishment, and the appeal to the people—were not in doubt, but the order in which they were to be posed to the Convention was important. The regicides wanted the questions of guilt and punishment decided *before* the appeal to the people. If Louis were found guilty (a judgment no deputy thought in doubt) and then sentenced to death (the logical punishment), the appeal to the people would have little significance. On the other hand, the antiregicides wanted the vote on the appeal to the people first, for if the appeal was carried, the *conventionnels* might be inclined to be more moderate in voting on the king's guilt and punishment.

The parliamentary fight over the order of the questions was therefore fierce. And as with everything in the trial Jacobins and Girondins struggled for supremacy, poring over the list of deputies counting votes, trying to guess how the majority of Marais deputies would vote. The majority of the *conventionnels* had not yet declared themselves but by January 14 there was a good deal of evidence available on which to base a prediction. For example, there were 406 published opinions in the trial—speeches either delivered at the tribune and subsequently published, or speeches which were never delivered but were published at government expense— which came from the pens of 291 deputies, or about 39 percent of the Convention. Seventy-eight of the eighty-three departments represented in the Convention had at least one deputy who had published at least one opinion. The views of a significant number of deputies and a majority of the departments were known, or partly known, before the voting began. Still these statistics are both a bit misleading and inconclusive. Many of the published opinions were ambivalent or deliberately obscure; there were even deputies who had published on more than one side of the issue. Moreover, the majority of the deputies had remained mute throughout the trial, neither participating in the debates nor publishing an opinion. How this quiet majority would vote would determine the outcome; and the time of persuasion was over.

Neither Jacobins nor Girondins were clairvoyant, and both factions assumed more support than they had. The regicides reasoned that the consistent failure of Girondin proposals during the trial, coupled with a growing skepticism about Girondin capacities for revolutionary leadership, meant that the antiregicides had little support in the Convention. The Jacobins further assumed that the political behavior of the Marais deputies would be consistent: having opposed Girondin proposals for a departmental guard, for punishment of the *septembriseurs*, for impeachment of the Duke d'Orléans, they would now oppose clemency for the king by voting for death and against the appeal to the people. But it is usually a mistake to assume that political behavior is rational and logical; and in an issue so emotional and personal as the king's fate it was an obvious mistake. But if the Mountain overestimated its strength, it was essentially correct in its analysis and made a prudent political decision on January 14, or at least a decision consistent with its mistaken evaluation. The regicides decided that Louis would be found guilty if the deputies were left free to vote. Not one of the great radical leaders—Robespierre, Saint-Just, and Marat particularly— participated in the debates that day. The only Jacobin of any importance who spoke was Georges Couthon, whose contribution was slight and who had not yet emerged as one of the leading voices of the Left. The regicides shrewdly avoided antagonizing the Marais with yet another diatribe on revolutionary justice and the machinations of the Girondins.

The antiregicides reasoned that the Convention had shown no particular enthusiasm for regicide and had in fact shown considerable uneasiness about unorthodox procedures. True, the majority had not supported any of the Girondin proposals, but neither had they supported any Jacobin proposals. The antiregicides assumed this meant that a majority of the deputies were reluctant to send the king to the guillotine, reluctant to support the Mountain. The antiregicides counted on the appeal to the people. Those who wanted to save the king, those who recoiled from the dreadful responsibility of voting on Louis's fate, those who were naturally timid would all support the appeal, and this support would save the king—for the antiregicides always assumed the primary assemblies were more moderate or more lenient than the Convention. In addition the appeal to the people promised options for the future; killing the king was definitive.

The debate on the order of the questions was disorganized and frequently out of control, the proposals bewildering in complexity and number. Thirty-two deputies spoke, roughly divided between regicides and antiregicides since the procedural rules of the Convention specified that a speaker for a proposition must be followed by a speaker against it. Several of the acknowledged leaders of the Girondins went to the tribune to make the case for putting the appeal to the people first in the order of questions: the Mountain leadership sat mute. Again, as during the original debates on the appeal, there was considerable confusion among the speakers on what the appeal meant; they were united only on its importance.

Early in the January 14 debates one agreement did emerge: the need for a roll-call vote. The arguments used to support this *appel nominal* were identical for regicides and antiregicides alike: the solemnity of the occasion and its enormous political importance. The issue of open voting versus secret ballot was a continual one for the Revolution, groping its way toward democratic procedures. In general the moderates favored a secret ballot, the radicals an open vote. The former insisted that a secret ballot saved the voter from the unfair pressure of his peers, from subsequent harrass-

ment because of his vote, and consequently guaranteed a free vote.
The latter insisted that a secret ballot encouraged selfishness and
irresponsibility. It was healthier for a man to stand up publicly
and be counted. Secrecy was the way of the court, but a revolutionary people should do their political business in the open. In
the November elections for mayor of Paris the Girondins had insisted on a secret ballot as a control on radical intimidation, the
Jacobins had insisted on a voice vote. But in the king's trial both
factions agreed that the voting must be open and by roll call. The
reason was simple: both Girondins and Jacobins believed the silent
majority would prefer the protection of a secret vote and both believed a secret ballot would lose them support in the Marais. Neither faction was sure how the majority would vote; the Jacobins
thought the obscure deputies potentially antiregicide, the Girondins thought them potentially regicide.

The proposals on the order of the questions and their wording
covered nearly every imaginable possibility. Some argued that the
Convention should vote only on the question of the king's guilt,
and if he were found guilty he would then suffer the penalty prescribed for treason in the Criminal Code: death. Some argued that
the appeal to the people must come first, for they understood the
proposition to mean that the nation must be consulted before any
other votes were taken. Others argued that the appeal was only a
ratification but still must come first in the order. Some wanted to
drop the vote on the appeal to the people altogether. A Girondin
sympathizer, Pierre-Claude-François Daunou, proposed the most
complicated procedures of the session. First the deputies would
have to decide if the king's judgment was a political act or a judicial act: were they trying the king or merely making a decision on
the nation's security? In the former case Daunou's proposal called
for eleven different votes, in the latter ten. The proposal won no
adherents. Nicolas-Marie Quinette, a moderate, thought the appeal to the people a political maneuver and wanted to avoid the
entire issue by voting only on Louis's guilt. This proposal was an
attempt to make Louis an ordinary citizen, subject to the same laws
and penalties as any other Frenchman.

The Girondins broke ranks on this issue. No two Girondin
spokesmen formulated the question of the appeal to the people in

the same way and a few even wanted it eliminated. Jean-Louis Carra, the intemperate editor of the *Annales patriotiques*, for example, sided with the Jacobins and insisted that the Convention vote only on Louis's guilt. Jean-Henri Bancal, the friend of Tom Paine—it was Bancal who translated Paine's speeches into French and delivered them to the Convention—and Brissot proposed that the first question should be "did the Convention have the right to judge the king?" Once this was decided the deputies could vote on Louis's guilt. The third question would be: "Has the Convention received from the people the mission of pronouncing on life or death?" The proposal fell, deservedly, still-born from the tribune. But it indicated that there were still deputies who believed the Convention could not try the king.

When all those who had requested a chance to speak were finished, the secretaries, doubtless as confused as their colleagues, read out the various proposals. This repetition only thickened the already impenetrable fog. The deputies responded by indulging themselves in a half hour of uncontrolled rancor. In the midst of the disorder, Defermon, a former president of the Convention, managed to propose a compromise: he called for a vote on which of the three questions would come first. The secretaries began calling the roll on Defermon's motion, but the Convention was immediately convulsed by disorder. During a brief lull in the tumult Barère and Barbaroux both suggested compromises and again the secretaries began calling the roll. Again anarchy replaced order. The president, Vergniaud, surrendered to the confusion and put his hat on his head, symbolizing that the session was suspended and could do no parliamentary business. After several minutes the deputies became aware of Vergniaud's action and settled down. Couthon, the courteous and mild-mannered Jacobin who was confined to a wheelchair by crippling meningitis, got the floor. "It is a very painful thing for the public welfare to see the disorders in which the Convention finds itself," he told the Convention. The session was more than three hours old and aside from agreement on the necessity for a roll-call vote not a single decision had been reached; there seemed no end in sight. Couthon called for an immediate roll-call on Louis's guilt. Once again order collapsed. Manuel proposed that the entire problem be turned over to a com-

mittee which would present the Convention with the order and
wording of the questions the following day. The disorder continued. Vergniaud, worn out by his fruitless efforts to control the
Convention, asked Treilhard, a former president, to replace him in
the chair. Treilhard could not enforce the chair's authority any
better than had Vergniaud.

As might be expected the factions used the occasion to calumni-
ate their opponents, which only added to the confusion. Pierre
Loysel, a Girondin sympathizer, deliberately baited the Mountain:
"If one should declare Louis guilty before the sovereign ratified
this judgment, one would assassinate him," he shouted. The insult, in the laconic words of the transcript of the session, brought
"violent interruptions and new murmurs from the extreme Left."
The demonstration set off by Loysel's impudence lasted only a
short time. The Convention was wearying of the incessant bickering and disorder. The deputies had worked themselves into a state
of excitement that had succeeded in exhausting their passion for
confrontation. Gradually they subsided into a state resembling
parliamentary order. Boyer-Fonfrède, one of the Girondin inner
sixty, proposed a compromise that finally was accepted:

> First question: Is Louis guilty? (yes or no)
> Second question: Whatever your decision, shall it be submitted to the
> ratification of the people? (yes or no)
> Third question: What punishment shall Louis suffer?

Approximately the same formulation had been proposed hours
earlier, but the Convention was not then ready to accept it. And
it was important that the compromise come from the Girondins,
the champions of the appeal to the people. The deputies voted
to accept Boyer-Fonfrède's formulation and the session ended at
9:30 P.M.

Like all compromises Boyer-Fonfrède's was acceptable rather
than satisfying. Neither Jacobins nor Girondins had won a clear
victory. By putting the question of Louis's guilt first the Convention declared itself sovereign, capable of judging the king without
first having to consult the primary assemblies. But by then deciding on the appeal to the people the Convention broke the continuity between verdict and punishment and in doing so contra-

dicted itself: the Convention was sovereign on the question of guilt, but not sovereign on the question of punishment. Furthermore, Boyer-Fonfrède's compromise made the appeal to the people into a ratification of the Convention's decision on punishment. This was Vergniaud's original conception but it was not shared by many supporters of the appeal. And there was also an implied contradiction in the appeal to the people as a ratification, a contradiction Robespierre had pointed out in December when he responded to Vergniaud. If the primary assemblies could only ratify the Convention's decision then their sovereignty was limited; this was a theoretical impossibility. Fortunately, the Convention was too tired and bored to take up the enormous question raised by Boyer-Fonfrède's formulation: could the Convention, by decree, limit the nation's sovereignty? Still, inclusion of the appeal to the people as the second question to be voted on was a victory for the Girondin and antiregicide feeling in the Convention. Whatever the verdict, punishment could not be imposed, assuming the appeal to the people carried, without consulting the nation, and this would inevitably mean delay.

The wording of the question on punishment was deliberately oblique, which did not trouble the deputies. The regicides had wanted a simple "yes" or "no" vote on the death penalty, which would have been consistent with the first two questions. Boyer-Fonfrède's formulation gave the deputies the responsibility, perhaps the agony, of formulating the sentence. In addition, it was decided that each deputy, on each of the three questions, would be permitted to explain (*motiver*) his vote, either orally or in writing. This proviso was particularly important for the question of punishment. This was the most difficult of the three questions and numerous deputies exercised the privilege of explaining why they voted as they did.

The wording of the third question, aside from the procedural problem just described, was a defeat for the regicides. Much, of course, depended on the outcome of the vote on the appeal to the people. But in order to vote for death the deputies had to vote unconditionally, that is, they could not attach conditions to their votes, whether of time, place, or manner. The antiregicides, on the other hand, had numerous choices since any conditional vote would probably be counted as antiregicide. In particular the third question offered the silent majority a chance to equivocate: they could vote for death and attach conditions that rendered their votes antiregicide.

On balance the antiregicides had the procedural advantage. They had two opportunities to vote to save the king, either by supporting the appeal to the people and then voting to spare Louis, or by supporting the appeal and then voting the death penalty, with conditions. And if the appeal to the people carried it would influence the vote on death. The Mountain was untroubled by this advantage. Its leaders had faith in the rightness of their views and in the inexorable march of logic that would lead Louis to the scaffold. All the proposals for sparing the king looked suspiciously like royalism. In addition, revolutionaries of every persuasion accepted as an article of faith that the rule of law was superior to the rule of men; and the rule of law meant equality before the law. If Louis was guilty of treason he must pay the price. The Mountain believed there was no satisfactory alternative to regicide and that the majority of *conventionnels* would agree.

The session of Tuesday, January 15, began at 10:43 A.M., a late start for the Convention. The long and bitter session of the previous day (and night) had exhausted the deputies, so that despite the importance of the business at hand many were unable to take their seats at the usual time. While the late sleepers and the stragglers drifted into the Manège the Convention concerned itself with routine business. Manuel, one of the secretaries, read the minutes of the January 14 session, which the deputies accepted. Bancal, another secretary, then read the minutes of the January 13 session, which were also adopted. Following these formalities the Montagnard Augustin Mallarmé rose to deplore the empty benches (it was already 11:00) and demand that the roll call begin at once. But the members present decided to pass to the routine reading of letters while waiting for the rest of their colleagues. We may leave the Convention to read its correspondence and briefly explain the system of voting by *appel nominal*.

The Convention included 767 deputies, the same number as the Legislative Assembly, in conformity with the law of January 15,

1790, on national representation. Of this number 749 represented the eighty-three departments of France; the other eighteen deputies represented the overseas colonies, although at the time of the voting in the king's trial none of the colonial deputies had yet arrived in Paris. The officers of the Convention, the president and the six secretaries, were responsible for conducting and tabulating the vote. Throughout Louis's trial, indeed since the opening of the Convention, the presidency and the secretaryships were dominated by the Girondins. For the *appels nominaux* on the king Vergniaud was in the chair and six Girondins were at the secretaries' table. This fact was bitterly resented by the Jacobins, who suspected that the Girondins were using their control of the offices of the Convention to gain factional ends. Just before the voting began on January 15 Louis Legendre, a former Paris butcher, challenged the impartiality of the secretaries: "In the various roll calls the secretaries have often been accused. I ask that four commissioners be named to act as a control." This first Montagnard call for an ombudsman to check the Girondin secretaries failed to win support in the Convention but underlined the obvious: votes in the *appels nominaux* were conceived as votes in the Jacobin-Girondin struggle as well.

The roll was called by department, in alphabetical order, beginning with Ain, Allier, and so forth. The members of each department delegation were called in the order of their election, which meant that those who had received the most votes at the time of their election came first. Robespierre, for example, had received the most votes in the Paris elections for the Convention and so his was the first name called for his department in any roll call. The delegations did not caucus; each deputy voted individually, unbound by the votes of his colleagues. And no delegation was permitted to cast a bloc vote. To give each of the departments the honor of voting first in a roll call the Convention had adopted a system of rotation used in earlier assemblies: each department, after it had voted first in a roll call, would be put at the end of the alphabetical list and the next department would then vote first on the next roll call. Thus the first *appel nominal* in the Convention had begun with Ain, the second with Allier, and by the time of the roll calls on the king the Convention had reached the letter G. The first *appel* in the king's trial began with Gard, the second would

begin with Haute-Garonne, the third with Gers, and so forth. But
on January 15, when two roll calls were taken one after the other,
both began with Gard, the result either of confusion or a deliberate
attempt to manipulate the voting. By giving the department of
Gard the honor of voting first in two roll calls the secretaries were
able to change the order and thus make sure that the third *appel
nominal*, on punishment, would be begun by Haute-Garonne. As
we shall see this was not a trivial matter and there is some plausi-
bility in Jacobin assumptions of a conspiracy. At any rate, the error,
if it was an error, was too useful to be dismissed as accidental.

To insure accuracy each deputy, when his name was called, had
to come to the tribune, declare his vote, and on his way back to
his seat check that the secretaries had correctly recorded it. Deputies could, if they wished, explain their votes at the tribune and
then deposit a written copy of their explanations with the secretaries so that it would be included in the official record of the session. None of these familiar procedures was altered for the voting
on the king, but because there was some confusion in the final
tabulations and because of the importance of the occasion, the
Convention published three official pamphlets, signed by the president and the secretaries, explaining and clarifying the results. No
other roll call during the Revolution was treated with such concern
for accuracy. Yet no other roll call remains, despite these efforts, so
confusing. It is difficult to arrive at the exact figures for the *appels
nominaux* on the king, for no two compilations agree exactly. Even
the Convention's explanation of the figures in three official pamphlets have discrepancies. In an effort to be faithful to the sources
I have decided to give the figures which the deputies heard from
the president when he announced the results.*

After the routine reading of letters the Convention decided that
the voting should begin at once. "Mention will be made," said the
Convention's decree on the *appels nominaux*, "in the list of those
absent by commission and of those absent without cause." Those
"absent without cause" would be censured "and the lists, with the
indications of absence, of censure, and the opinion of each [dep-

---

*The figures given in the text are taken from the *Archives parlementaires* and the
Moniteur, the official and semiofficial transcripts of the session. These are the totals
the deputies heard. The whole question is analyzed in the Appendix to this history.

uty] will be printed and sent to the departments." This last pro-
vision was in keeping with the publicity that had marked every act
in the trial: no deputy would be permitted to escape his responsibility to the Convention, his constituents, or the Revolution. This
insistence on openness, as Barère had argued on January 4, was
the best guarantee that the king had received a fair trial. Vergniaud, the president, then announced the calling of the question:
"Is Louis Capet, *ci-devant* king of the French, guilty of conspiracy
against the liberty and attempts against the security of the state?
Yes or no." The secretaries began calling the roll.

Most of the deputies were satisfied with a simple "Yes" or "No."
Still, dozens of deputies could not resist the temptation to give the
reasons for their choice, and these explanations, in abbreviated
form, reflect all the issues of the trial. Here we can only glance at
several of the opinions and personalities in a perhaps vain attempt
to convey the drama, the range of opinion, in the *appels nominaux*.

Several deputies abstained, some for personal reasons, others
for political reasons. Antoine-Hubert Wandelaincourt, a priest
who had embraced the Revolution and become the constitutional
bishop of Haute-Marne, told the Convention he had not received
from his constituents "the right of pronouncing in a criminal case."
Wandelaincourt, like several others, insisted he had been elected
to the Convention to make laws, not judge criminals. Joseph-
Jérôme Lalande, an astronomer and one of the founders of the
important Paris masonic lodge Neuf sœurs, also abstained: "Neither yes nor no. I am not a judge," he announced. Antoine Conte,
one of a group of 118 deputies whose perpetual silence earned
them the jibe that they were "known only to the cashier of the
Convention," made the same distinction between legislator and
judge, but cast an ambiguous vote that the secretaries decided to
count as a vote for guilt: "yes as legislator: as judge I have nothing
to say."

Morisson, whom we met on November 13 as the first deputy to
defend Louis in the Convention, refused to participate in any of
the roll calls. He remained true to his conviction that the king could
not be tried because he was immune under the constitution of
1791. For Morisson, the entire trial had been illegal. Jean-Baptiste
Noël also abstained: "I have the honor of pointing out that my son

was a grenadier in the battalion of the Vosges. He died on the frontier fighting the enemies that Louis is accused of having raised against us. Louis is the primary cause of my son's death. Delicacy forces me not to vote." Noël repeated this touching response on all the *appels nominaux* in the trial. But there were those with less delicacy. The Duke d'Orléans had no difficulty voting his cousin guilty.

The roll call on the king's guilt was over in a relatively short time. Vergniaud consulted briefly with the secretaries then told the Convention: "I am going to announce the results of the *appel nominal*. I invite the members and citizens to hear the results in the calm that is appropriate to the situation." The secretaries computed the Convention's membership at 745 deputies. Twenty were absent on official business. Five were absent because of illness. One was absent "without known reason." Twenty-six deputies had made "diverse declarations," that is attached some condition or refinement to their votes, which left 693 deputies who had voted "yes" the king was guilty as charged. Not a single deputy had voted "no." "Thus," Vergniaud announced, "the National Convention declares Louis Capet guilty of attempts against liberty and of conspiracy against the general security of the state." The declaration of guilt was nearly unanimous. The secretaries, with some justification, decided to count the twenty-six "diverse declarations" as either votes for guilt or invalid votes, since seventeen of the deputies who voted in this manner declared Louis guilty but refused to vote him guilty because of legal or personal scruples. The Jacobins had been correct: Louis was thought guilty by the entire Convention. It remained to be seen if the deputies were consistent and would condemn the guilty king to death.

Without a break the Convention passed to the second roll call: "The judgment that will be rendered on Louis, shall it be submitted to the ratification of the people united in their primary assemblies? Yes or no." This vote on the appeal to the people, in its definitive formulation, had little to do with Louis's fate, but it was the crucial vote in the political contest between Jacobins and Girondins. The Convention was being asked to decide its political future by choosing between two diametrical views of the trial and the Revolution. "Never," writes Jean Jaurès, "did the Revolution run a greater danger." Jaurès, one of the few historians of the Revolution with vast political experience as a deputy and party chief, believed, as did the Jacobins, that the "approval of the appeal to the people meant the loss of revolutionary France." Mallet du Pan, a contemporary journalist, put it bluntly: "Most who voted to send the judgment of the king to the people did so not by any sentiment of justice, of humanity, of compassion for this unfortunate prince; but solely for political reasons. In a word, to spare the Convention the odium of being regicide."

The roll call on the appeal to the people was long and tedious. Many deputies chose to explain their votes, often at great length. They did not hope to persuade their colleagues or alter the outcome; rather they used the occasion to justify themselves and excoriate their enemies. In the dozens and dozens of explanations we see the conflicting pull between personal and group loyalties, and between political conviction and expediency. The vote on the appeal to the people, like the issue itself, was confused and confusing. Some had been persuaded by Barère's great speech, or perhaps by his plea for united action. Some already knew how they would vote long before Barère went to the tribune. Some could not disentangle the implications of the appeal from their own desire to avoid the responsibility of sending Louis to the guillotine. Some continued, despite the wording of the appeal to the people, to see it as a vote on the people's sovereignty and the nature of a representative government. Support for the appeal came from unexpected quarters; so too did opposition.

The most striking feature of the roll call on the appeal was the difference between what men had said in the debates on the issue and how they voted on January 15. A number of the original supporters of the appeal to the people deserted the cause. Still others tried to insist that their vote was not politically motivated. Cambacérès, for example, said he voted against the appeal because "the decree by which we constituted ourselves Louis's judges" had not been sent to the primary assemblies for ratification. Such a proposal, he conveniently forgot, had never been made during the debates. But one reason was as good as another. It was the vote that counted. Lanjuinais voted for the appeal, which was expected, but he voted ambiguously: "I say yes if you condemn Louis to

death; in the contrary case I say no. I hear it said that my vote will
not be counted. Since I want it counted, I say yes." Lanjuinais
had voted Louis guilty. Now he wanted to use the appeal to save
the king from death. A number of deputies experienced a similar
dilemma and believed that the only way to save Louis was to support the appeal to the people. The Girondins had consistently denied that the appeal was designed to save the king, but the deputies who voted with Lanjuinais did not agree.

Philippe-Laurent Pons, a lawyer who scribbled verse in his spare
time, told the Convention he had been "enlightened by diverse
opinions, and especially by Barère's" and he voted against the
appeal. Some voted out of class bias, like Louis-Joseph Froger-
Plisson, one of the few rich landlords who sat in the Convention.
His scorn for the lower classes who infested the primary assemblies—"composed only of farmers, of artisans, who cannot have
any political knowledge"—would not allow him to send them any
important measure for ratification. Some took the occasion to
flaunt their revolutionary credentials. Armand-Constant Tellier
voted against the appeal by telling an anecdote: "The electoral
assembly of my department [Seine-et-Marne] decided, almost
unanimously, that it would have constructed a cannon of the cali-
ber of Louis XVI's head, and shoot it at the enemy should they
penetrate French territory." Without irony Tellier interpreted this
to mean that his constituents opposed the appeal to the people.
Seine-et-Marne, incidentally, was not the only department to express its hatred of Louis by giving free rein to a macabre imagination. Louis's head seemed an ideal cannon ball as it seemed an
ideal bowling ball to Hébert's folk hero, Père Duchesne. The verbal
violence of the Revolution often took the form of images of canni-
balism or mutilation, although there was considerable variation
over which organ or part of the body was most appropriate for an
outrage.

Although the appeal to the people had been presented and
understood as a factional issue, there was little correlation between
political allegiance and the voting on the appeal. For one reason or
another, between December 27, when the appeal was proposed,
and the voting on January 15 a number of deputies changed their
minds. Even a number of Girondins voted against the appeal.

There was no party discipline because there were no parties. Charles-Antoine Chasset, a Girondin who later deserted the Convention to join the counterrevolutionaries in Lyon, voted against: "As representatives of the people, as politicians, we have been sent [to the Convention] with unlimited powers. I say no." Jean-Antoine-Nicolas Condorcet, the last of the great French philosophers of the Enlightenment tradition, also deserted his Girondin friends. Condorcet was more influenced by his conscience than his political loyalties: "I would want the execution [of the decree against Louis] suspended until the constitution could be finished and published, and the people would have pronounced in their primary assemblies, according to the forms of the constitution. But being consulted today . . . whether or not there should or should not be an appeal to the people, I say no." The convoluted expression of his opinion indicates the difficulty Condorcet had in voting throughout the trial. His reticence and thoughtfulness speaks well of him as a man if not as a political ally.

Some deputies—Jean-Baptiste Treilhard is a good example—rejected the appeal for practical reasons: "I long believed the measure of the appeal to the people good but the inconveniences that seem to be attached to it oblige me to say no." Some voted one way and then seemed to support the opposite position in their explanation. Pétion voted for the appeal but could not resist a childish insult cast at the Jacobins: "My opinion not being that of the majority, what I would wish for the public tranquillity is that the votes opposed to those of the minority might be even more numerous than they are. But the decree being rendered, there is no member in this assembly who does not have a sacred duty to obey and to defend it. I say yes." French, with its subjunctive mood, which seems to defy translation into English, is admirably suited to permit and even encourage tentative expression and many, like Pétion, used the subjunctive as a means of approximating their feelings. Saint-Just, of course, was not troubled by ambivalence: "If I did not hold from the people the right of judging the tyrant, I would hold it from Nature. No." This is what he had argued on November 13; and nothing had happened in the trial to change Saint-Just's mind.

As soon as the votes were tabulated Vergniaud announced the

results. Of 745 deputies 717 were present for the roll call. Ten abstained for one reason or another, twenty were absent on mission, five were ill, and three were absent without known reason. There were 424 votes against the appeal, 283 votes for. "I declare, in the name of the Convention," said the president, "that the judgment against Louis Capet will not be sent to the people for ratification."

The majority of the Girondin leadership had supported the appeal, but, as noted above, there were some significant desertions. Enemies of the Girondins variously interpreted the defeat of the appeal to the people. Some saw it as evidence of Girondin incompetence; others as an indication of Girondin cynicism or duplicity; still others as a just retribution for Girondin ambition and arrogance. Whatever the interpretation, it was clear to all that the defeat of the appeal seriously compromised the faction. It was the first *formal* test of strength between Jacobins and Girondins, the first vote on an issue that was perceived as essentially factional. Not only had the Girondins failed to attract a significant number of Marais deputies to their cause, they had also failed to vote as a bloc. Even the delegation for the Gironde, which included several important leaders of the faction—Vergniaud, Guadet, Gensonné, Grangeneuve, Ducos, Boyer-Fonfrède, Lacaze, and Bergoeing—split on the appeal to the people: five voted for the appeal, seven against.

The Girondin speakers for the appeal to the people had painted a picture of civil war if the appeal failed, yet exactly those departments where the threat of civil war was greatest—Maine-et-Loire, the Vendée, Charente-Inférieur, Indre-et-Loire—voted overwhelmingly against the appeal (forty-two to five). Similarly, those departments on the frontiers of France who would suffer the ravages of war which Brissot had promised if the appeal failed, rejected it. In like fashion the presentation of the appeal as anti-Jacobin, anti-Paris, antiradical, attracted few supporters, although the Convention as a whole was not pro-Jacobin, pro-Paris, or proradical. Whether in defeating the appeal the majority of deputies deliberately opted for Jacobin leadership of the Revolution or were consciously expressing their distrust of the Girondins, is academic. The critical fact is that the Girondins had lost a crucial vote and had probably lost their chance to control the Convention, destroy the Mountain, and moderate the Revolution. It is not so much that the Jacobins won the initiative in the trial and the Convention when the appeal to the people failed as that the Girondins had lost it. The deputies had voted against the appeal in large part because they thought it a dangerous or impractical or unnecessary measure, not because they were Jacobins or Jacobin sympathizers. But in rejecting the appeal they inevitably gave the Jacobins a vote of confidence.

The Montagnard Lebas wrote his father immediately after the voting on January 15, the appeal to the people failed "to the great astonishment of both sides." And the failure of the appeal marked not only the ascendancy of the Mountain, but also Louis's end. The deputies were now free to vote on Louis's punishment, knowing that their votes would be definitive. As we have seen, all the schemes for saving the king's head depended on the appeal to the people. On January 15 all these schemes collapsed. The Convention had announced to France and to the world that it alone would judge the king; and most contemporaries believed this meant the death penalty. Those in the Convention sympathetic to the king's plight now had to vote for some penalty other than death. But in doing so they would publicly announce that although they considered the king guilty of treason, and although any other man found similarly guilty would go to the guillotine, Louis was somehow different. The laws that governed France somehow did not apply to Louis. To spare Louis from the punishment prescribed for treason looked suspiciously like saying what the royalist apologists had said for centuries: the king was unique, above the law, perhaps a semidivine creature who must answer only to God. Here was a dilemma to inflict sleeplessness on hundreds of deputies, for the next day they had to return to the Manège to vote on Louis's punishment.

CHAPTER X

The Vote on Death

THE MANÈGE, JANUARY 16–17, 1793

HE SESSION of January 16 began at 10:30 A.M. with the customary reading of minutes and official correspondence. Once these preliminaries were done with, the Convention would turn to the business of the day, the third *appel nominal*, the king's punishment. The deputies were nervous and with glee tried to frighten each other with rumors of assassination and insurrection. An unidentified deputy told his colleagues that Charles-Michel Villette, a marquis, a retired soldier, and an extremely rich man who represented Oise, had been threatened with death if he did not vote to send the king to the guillotine. Another deputy announced that he had heard rumors of cannon being moved from the suburb of Saint-Denis to be used against the Convention if it failed to condemn Louis. Another deputy complained that lists of those who had voted for the appeal to the people were being hawked in the streets of Paris as proscription lists of the royalists and aristocrats in the Convention. No one had yet made a motion that the Convention begin the roll call on Louis's punishment, and the hours slipped by as the deputies described the potential dangers being prepared for them. To calm their nerves and dispel the phantoms of their imaginations, the *conventionnels* proposed a series of fantastic draconian measures designed to insure tranquillity during the voting. Some called for federal troops to guard the Manège; some wanted assurances from the municipal authorities that there would be no uprising.

It was almost midday and the Convention was on the verge of hysteria, willing, even anxious, to believe the wildest rumors. The municipal authorities were sent for and asked to prepare a report on the state of Paris. Meanwhile the Convention appointed an executive council, drawn from the ministers and headed by Joseph Garat, minister of justice, to make a separate report and investigate the various rumors. While waiting for these reports the Convention listened to several more lurid rumors. In the early afternoon Garat returned to the Convention, a short time before Mayor Chambon arrived with his report. Garat told the deputies that the cannon being moved from Saint-Denis presented no threat to the Convention. These were heavy siege guns and there were no crews to man them. The Convention was too distracted to ask why the guns were being moved in the first place, with or without their crews. Rumors were explained away as carelessly as they had been created; the deputies were willing to accept almost any explanation, as long as it came from the authorities.

Following the report on the Saint-Denis cannon, the Convention heard the mayor's report on Paris. Chambon assured the deputies that all necessary steps had been taken to assure tranquillity, yet nasty reminders remained of the instability of Paris. There had been a royalist demonstration at the January 14 performance of *The Friend of the Laws*, broken up only when General Santerre arrived with troops and artillery. A repeat performance was expected if the play remained open. And there were persistent rumors of another prison massacre. No evidence existed that men were planning another purge of the prisons, but fear often fixes its attention on the most frightening and chilling possibilities. The whole emotional issue of the September Massacres had not been debated in months, but it had not vanished from men's minds. Paris was thought capable of any and every imaginable atrocity. Gensonné, the duck of the Gironde, articulated the common belief that any action helps dispel fear. He called for a daily account of "the measures taken to assure public tranquillity" and wanted the Convention to authorize an armed force "in case of negligence by the constituted authorities." The deputies supported the proposal for regular reports but ignored the call for an armed guard. Prison massacres, insurrections, armed guards, the debates in the Convention on the

morning and afternoon of January 16 recapitulated the debates that
had troubled the Convention in the first weeks of its sitting. And
no one in the Manège seemed anxious to get on with the voting.

It was late afternoon when Garat returned to the Convention
from his second personal tour of Paris. He had visited the mayor
and while on his way to Chambon's house found Paris "perfectly
tranquil." He reported that at the Hôtel de Ville, the home of the
Commune, men were going about their tasks as if January 16 were
just another day. The mayor he found at home, "tranquil in the
midst of his family" and seeing no need for emergency measures.
Garat concluded his report by assuring the deputies that they had
nothing to worry about, the various rumors had no basis in reality.
But before the Convention was willing to pass to the order of the
day, the voting, it was again distracted, this time by a new parliamentary maneuver. It was late afternoon, and late in the trial, but
those who wanted to save the king had not given up. The Girondin Lanjuinais got the floor and called for a two-thirds majority in
the vote on Louis's punishment. The Convention, he argued, exploiting the fears of his colleagues, was "threatened by the poi-
gnards and cannon" of the Mountain. Justice and humanity, as he
put it, demanded a two-thirds rule. The logic of the argument is
difficult to follow, but as with all the other Girondin attempts at
delay this one seemed to spring from a praiseworthy, albeit excessive, concern for proper forms. But it actually arose from another,
less disinterested source. Lanjuinais wanted to save Louis from the
regicides by insisting they win a majority larger than that required
for any other parliamentary business. France did not have a two-
thirds rule, and consequently Lanjuinais's proposal would have
required the creation, by Convention decree, of a new regulation.
Every decision previously taken by every revolutionary assembly
had been decided by a simple majority of those present.

It does not necessarily follow that because Lanjuinais was a Girondin, one of the inner sixty, his proposal was a Girondin proposal. In a political situation where parties are so amorphous as to
be nonexistent, and especially in a situation so emotionally charged,
we cannot attribute the proposals of individuals to the faction they
support. Yet almost all the proposals for further delay, for new
parliamentary procedures, in short all the proposals designed in

one way or another to save the king, came from prominent Girondins. Lehardy, another Girondin, supported Lanjuinais and added that the deputies should be given only two choices in the roll call: death or deportation. Not only did Lehardy's proposal attempt to reverse the Convention's earlier decision on the wording of the questions to be voted, but it was offered as yet another means for saving Louis. To make the question one of either death or deportation, Lehardy reasoned, would attract more antiregicide votes, since it would eliminate the possibility of conditional votes. Men who might have voted for death because they believed Louis had to pay the price of his crimes, and then attached conditions because they were reluctant to bear the responsibility of his death, might now vote for deportation. Lehardy wanted to force men to choose, believing that such a forced option would save the king. The Mountain responded by reminding the deputies that Louis had been found guilty of treason, and not only was a two-thirds majority an exception to parliamentary procedures, but it was unnecessary to vote at all on Louis's punishment. The Convention had only to open the penal code, read out the penalty, and send the king to the guillotine.

The Convention was on the verge of collapse. Regicides and antiregicides were locked in yet another struggle which seemed likely to abort the roll-call vote. The entire morning and most of the afternoon had been lost to fear and rancor. But Danton, just returned from the victorious revolutionary armies in Belgium, threw his enormous energy and passion, assisted by the most respected pair of lungs in the Convention, into the debate. "It has been argued," he declared, "that such was the importance of this question that it was not enough to settle it in the ordinary way. Why, I ask, when it is by a simple majority that the affairs of the entire nation were decided, when it was a question of abolishing the monarchy, no one even thought of raising this question, that some want to decide the fate of an individual, a conspirator, with more rigid and solemn procedures." Danton's passion and logic swept away all the antiregicide objections. The Convention passed to the order of the day, thus declaring that a simple majority of those present—which was 361 votes—would decide Louis's fate. No further mention was made of Lehardy's proposal to change the wording of the question on punishment. It had taken the Convention almost ten hours to reach this obvious conclusion. It was 8:00 P.M. on January 16 when the roll call began.

It was a dreary winter night in Paris with a heavily overcast sky. The pathetic lighting in the Manège scarcely dispelled the gloom, and made faces appear even more somber than the occasion itself. Once begun the roll call would continue until completed, through the night and on into the next bleak winter day. One by one the departments were called. One by one the deputies, in the order of their election, mounted to the tribune and declared their votes. An enormous number of deputies, perhaps the majority (or so it seems), chose to explain their vote, to their colleagues, their constituents, to France, to the world, and perhaps most of all to themselves. Here was another aspect of the public nature of the trial: the entire roll call would be reported, verbatim, in the next day's newspapers. "It was," wrote Brissot with his customary excitement issuing in exaggeration, "the most imposing spectacle that men had ever witnessed, seeing more than seven hundred citizens, chosen by twenty-five million of their fellows to exercise their powers, mount, each in his turn, to the tribune, and express his opinion on the fate of the man who had ruled, a short time ago, the destinies of a great nation." The roll call on Louis's fate was a great republican ritual for Brissot. "The patriotism and the probity of the majority, the enlightenment of most, the talents of several, added new interest to the importance of the occasion. Oh," he rhapsodizes, "if the entire nation could have heard its representatives."

Other witnesses were less grandiloquent. Louis-Sébastien Mercier, a deputy from Seine-et-Oise who had discovered his true métier as a journalist and social critic, was a violent antiregicide whose sardonic cast of mind and gift for satire kept him free of factionalism: he despised Jacobins and Girondins equally. People, he writes sourly, may talk about "a kind of religious dread" that pervaded the Convention on January 16–17, but the scene enacted during the voting was cruel and grotesque. "The back of the hall was transformed into a theater box where the women, in the most charming state of undress, ate ices, oranges, drank liqueurs. People went to bow to them, people returned [to their seats]." The surrealism of the scene inspired Mercier, whose verbal portraits remind one of Daumier's cartoons of the nation's representatives during the reign of Louis-Philippe in the nineteenth century: the dowager Duchess d'Orléans, "the Amazon of the Jacobin bands," jeered "when she didn't hear the word 'death' resonate harshly on her ears." The public galleries were filled with "strangers and people of every estate. They drank wine and brandy as if they were in a bar reeking of smoke. The betting [on the outcome] was going on in all the neighboring cafés." On the floor of the Convention, on the deputies' benches, Mercier saw the same grim burlesque. "The boredom, the impatience, the fatigue could be read on almost every face. Each deputy mounted in his turn to the tribune and said to whoever was near, 'Is it my turn soon?'" Mercier preferred to fix his attention on the grotesque; perhaps he could not bear what was happening at the tribune.

Both impressions, Brissot's fervid and abstract celebration of the deputies announcing the nation's will, and Mercier's bitter picture of ordinary men and women behaving like a drunken mob, are true. The heroic and the commonplace, the solemn and the silly, rubbed elbows in the Manège, whose odors and vapors and lurid light gave the entire scene its phantasmagoric dimensions. But let us return to January 16–17 and more prosaic sources.

Secretary Manuel began reading the roll with Haute-Garonne. The first deputy of the delegation, Jean Mailhe, whom we last met in November as the chairman of the Convention's Legislative Committee, mounted to the tribune and cast the first vote:

> By a consequence that appears natural to me, as a result of the opinion I have already given on the first question, I vote for death. I will make a simple observation: if death has the majority I believe it would be worthy of the National Convention to examine if it might be useful to delay the time of execution. I return to the question, and I vote for death.

Mailhe's notorious vote, so deliberately ambivalent, was an attempt to be on both sides of the fence at once. The vote meant that before the death penalty was inflicted on Louis the Convention would first have to consider a delay. And if it considered a delay a reprieve became possible. In fact Mailhe was proposing that the vote on Louis's punishment must be followed by another vote.

The appeal to the people had been defeated, but Mailhe was offering the Convention yet another chance to avoid killing the king. Mailhe's ploy, like Lanjuinais's on a two-thirds majority and Lehardy's on changing the wording of the question, sprang from the same urge: to save Louis from the guillotine. Since virtually all the deputies had voted Louis guilty, and since many were reluctant to condemn him to death although under the law he deserved death, they had to resort to strategies such as the Mailhe amendment, to avoid looking foolish. The only means of rescuing the king, the only means of keeping their hands innocent of Louis's blood, without voting for some penalty other than death, was to find some. means of combining regicide and mercy. Mailhe's was the last such attempt in the trial, and if he attracted few supporters—only twenty-six deputies voted the Mailhe amendment—he had the satisfaction of maintaining a clear conscience in whatever future might befall revolutionary France. But he purchased his clear conscience dearly. A number of contemporaries thought his vote represented a conspiracy to save the king, and that he had been paid, probably by the Spanish, to vote as he did.

Mailhe's motives are obscure, for he was a secretive and sly man. Marc-Antoine Baudot, a doctor who became a zealous Montagnard, suspected him of selling out for 30,000 francs of Spanish gold, and that the Mailhe amendment was partial payment. Others thought Mailhe's vote was part of an elaborate plot to save the king which involved the Girondin secretaries. Instead of beginning the two roll calls on January 15 with two different departments, it will be recalled, they began both with Gard. This meant that Haute-Garonne and Mailhe would vote first on January 16. The suggestion is plausible but not provable, although so shrewd a political analyst as Jean Jaurès accepts this explanation. But if there was a conspiracy it was singularly inept and unsuccessful, and if the Spanish had paid 30,000 francs for the Mailhe amendment, they hardly got their money's worth. Those who were determined to save Louis at any cost could best do so by voting for imprisonment or deportation. They had no need of the Mailhe amendment. In general those who were reluctant to have the king's blood on their hands either cast a vote for death that was so hedged with conditions that it was counted as antiregicide, or simply voted for some penalty other than death. The Mailhe amendment did, however, have one advantage, and perhaps this is all the Spanish and the antiregicides hoped for: it necessitated another roll-call vote after Louis's punishment had been decided—and as Baudot rightly said, "in revolution time is enough."

The Mailhe amendment, then, functioned as a modified appeal to the people. But instead of the primary assemblies ratifying the decision of the Convention, the deputies themselves would have a chance to do so when they voted on reprieve (*sursis*). Only four of the most influential Girondin leaders voted the Mailhe amendment: Buzot, Vergniaud, Guadet, and Pétion. There is absolutely no evidence, no suspicion, that they too might have accepted Spanish gold. Only one member of Mailhe's own delegation, Claude-Louis-Michel DeSacy, voted with him: "If the majority is for this penalty [death], I would ask, like Mailhe, to present observations concerning the time of execution." The amendment failed to attract antiregicide deputies, appealing only to those, like Mailhe himself, who believed the king deserved death but could not bring themselves to vote it unequivocally. The timid, the reluctant, the confused embraced the Mailhe amendment; regicides and antiregicides voted their opinions without using the amendment.

The department of the Gironde came third in the roll call. Vergniaud, who yielded the president's chair to Barère in order to cast his vote, was the first deputy of the delegation. He had voted for the appeal to the people as "a duty to the Convention." Now he reversed himself but did so cautiously; Vergniaud voted the Mailhe amendment.

> The law speaks. It says death. But in pronouncing this terrible word, worried about the fate of my country, about the dangers that menace liberty itself, about all the blood that might be shed, I express the same wish as Mailhe, and ask that it [the death penalty] might be submitted to discussion by the Assembly.

Vergniaud's vote caused a stir. Jean-Baptiste Harmand, a Marais deputy, rushed to the tribune to confront Vergniaud, who had told him the previous evening that he could not, would not, vote for death. "What happened," Harmand blurted out. "How can it be that you have changed your mind in so short a time?" Vergniaud answered with olympian calm: "I did not believe myself able to put the public good in the balance with the life of a single man, that is all."

When the roll call began Louis's lawyers were standing in a narrow stairway leading to the public gallery. Malesherbes asked which letter would begin the *appel nominal*. "G" he was told. "Good," said DeSèze, "that is the Gironde. Vergniaud's vote is favorable to us, and his influence will lead the others." "This is not the Gironde," moaned Malesherbes when he heard the great orator vote the Mailhe amendment, "it is impossible." "Alas, all is lost!" sighed DeSèze.

Guadet voted with Vergniaud, but the rest of the Gironde deputies broke ranks. Gensonné voted for death and attacked the Mountain: "To prove to Europe and the world that we are not the instruments of a faction, and that we make no distinction between scoundrels, I ask that after the judgment of Louis we concern ourselves with the measures to be taken with regard to his family, and that you order the Minister of Justice to bring the assassins of September 2 to justice." Grangeneuve voted for imprisonment, Lacaze for imprisonment followed by banishment, Bergoeing for solitary confinement. Duplantier, the last deputy for the Gironde, also voted the Mailhe amendment. The remaining deputies—Jay, Ducos, Garrau, Boyer-Fonfrède and Deleyre—voted unconditionally for death.

By midnight the roll call had reached Loir-et-Cher, the eleventh department on the list. But the series was briefly interrupted as the deputies listened to a letter from their executive council on the state of Paris. The council had toured "the most populated quarters of the city," a euphemism for the most potentially explosive quarters, and found "complete calm and tranquillity." The Convention was reassured and returned to the voting. Vergniaud remained with his friends on the Gironde benches, unwinding from the enormous strain of chairing the session. When the roll call reached Hautes-Pyrénées, the thirty-fourth department on the list, Barère returned the chair to Vergniaud and cast his vote for death. Barère's announcement that he was yielding the chair gave the deputies a chance to let off steam. The fatigued yet tense deputies joked, shouted, left their places to stretch their legs, compared

tallies on the voting. Three hundred five deputies had already voted and the regicides had a slight edge over the nonregicides.

By the early hours of the morning of January 17 the vote had see-
sawed with no clear majority, no obvious trend. By the time the
roll call reached Paris (thirtieth on the list) the voting was so close
that it was impossible to predict the outcome. Paris, as expected,
voted overwhelmingly for death, 21 to 3. Robespierre voted first,
and lectured the weary deputies. "The sentiment that led me to call
for the abolition of the death penalty [in the Constituent Assembly]
is the same that today forces me to demand that it be applied to the
tyrant of my country, and to royalty itself, embodied in his person." Those who had refused to abolish the death penalty and now
refused to vote it for Louis were, for Robespierre, the true hypo-
crites. "All that I know," he continued, "is that we are the
representatives of the people, sent here to cement public liberty by
the condemnation of the tyrant, and that is enough for me . . . I do
not recognize a humanity that massacres the people and pardons
despots." The other Paris deputies were less verbose, less given to
paradox. Danton, with his customary vigor, scorned those who
said they could not vote for death because they were not judges: "I
don't understand this crowd of *men of state* who forget that one
doesn't come to terms with tyrants, who forget that we have
nothing to expect from the rest of Europe except force of arms. I
vote for the death of the tyrant."

The votes of the other Paris Montagnards were predictable, and
many deputies lost interest as the Paris deputies mounted the tribune. But as Philippe-Egalité, the last member of the deputation to
vote, made his way to the tribune, silence fell over the Manège.
The master schemer, forced to declare himself, voted for death:
"Solely concerned with my duty, convinced that all those who
have attacked or will attack the sovereignty of the people deserve
death, I vote for death." The deputies booed and hooted the Duke
back to his seat, but no one was very surprised by the vote. The
Duke d'Orléans would not enjoy the fruits of his apostasy: he himself went to the guillotine several months after his cousin, his
death a small consolation to royalists.

The voting continued for more than thirteen hours, through the
night and into the bleak dawn of another winter day. The deputies

dozed at their places rather than leave the hall. Women in the gallery compared pinholes in playing cards they used to keep a tally of the votes. When Vergniaud called the department of Gard, the last on the list, 712 deputies had voted; 359 for death, 353 for some other penalty. The simple majority was 361. Leyris, the first deputy for Gard, voted for death. The regicides were one vote short. Bertezène, who followed Leyris to the tribune, voted against death. Jean-Henri Voulland, the seven hundred fifteenth deputy to vote, a protestant, a lawyer, and a Jacobin, cast the deciding vote: death. The rest of the Gard delegation voted antiregicide. When Chazal, the last Gard deputy, had voted, Vergniaud announced the end of the roll call. The six secretaries began tabulating the vote, comparing lists.

Vergniaud announced that two letters had been deposited with him: one from Louis's lawyers requesting a hearing; the other from d'Ocariz, the Spanish *chargé d'affaires*. Did the Convention want to hear these letters? "What," Danton bellowed at the Convention,

> Spain didn't recognize our republic and they want to dictate laws to us! They didn't recognize us and they want to impose conditions, participate in the judgment that our representatives are about to render! Let the people hear this ambassador if they want; but let the president make a response to him worthy of the people whose organ he is. And let him say that the victors of Jemmapes will not give the lie to the glory they have won, that they will again produce the forces which have already vanquished, in order to exterminate all the kings of Europe who conspire against us.

Danton's advice was simple: "Reject, reject, citizens, all shameful propositions. No dealings with tyranny. Be worthy of the people who have given you their confidence and who will judge their representatives if their representatives have betrayed them." The exhausted deputies were in no mood for debate and certainly no one was willing to take on an opponent as formidable as Danton. Gensonné and Carra, two Girondins seldom on the same side of any issue as Danton, supported his heroic plea. The Spanish government could not meddle in French affairs. The Convention agreed. Robespierre, his green-tinted glasses pushed up on his forehead, called for the results of the vote. Afterward the deputies could decide if they wanted to hear Louis's lawyers.

While the deputies discussed Robespierre's motion an apparition was carried into the Manège. Gaspard-Severin Duchastel, in nightcap and nightgown, shaking with fever, was borne into the hall on a litter. In a trembling voice he demanded the right to vote with his deputation, Deux-Sèvres. The Convention laughed at "this kind of ghost," but it was no laughing matter. The voting was finished. No one yet knew the results but all knew that the outcome was very close. Duchastel's vote might well be significant; and he was a Girondin. He had not participated in any of the roll calls on the king, and he would return to his sickbed immediately after casting his vote on punishment. Someone—rumor said Gorsas and the rumor is plausible—had literally dragged Duchastel from his bed so he could vote against death. The bleary-eyed deputies mustered enough energy to throw themselves into yet another acerbic debate. Duchastel's vote could not be counted because the roll call was officially closed. Duchastel's vote must be counted because the roll call was not officially closed until the final tabulation had been announced. Duchastel himself, hardly able to speak above a whisper, defended his right to vote. He had come at great personal risk to exercise his privilege as a deputy. The Montagnard Garrau, who had himself voted for death, pleaded for Duchastel: "Had he voted for death, I myself would have demanded the obliteration of his vote. He has voted for clemency and I ask that his vote be counted." The Convention accepted Garrau's curious logic and counted Duchastel's vote.

The secretaries were still tabulating the roll call when Garrau again got the floor. He called for a "very precise" definition of Mailhe's vote. The Convention had to know if Mailhe's conditions were intrinsic or extrinsic to his vote for death. Was the Mailhe amendment a regicide vote? Garrau insisted that Mailhe himself return to the tribune and clarify his position. Mailhe's understanding of clarification was to "repeat the vote that I gave yesterday" without "changing a word or a single letter." He repeated his ambiguous vote: "There, on my honor, is what I said yesterday." And it was. The final decision on the Mailhe amendment was left to the secretaries and the president.

It was nearly 9:00 A.M. The secretaries were still busy tabulating the vote when Manuel, one of them, suddenly left the table and tried to leave the hall by way of the exit on the Jacobin side. Dismayed at the results of the roll call Manuel tried to flee. He was thwarted by a violent tumult that broke out on the Mountain benches and reluctantly retreated to the other side of the hall, departing by a door on the Girondin side. The next day he submitted his resignation and retired to his native Montargis. His departure on January 17 set off an enormous disturbance in the Manège. Vergniaud put on his hat, suspending the session. "Arrest Manuel," shouted the Mountain. Vergniaud, over the din of insults, reminded the Convention of "the dignity that is called for in the imposing circumstances in which we find ourselves. If someone has a complaint to make, let him ask for the floor and it will be given to him." Some semblance of order returned. Vergniaud removed his hat, the session continued. Châteauneuf-Randon made a motion that Manuel be recalled by the president. Gorsas, another secretary, tried to explain Manuel's behavior. In the midst of this explanation Manuel returned, as unexpectedly as he had left. Mercier says Manuel tried to filch "some votes favorable to the unfortunate king" and was almost killed in the hall. But the explanation makes little sense. There were no deputies in the hall who had not voted, although it is possible that Manuel, confused and angry, was on his way to drag some other sick deputy from his house to the tribune. The whole episode came to nought, for the vote on Louis's punishment had been tabulated.

"Citizens," announced Vergniaud, "I am going to proclaim the results of the vote. You have exercised a great act of justice. I hope that humanity will lead you to maintain the most profound silence. When justice has spoken, humanity must have its place."

Of the 745 deputies one was dead, six were ill, two were absent without cause, eleven were absent on mission, four abstained. Thus there were 721 voters and 361 was the simple majority. One deputy voted for death, reserving to the people the right of commuting the sentence. Twenty-three voted for death using the Mailhe amendment. Eight voted for death but with the condition that all the Bourbons must be expelled from France. Two voted for imprisonment for life in irons. Two voted for death with the condition that the sentence be carried out only after peace was restored, at which time the sentence might be commuted. Three hundred and nineteen voted for imprisonment until the end of the war, when the king would be banished from France. Three hundred and sixty-one voted for death without conditions.

It was 10:00 A.M. The Convention had been sitting for thirty-six consecutive hours. Profound silence reigned during Vergniaud's announcement. "I declare," said Vergniaud, "in the name of the National Convention, that the punishment it pronounces against Louis Capet is that of death."

The English regicides who signed Charles I's death warrant spattered ink on each other after they had signed that dreadful document. The *conventionnels* instead decided to hear Louis's lawyers. Vergniaud summoned them to the tribune. DeSèze, who had stood throughout the thirteen hours of voting, along with Malesherbes and Tronchet, mounted the tribune to read a letter from the king:

> I owe to my honor, I owe to my family, not to accept a judgment that accuses me of a crime that I cannot reproach myself for; consequently I declare that I give notice of the appeal to the nation itself of the judgment of its representatives. By this letter I give special power to my official defenders and expressly charge their fidelity with making known to the National Convention this appeal by all the means that might be in their power, and of asking that it might be mentioned in the minutes of the Convention.

The deputies were outraged. Here was the old Louis, the absolutist king who commanded rather than asked, a man accustomed to giving orders and having them obeyed without question. DeSèze argued that humanity itself demanded that the king not be executed by so small a majority. Tronchet argued that a two-thirds majority was necessary to send Louis to the guillotine. This would mean an additional 120 votes for death. Malesherbes, so distraught he could hardly speak, pleaded painfully for the king's life.

> I am not capable of improvising . . . I see with sadness that I have not had a moment to present you with reflections capable of touching an assembly . . . I have observations to make to you . . . Citizens, excuse my difficulties . . . I have had occasion, during the time that I belonged to the legislative corps, to prepare, to reflect on these ideas. Will I have the unhappiness of losing them if you do not allow me to present them to you, in this place, tomorrow?

The old man was deeply shaken. His emotional state was expressed in choked phrases. He was on the verge of sobbing. More than any set speech he might have delivered his emotional outburst impressed the Convention; but it changed nothing.

Louis's tactless and desperate letter, however, did bring back the entire question of the appeal to the people. No episode in the trial, no proposition, could be laid to rest, it seems, until it was at least twice rejected. Louis saw the appeal, as did its original supporters, as a means of avoiding death. But his call for an appeal to the people was cynical if understandable. Louis, in his eighteen years on the throne, had never consulted his subjects. The sole exception was in the spring of 1789 when he called for the *cahiers de doléances*. And at the *séance royale* it was clear that he was willing to consider only such advice and complaints as harmonized with the reforms he himself had decided to make. Now he wanted the nation he had so consistently ignored to save his head.

Louis's letter was the *cri de cœur* of a man in mortal danger. The royal plea for clemency was brutally silenced by Robespierre, taking part in the debates for the first time since January 14. Such an appeal is "contrary to the principles of public authority, the rights of the nation, the authority of its representatives." Guadet, who had fought, throughout the trial, to destroy Robespierre and the Mountain, supported his arch-enemy for the first time. The appeal to the people had been defeated by a clear majority more than sixty hours ago. It was dead and beyond resurrection. All the deputies had now to decide was the time and place of execution. Guadet asked that this decision be postponed till the following day. The Convention agreed.

This marathon session, probably the most extraordinary parliamentary session in French history, was over at 10:30 P.M. on the night of January 17. The deputies had just voted to send their king to the guillotine. Now, as they stumbled out into the winter night, they sought sleep.

CHAPTER XI

The King Must Die

THE MANÈGE: JANUARY 18–20, 1793

N THE MORNING of January 18 the deputies returned to their places. They hadn't had much rest but in the relative calm of a new day they began discussing the need for a recount and the publication of the corrected vote. A number of deputies were unhappy with the bookkeeping of the secretaries. Some had kept private tallies which did not square with the announced results. Others, like André Dumont, had had their votes incorrectly recorded—he was a regicide yet was counted with the antiregicides. A few wanted merely to refine the explanations for their original votes. For this last group of deputies the stenographic record of the session functioned like the *Congressional Record*: a deputy could have it reflect what he wanted people to believe he had said. And there were some who had voted death conditionally but who now wanted to separate the conditions from their votes. All of this discontent the Mountain wanted to use to make a case against the Girondins, to prove deliberate tampering. The majority of deputies were interested only in having the vote corrected.

Jean-Augustin Pénières-Delzors, a Girondin from Corrèze, suggested a procedure for verifying all the votes. He wanted the roll called out again, along with the recorded vote, so that each deputy could certify whether or not his vote had been correctly recorded. The procedure would have been tedious and would have given the deputies a license to squabble with each other and with the secretaries. Besides, not all the deputies who voted on January 16–17

were at their places on the eighteenth. But most important, the
Convention had no desire to relive the agony of January 16–17.
Thus a compromise was reached: all those deputies who asked to
clarify their votes were allowed to do so, and individual deputies
who were concerned that their votes had been incorrectly recorded
were allowed to check the lists. The secretaries then decided that
the Mailhe amendment votes would be counted as regicide. In the
original announcement of the total the Mailhe amendment votes
had been counted as antiregicide. No one protested the decision
and the majority for death was augmented. Mailhe himself was
absent on January 18, which spared the Convention yet another
verbatim repetition of what he had said on January 16 when the
voting began.

Once these adjustments were made Vergniaud announced the
corrected tally. Twenty-eight deputies had not voted for one reason or another. There were thus 721 votes cast, with a simple majority remaining 361. Two had voted for imprisonment in irons; 319
had voted for diverse punishments other than death; 13 had voted
for death with reprieve; 26 had voted the Mailhe amendment; and
361 had voted for death unconditionally. There were, in the new
tally, 387 votes for death and 334 votes for some penalty other than
death. The Convention then decreed that a pamphlet containing
this revised tally be printed and distributed throughout France,
over the signatures of the president and the six secretaries.

Almost all the difficulties in the voting sprang from the Convention's decision to allow the deputies to determine the nature of
punishment. A simple "yes" or "no" vote on the third *appel nominal* would have eliminated most of these confusions. But for such a
momentous decision the deputies were reluctant to accept such a
choice. They wanted at least the illusion of making a free choice, of
exercising the individual judgment that was fundamental to all the
men of the revolutionary generation. In general the regicide votes
were unambiguous. The majority of regicides were satisfied with
the chilling words, *la mort*. Even those who could not vote *sans
phrase* were forthright: "Since Louis XVI was the enemy of the
people, of its liberty and happiness, I vote for death." So spoke
Saint-Just, voting with the Aisne delegation.

But for many who lacked the comfortable security of a compelling ideology, who were tugged at by myriad feelings and loyalties and habits, it was painful to vote precisely. No recounting of their confused or ambiguous votes, no opportunity to rephrase their votes, was likely to dispel their uncertainty. But there was no need for yet another agonizing analysis of the vote, yet another recount. Mailhe had implicitly called for a fourth *appel nominal*. The deputies would have another chance to undo or modify their votes by voting on the question of a reprieve for the king. The Mountain was furious. For months it had insisted that no trial was necessary, and only reluctantly had it capitulated to majority opinion. But now, with the king condemned to death, it had to endure still another vote, another delay, another possibility that the king might be saved. The king's trial was not yet over.

The emotionally drained and physically exhausted deputies still had enough reserve energy to continue the struggle over the king. Robespierre threw himself into the debates, calling for the immediate execution of the condemned king. Any delay would be cruel and would nullify the will of the majority. Aubin Bigorie du Chambon (not to be confused with the mayor of Paris), one of the Girondin inner sixty, responded by calling for a compromise in the form of an adjournment, the old Girondin tactic of delay and obstruction. All the old wounds were opened. Marat and Lanjuinais, from opposite sides of the hall and the issue, rushed to the tribune. Deputies hurled insults at each other. The weary president once again put on his hat to suspend the session. But the bickering and disorder continued for hours. The exhausted and exasperated Vergniaud yielded the chair to Treilhard, who himself surrendered to the anarchy at 10:30 P.M. and adjourned the session.

But passions were not to be regulated by parliamentary rules. The Mountain refused to recognize the adjournment. About 300 deputies stayed in the hall. Treilhard ignored both them and their taunts, left the chair, and walked out. The disgruntled Mountain and its sympathizers were in possession of the Manège and proceeded to conduct a rump parliament. Lacombe Saint-Michel mounted to the tribune and read to his auditors the rules of procedure governing any dispute over whether or not the session was adjourned. Lacroix illegally assumed the president's chair and told the tumultuous Mountain that it had no right to deliberate without the president, the secretaries, and the other deputies. Couthon shouted back, with the Mountain as a claque, that those present would remain in the Manège and at their places since the country was in danger and patriotism demanded vigilance. For the next hour and a half the rump session continued, unruly and noisy. Around midnight the commandant of the Paris National Guard, Santerre, appeared and made a rousing speech. The people, he declared, would see justice done the following day. Exhausted, and apparently pleased with their show of strength and the assurance of a lynching if the Convention refused to carry out the death sentence, the Mountain cheered Santerre and then left the hall.

The next morning, January 19, the Convention convened at 10:30. Discussion of reprieve began at once. All the familiar arguments and antagonisms were replayed. Buzot called for the exile of all the Bourbons before Louis's execution. Thuriot threatened the Convention with another September Massacre if Louis were not immediately executed. Casenave made a muddled speech calling for delay until the constitution had been approved by the country. Barbaroux reiterated Buzot's arguments. Guffroy accused the secretaries of "having knowingly altered the votes of a great many voters." Condorcet proposed an end to the death penalty for all private crimes and a discussion of whether it would be retained for "crimes against the state." Brissot rode his hobbyhorse about what Louis's execution would mean to the allied European powers. The question of reprieve was turning into a rehash of the entire trial, with the possibility that this final vote could reverse the decisions so painfully reached by the deputies.

Tom Paine, the hero of the American Revolution who had been made an honorary French citizen and elected as deputy by several constituencies (he decided to represent Pas-de-Calais, Robespierre's old department), was recognized by the president and stood mute at the tribune while Bancal read his prepared speech in French translation. Marat, from his perch atop the Mountain, interrupted: "I maintain that Thomas Paine cannot vote on this question. Being a Quaker his religious principles are opposed to the death penalty." Marat had not thought fit to raise this objection on January 16–17 when it would have been more appropriate. Bancal ignored Marat and continued reading Paine's proposal that Louis be banished to America for life. This was the speech Paine had promised the American ambassador, Gouverneur Morris, he would deliver. Thuriot shouted that this could not be the true opinion of Paine. It must be a faulty, deliberately faulty, translation. Marat immediately appropriated this view: "It is a wicked and misleading translation." Marat was one of the few deputies in the Convention who knew English, but he had not seen the speech, either in French or in English. Garrau, another English-speaker, said he had seen Paine's original and vouched for the translation.

Paine had enormous prestige in the Convention although his active participation was pathetic. He did not know enough French to join in the debates, and he naturally attached himself to men who knew English. These, like Bancal, were mostly Girondins, and Paine became identified with the faction. His speech made little impression on the Convention, despite the irony of sending Louis to live out his days in a republic that he himself had helped create. But the struggle was again under way. Men were still willing, even anxious, to trudge over the same ground that they had covered in the previous four months. If they could not convince or persuade, they could at least try to wear down the opposition, and delay was still a useful tactic for those anxious to keep Louis from the guillotine.

As on January 4, in the midst of the debates on the appeal to the people, it was Barère's intervention that saved the Convention from another fruitless and bitter and endless struggle. Once again he was able to summarize all the arguments and appear before his colleagues as the disinterested voice of reason. Any reprieve for Louis, Barère argued, would make the Convention's work impossible. Any reprieve would be "horrible and machiavellian." It would inaugurate a "new diplomacy" that would "stipulate the health or the banishment of a condemned man as the first article of a treaty." The sword would be held suspended over Louis's head for months. At each movement of the enemies of France the

Convention would say to the miserable king, who was, of course, unable to control the crowned heads of Europe, "your head will fall." "Citizens, do you want to expose this head to the chances and the conjectures of military events?" Such behavior is unworthy of republicans. The royal superstition must be destroyed now and definitively, for the health and safety of the republic itself. And in destroying the royal superstition the deputies must face the inevitable and disagreeable result of offending the governments of Europe. But to grant Louis a reprieve would be to deal with him and with the remaining European monarchies "in the manner of tyrants."

Barère's intervention was crucial. He offered no new arguments, no new subtleties. But he "showed, with his close dialectic, that a reprieve was as impolitic as it was immoral and cruel. He showed also that [the difficulties] lay in our divisions, our suspicions, our panicky fears and petty intrigues," as the deputy Romme noted in his diary. At the end of his speech Barère called for an immediate roll call on the question of reprieve: "Will there be a reprieve in the execution of the judgment of Louis Capet? Yes or no." The *appel nominal* began at once with the department of Gers.

The Girondins again split. Guadet and Bergoeing, Brissot and Pétion, voted for reprieve, Vergniaud and Gensonné, Ducos and Boyer-Fonfrède against. Lacaze and Grangeneuve, among others, abstained. But the Mountain was consistent, as it had been throughout the trial. Almost to a man it voted against reprieve. Many Marais deputies who had cast antiregicide votes in the third roll call now voted against the reprieve; others simply abstained. In general those who had wanted to send Louis to the scaffold on January 16–17 rejected the reprieve, while those who had voted to spare him in the third *appel nominal* now voted, following no particular pattern and appearing inconsistent, to carry out the death sentence. The roll call ended at 2:00 A.M. on January 20. The president, Vergniaud, announced the results. Twenty-one deputies were absent because of illness; seventeen were absent *en mission*; eight were absent without cause; twelve abstained; and one deputy was dead. There were thus 690 votes cast, the fewest of the four roll calls, and the simple majority was 346. 310 voted for reprieve; 380 against. The margin of victory for the regicides was unquestioned and unambiguous. Vergniaud made the official announcement:

> The National Convention decrees that there will not be a reprieve in the execution of the judgment of death that it rendered against Louis Capet, last king of the French, on the seventeenth of this month.

On the motion of Cambacérès the Convention adopted four articles, fixing the king's fate in the stilted language of an official proclamation:

> I. The National Convention declares Louis Capet, last king of the French, guilty of conspiracy against the liberty of the nation and of attacks against the general security of the state.

> II. The National Convention decrees that Louis Capet will suffer the death penalty.

> III. The National Convention declares null the act of Louis Capet, carried to the bar by his counsels, called "the appeal to the nation of the judgment against him rendered by the Convention" and prohibits to any person whatsoever to reintroduce this appeal, under pain of being pursued and punished as guilty of attacking the general security of the republic.

> IV. The Provisional Executive Council will notify during the day, will present itself to Louis Capet, and will take the measures of security necessary to insure the execution within 24 hours . . . and to render an account of everything to the National Convention immediately after it will have been done.

The session ended at 3:00 A.M., Sunday, January 20, 1793.

Danton was right when he told Théodore de Lameth, in October, that if the king came to trial he would perish. Not only would a trial commit the deputies to the inexorable logic of crime and punishment, force them to condemn the king or condemn the Revolution, but regicide feeling was widespread in the Convention and the final solution to the question of the king was more practical than any halfway measure. If the king lived the royalists would be given hope, plots to reestablish the monarchy would plague the republic, and the crowned heads of Europe, Brissot's analysis notwithstanding, would have a pretext for war and conquest. Both

Jacobins and Girondins understood the problem. The Jacobins insisted the king be condemned, by a trial if necessary; the Girondins sought to save Louis by aborting the trial. However anarchic or individualistic the voting on the king's fate may have been, the deputies had only two choices: life or death.

Once the king was declared guilty by almost all the deputies, once the appeal to the people was rejected, the king was dead. The range of opinions expressed in the third *appel nominal* is enormous, covering almost every imaginable variation, but at base there were only two possible votes, regicide or antiregicide. All the conditional votes, all the attempts to vote for the death penalty without inflicting it on the king, were attempts to avoid the dreadful choice the Convention forced upon itself. And these votes failed in their purpose. They might just as well have been abstentions for they did not influence the outcome. The only votes that mattered, except in psychological and ethical terms, were the votes for or against death. And the majority declared for death. The *conventionnels* knew this, knew what they had done and what it meant. The regicide Dubois-Crancé gives the most extreme interpretation of the voting: "One can even say that, at base, there had been unanimity, for very few voted for solitary confinement pure and simple." Exaggerated but not untrue. There was only one regicide vote, *la mort*, with or without explanation. But there were literally dozens of antiregicide votes. Men had ample opportunity to vote to spare Louis. This was the position of the Restoration government that returned to France with Napoléon's defeat.

The restored Bourbons, in the person of Louis XVIII, Louis's brother, were anxious to forget the unforgettable, to obliterate the past. Immediately after giving Louis XVI a belated state funeral, the Restoration drew up a bill of exile for the remaining regicides. The restored royalists, of course, took the widest possible definition of a regicide. All those who had voted death unconditionally (361); all those who had voted the Mailhe amendment (26); all those who had voted death with conditions (46); and all those not included in any of these categories but who had voted against reprieve (22)—were considered regicides. In all, 455. In their retrospective vengeance the restored Bourbons recognized the collective responsibility of the Convention and with Article VII of the law of January

12, 1816, sent those regicides still alive and still in France into exile. Ironically the restored monarchy thus rejected a favorite royalist myth: Louis XVI had been killed by the smallest possible majority of the Convention, by a single vote. And if the Restoration identified 455 regicides it consequently thought that only 286 deputies were antiregicide. Fewer than 40 percent of the deputies had voted unequivocally against death. The Restoration figures support Dubois-Crancé's analysis. There is, of course, an inconsistency here. Why didn't the Restoration consider as regicides everyone who voted Louis guilty? Such a blanket condemnation would have made sense to Danton, not to mention countless royalists. But even the Restoration chose to accept the Convention's distinctions, just as Louis himself had accepted their offer of a trial. The Restoration, apparently, could live with the contradiction that a king could be tried and found guilty of treason by his subjects, yet not be punished with death. Royalist ideology had so decayed by the nineteenth century that such sophistry was possible.

Although only regicide and antiregicide votes counted, there were four distinct categories of votes: those who voted unconditionally for death; those who voted conditionally for death; those who voted unconditionally against death (banishment or imprisonment, or a combination of the two); and those who voted uniquely. The confirmed regicides voted for guilt, against the appeal to the people, for death, and against reprieve. The confirmed antiregicides voted for guilt, for the appeal to the people, against death, and for the reprieve. All the other possible combinations were expressions of confusion, or timidity, or perhaps even factional loyalty. The four roll calls on the king split the Convention into regicides and antiregicides, or *appelants* as the latter were called. The two groups were irreconcilable and since the regicides were in the majority it was only a matter of time before they solidified their hold on the Convention and the Revolution, eventually purging the assembly of the *appelants*.

To understand the motives of the deputies it would be necessary to know each of them intimately. What moved this or that deputy to vote as he did? Was he persuaded by the political arguments of his colleagues, or did he vote for personal reasons? We shall probably never know. But if we cannot explain each and every vote, we can look at what groups of men did, and try to understand their public as opposed to their private motives.

The old Girondin charge that the Convention was intimidated by Paris and could not deliberate freely was disproved by the voting. None of the deputies who swore they would vote for clemency, even if it meant their lives at the hands of a Paris mob, was touched. Ironically enough the only deputy to die for his vote was an aggressive and ferocious Montagnard, Michel Lepeletier de Saint-Fargeau. He voted for death and against reprieve and was stabbed to death in the café in the Palais-Royal which he frequented, on January 20, by a certain Pâris, a former royal guard who saw himself as the avenger of the royalist cause. Lepeletier's assassination only strengthened the regicide cause, by this time identified with the Jacobin cause. His martyrdom gave the Mountain a useful opportunity for propaganda. Lepeletier was given an elaborate state funeral, something that was deliberately denied Louis XVI. The Jacobins were not above flaunting their grief for political advantage. This does not mean that many deputies did not feel intimidated in Paris, but it does mean that their fears were unrealistic, irrational. The *appelants*, as it turned out, had a good deal to fear and many of them would pay in blood for their votes. But not at the hands of a Paris mob or a fanatical revolutionary assassin. They would pay at the hands of their regicide colleagues.

Both factions, Jacobins and Girondins, were fairly consistent throughout the voting and the trial, with a few notable exceptions. Isnard, for example, one of the inner sixty, sounds like a Jacobin fire-eater: "If I had the fire of heaven in my hands I would strike down all those who might attack the sovereignty of the people. Faithful to my principles, I vote for death." And Lasource, another Girondin leader, was only a bit less dramatic: "It is necessary that Louis reign or that he go to the scaffold." Not all the regicides were Jacobins then, but all Jacobins were regicides.

One might expect the regicides themselves to provide the reasons for the outcome of the trial. This was a generation of men who delighted in self-advertisement, who spoke and wrote incessantly, who could not restrain their urge to analyze and explain. But long after the voting was finished, long after Louis was dead, when men had the leisure to come to terms with themselves and the past by writing their memoirs, they were reluctant to talk about what they had done and why they had done it. Part of the reason was the precariousness of political life during the revolutionary period. Those who survived the Convention and who served in the reactionary governments that ruled France—whether the bourgeois republic of the Thermidorians or the Directory, the bogus republic established by Napoléon or the Empire which he quickly established, not to mention the Restoration—were usually anxious to forget their radical past. In a hostile political climate being a regicide was not something to celebrate. "Here is presented the most tragic event of the Revolution," writes Thibaudeau in the chapter of his *Mémoires* devoted to January 21, 1793. "Despite the almost thirty years that have elapsed, this subject still cannot be broached." Another regicide, Carnot, told his son that he "would have supported willingly not an acquittal (which would have been a bill of innocence applied to treason), not the appeal to the people (a cowardly ruse, a greater error), but a reprieve which could have been followed one day by popular clemency." But Carnot chose to forget that he had voted against reprieve on January 20, 1793. Still, if the surviving deputies refused to talk in detail about what had happened, what they had done, none of them tried to obliterate the memory of the Convention, none of them were piously contrite. They accepted the collective responsibility for Louis's death and lived with it. In general only those contemporaries who did not have to stand up and be counted on January 16–17 were willing to deplore what had happened and insist they would not have done what was done. Joseph Garat, for example, the minister of justice who carried out the Convention's sentence and who died in the comfort and security of an academic position, cursed the verdict and the violations of legal procedure during the trial. But in January 1793 he prudently kept his objections to himself, and he kept his ministerial portfolio.

Despite the apparent dominance of brilliant personalities, despite the individualism of the voting, despite the bitter factional struggles, it was the Convention as a whole that spoke, with a collective voice that was unmistakable. And once Louis had been condemned to death the *conventionnels* refused to reverse the decision by voting for reprieve. So sure were the regicides of their victory that the Jacobins sent two of their deputies *en mission* before the final vote on reprieve. The unusually high number of abstentions in the fourth *appel nominal* also testifies to the willingness or resignation of the deputies in accepting the king's death. Louis could easily have won a stay of execution had the 334 antiregicide votes, along with the 26 Mailhe amendment votes, supported the reprieve. But those who had voted to save the king on January 16–17 voted to let him die on January 20. Mailhe himself voted against reprieve.

What mattered most was that the Convention had been through its greatest crisis and was still intact. The Jacobins were, it is true, now the dominant faction, but their ascension was incomplete in January. It would be months before they could dominate the Convention completely. And their victory in the king's trial was not the triumph of truth over falsehood, or rather political consistency over political flabbiness. The Jacobins triumphed, and Louis died, because they were able to articulate what the majority of the deputies felt yet could not express, and because their opponents, the Girondins, had bungled the trial. The struggle of the factions is inseparable from the king's trial and it is probably the most significant place to study the fight for supremacy in the Convention. Unlike any other episode in the Convention's history—or for that matter in the parliamentary history of the Revolution—the king's trial reached into the farthest corners of the Assembly. Men whose political lives were otherwise obscure were forced, or felt compelled, to participate. More than 70 percent of the deputies spoke on some aspect of the trial. It was the first and last time in the Revolution that the majority of deputies were so deeply involved. So this first triumph of the Mountain was more significant than a mere tactical skirmish. When the Convention sent Louis to his death the overwhelming majority of the *conventionnels*, reluctantly to be sure, gave their support to the Jacobins, indicating that they accepted the inevitability of Louis's death and, implicitly, the necessity for Jacobin leadership.

This is not to minimize the sincerity or the agony of those deputies who abhorred the death penalty, who could not, for philosophical, or emotional, or personal reasons send the guilty king to the guillotine. But such men were not made for the brutality of revolutionary politics. The tough, the committed, and even the insensitive understood the choice confronting them; the others may have understood, but could not act. And in politics, especially revolutionary politics, *il faut choisir*.

The regicides had insisted, in Michelet's colorful phrase, that "the death of this living God would pass without miracle, without thunder and lightning." When the Convention unanimously declared Louis guilty it established the principle of its sovereignty and the accountability of kings. When it voted Louis's death it said, in a manner beyond dispute or modification, that, as Robespierre put it, "the king must die for the Revolution to live." The people's quarrel with their king had been settled.

The king first heard his sentence from Malesherbes, who rushed to the Temple on the morning of January 17, immediately after the results of the third *appel nominal* were announced. The loyal old man reached the prison in a state of nervous excitement. "All is lost, the king is condemned," he blurted out to Cléry. He entered Louis's apartment to give him the dreadful news. The king was seated in semidarkness. A single lamp burned on the fireplace mantel, but did nothing to dispel the gloom of the old fortress. Louis, his elbows propped on the table, his head buried in his hands, looked up when Malesherbes entered. Between sobs Malesherbes delivered his tidings to the king. Louis stared dumbly up at him, then slowly got to his feet. Passionately and spontaneously Louis embraced the old man, trying to comfort him. Malesherbes tried to fall to his knees before his sovereign; Louis held him close. "For two hours," the king mused, embracing Malesherbes, "I have been trying to think if, in the course of my reign, I did anything that deserved the slightest reproach from my subjects. Alas, M. de Malesherbes, I swear to you with all the sincerity of my heart, as a man who is about to appear before God, I have always wanted the happiness of the people." Louis, in extremis, responded as he always had—when captured in Varennes, when the Paris crowd invaded the Tuileries, when he was interrogated by the Convention, when he presented his defense—with a mixture of self-righteousness and incomprehension. To the end he never felt a sense of guilt, protected as he was by a theory of kingship, reinforced by religion, that was always reassuring.

The king was more touched by the old man's grief than his own fate. There would be time enough to search the terrors of his mind. For the moment Louis was relieved that his ordeal was almost over. For the first time since August 10, 1792, he knew his fate. "So much the better; that [the judgment] frees me of uncertainty," he told Malesherbes. The king remained pensive and rooted for a long time, still clinging to his lawyer and friend. Then he abruptly started pacing back and forth. He was in a state of shock. Only slowly did the mindless pacing restore his equilibrium. Then, with one of those sudden fits of resolution and energy that usually surprised everyone, Louis initiated the preparations for his death. He sent Cléry to the Temple's library to find the volume of Hume's *History of England* dealing with the death of Charles I. His preparations for death were simple, practical, and methodical. Religion and family, his two comforts in life, had now to bear the burden of sustaining Louis's spirit. He made arrangements for a confessor, and for his family, prepared letters for the Convention and the Commune, provided for his servants as best he could, and for the next few days read Hume's fifth volume. He also intensified his reading of spiritual works and talked often and intimately with Cléry, his valet. He believed he had been condemned to death by only five votes, which is the report Malesherbes brought him, and he attributed his condemnation to the Paris delegation and "the assassins devoted to the Duke d'Orléans." It was more comforting to attribute his sentence to his cousin's ambition and the machinations of a few radical deputies than to acknowledge the collective responsibility of the Convention, indeed, of the nation in revolution. Louis could understand ambition and demagoguery and power. He could not understand what his subjects considered justice. "What have I done to my cousin to make him pursue me like this?" Louis lamented, and then sighed with resignation, "Ah, he is more to be pitied than me; my position is sad, without doubt, but his is sadder still. No, without a doubt, I would not want to change places with him."

The Commune too began preparations. As soon as the results of the third *appel nominal* were announced, and before the vote on reprieve, the General Council of the Commune and the mayor of Paris issued a joint order: Louis would be guarded at all times and security measures at the Temple would be strictly enforced. "As a sign of rejoicing the streets of the city of Paris will be lighted today," the Commune further decreed. The Council also named Jacques Roux, the passionately radical ex-priest, and Jacques-Claude Bernard, as its official representatives at the execution. They would be charged with accompanying the victim to the scaffold and making an official report. Two men more hostile to the king and the monarchy could not have been found by the General Council, which also decreed that the faithful Cléry, under supervision, would be allowed to remove from the Temple some linens for himself and the surviving members of the royal family before Louis's apartment was sealed up. Still worried that the king might attempt suicide to escape the guillotine, the Commune asked the Convention to ratify its stringent security measures about visitors, sharp instruments, and a twenty-four-hour guard.

Military preparations for the execution were also begun on January 17. Commandant Santerre sent the General Council his report on the preliminary measures he had taken. "The day of the execution of Louis Capet the place of the Carrousel [in the Tuileries gardens] and its environs will be bristling with cannon. All the sections will guard their respective neighborhoods. Care will be taken to break up groups of people and disperse them, and to discover their motives in gathering." In addition, as on December 11 and 26 when Louis left the Temple to appear before the Convention, virtually every soldier and national guardsman and federal in the city would be armed and on active duty, and every section would see to it that its armed members were in the streets or on alert. Literally thousands of armed men would be mustered to see Louis to his death. Essentially the same orders of the day that had been followed on December 11 and 26 would be in force on January 21, and Santerre carefully issued the necessary documents and sent them to each section; at the same time special cards of identity were prepared and ammunition was issued. Paris was ready to kill the king.

CHAPTER XII

The March to the Scaffold

PARIS, JANUARY 20–21, 1793

HE ROADS are closed behind us," wrote the regicide Lebas to his father on January 20. "We must go forward whether we like it or not. Only now can we say we will live free or die." The Convention made its preparations.

Garat, the minister of justice, was sent to the Temple as the Convention's representative on January 20, charged with informing Louis of his fate. He left the Manège and arrived at the Temple around 2:00 P.M. Louis listened thoughtfully and silently as Garat read the official proclamation of his condemnation. The king made no response. He walked over to where his briefcase lay on the table and removed from it a letter in his own hand, which he gave to Garat. It was addressed to the Convention:

> I ask the Convention for a three-day delay in order to prepare myself to appear in the presence of God. I ask the Convention for the right to see, without restrictions, the person [his confessor] whom I will indicate to the Commune and ask that this person be protected from all fear, from all uneasiness, in rendering this act of charity toward me. I ask to be free of constant surveillance . . .

In the original holograph of the letter, preserved in the French National Archives, the words "of the National Convention," which occur twice, are crossed out by the king. To the last Louis remained polite toward his enemies, but he would not legitimize them with an official title; for him the Convention was not the government of France. In the three-day interval he sought, Louis wanted "to be able to see my family when I ask to, and without witnesses." He closed by asking the Convention to care for his family and allow them to retire "to a place it considers proper." But only Madame Royale, the king's daughter, would survive the Revolution.

These final words to the Convention are those of a feudal monarch anxious to fulfill his obligations toward his clients, those who had served him or defended him, those who had remained loyal when the rest of the nation deserted its king. "I recommend to the charity of the nation, all those attached to me. There are many who have put all their fortunes in their duty and who, no longer having a position, might be in need." Cléry was first among these but he was not alone, for dozens of domestics, many of them grown up in the royal service, remained alive and compromised for their loyalty to their master. Among such dependents were "old people, women and children, who have only [their positions] to live on." The place for the date at the head of the letter was left blank: "At the tower of the Temple, the ____ January 1793," a poignant indication of a hopeless hope that the reprieve might be accepted, or a foolish desire to be precise, for the letter had been written a couple of days before Garat was sent to the Temple.

The Convention was asked to look after the future; the Commune controlled the present. Louis had also written to the General Council asking for a confessor of his own choice, Henry Essex Edgeworth de Firmont, an Irish priest living in Paris. Edgeworth was the son of an Anglican Irish clergyman but had converted to Catholicism and studied at Toulouse with the Jesuits. He took the name de Firmont when he was ordained but declined an Irish see, preferring to work with the Paris poor. He entered the seminary for foreign missions in Paris and in 1791 became the confessor of Louis's pious sister, Madame Elisabeth. In revolutionary Paris, indeed in revolutionary France, at least since the stringent anticlerical legislation of 1790, it was illegal and hence dangerous for priests to administer the sacraments if they had not sworn an oath to the civil constitution. This made it extremely difficult for a devout Catholic to find a priest who was willing to take the risk. Sacraments received from revolutionary clergy were considered suspicious and perhaps inefficacious by the pious. But Edgeworth was a foreigner and immune to the harsh anticlerical laws. He lived quietly in Paris and preserved a reputation for piety and priestly purity. Madame Elisabeth, who was au courant in such matters, had recommended him to Louis. After accompanying the king to the scaffold Edgeworth entered the service of the Count of Provence, Louis's exiled brother and the future Louis XVIII, becoming his private chaplain. Eventually he accepted a pension from Pitt out of fear of being a burden to his new royal master. He died, in 1807, of a fever contracted while attending French prisoners at Mittau.

In addition to requesting the services of Edgeworth, Louis asked the Commune, in the same letter, to permit him to see his family freely and without witnesses "because in the situation in which I find myself, it is painful not to be able to be alone" with them. He added a postscript requesting that he be allowed to see his lawyers. Garat saw to it that the two letters, to the Convention and the Commune, were delivered. He himself carried the king's letter to the Convention and read it to the deputies, who decided that Louis would be permitted to have Edgeworth as his confessor and to see his family in privacy. The Executive Council of the Commune was authorized to tell the prisoner that "the nation, always great and always just, would concern itself with the future of his family." The deputies rejected Louis's request for a three-day reprieve: the king would die within twenty-four hours.

While the king negotiated with his captors the city of Paris was calm. The newspapers were more agitated than the population, and made a point of assuring their readers that the guillotining of the king would pass without incident. The *Annales patriotiques* scoffed at the "sinister predictions" of a royalist uprising; Paris had never been more tranquil. Indeed, the article continued, Louis's death was likely to cause less stir than the execution of any other criminal. The people of the city had begun by despising their king. During the trial they had come to resent him. And now the demystification of the monarch and the monarchy was complete: the people saw, in place of an anointed king, only a man, a guilty man, about to pay for his crimes. The *Annales patriotiques* concluded its analysis by assuring its readers that although there might

remain a few "royalist fanatics," a few "superstitious monarchists," they presented no threat to the general population. The dis-
ease of royalism was not contagious; there would be no epidemic.

Edgeworth arrived at the Temple on January 20, in the afternoon. The king spent a large part of his time with his confessor.
What remained was devoted either to his family or to solitary reading. The king's family, according to Madame Royale, did not hear
about the death sentence until the evening of January 20; her father
had kept the news from his family for almost three days, to spare
them anguish. Such concern is entirely within Louis's character,
but that the family did not hear the news from one of the Temple
guards, some of whom went out of their way to be cruel, seems unlikely. At any rate, around 7:00 on the evening of January 20 the
guards came to the queen's apartment and announced that by decree of the Convention the royal family could see the king that
evening. They had not been permitted to see Louis from the time of
his defense before the Convention. Louis arrived immediately after
the announcement. He spent the next hour and a half with his family. At 8:30 he retired, with his confessor, just before his dinner was
served by Cléry. "The king ate little, but with a good appetite,"
Cléry reported. The general injunction against sharp instruments
in the Temple, long in force and scrupulously observed in these
final days, meant that Louis could not have a knife with his meal.
Cléry prepared a meal that could be eaten with a spoon. "Do they
think me so wicked that I would try to take my life?" he lamented
as he ate his meal of soft foods. Suicide was unthinkable for Louis.
In this as in so much else about his religion, he believed profoundly in the obligations of his cult. He could not and would not take
his own life and suffer the consequences of eternal damnation.
And he resented the assumption that he might kill himself just as
he resented the humiliation of having to eat, like a child, with a
blunt implement.

After this outburst, the king ate in complete silence. For his last
supper Louis had a pan-fried chicken, a few little pastries, some
boiled beef, and a purée of turnips. He ate two chicken wings,
some vegetable, two glasses of wine cut with water, and a piece of
sponge cake with a glass of Malaga wine for dessert. Immediately

after dinner he retired to his alcove with Edgeworth. He prayed for a time with his confessor and then, around 9:30, had his final meeting with his family. Marie-Antoinette, Madame Elisabeth, and the two children, each of them led by the hand by one of the women, were escorted to Louis's apartment. They all threw themselves into the king's arms and he lavished kisses on the children. They moved into the dining room and Cléry, for the first time in the Temple, closed the door behind them. Cléry himself remained outside, with the guards. The door to the dining room, however, had a small window so that this final leave-taking could be seen but not heard. Louis was seated with Marie-Antoinette and Madame Elisabeth to his right and left, respectively. His daughter stood in front of her father, his son between his legs. Louis kissed and fondled the children, sobbing intermittently.

At 10:15 P.M. Louis arose to leave. Cléry opened the door and heard the final words of the king to his family: "I assure you that I will come to see you tomorrow morning at eight." "Do you promise?" the royal family asked, almost in unison. "Yes, I promise." "Why not at seven," begged the queen. "Very well, at seven then. Adieu! . . ." Louis backed toward the door. Madame Royale flung herself toward her departing father and collapsed at his feet. Louis picked up the little girl as Cléry rushed into the room to take the swooning child from the king's arms. Louis quickly embraced his family, turned, and left the dining room.

The king was shaken. He immediately retired to his study alcove with Edgeworth for fifteen minutes of prayer. When the two men emerged Edgeworth set out at once for the General Council of the Commune, sitting in the Hôtel de Ville, to ask for the things he needed to celebrate mass in the morning. Louis refused to prepare for sleep until Edgeworth had returned from his mission. When he did return the priest assured Louis that the Commune had told him all the requested items would be provided. After this hasty exchange of information, the two again retired to the king's alcove to pray. At 12:30 A.M., slightly later than the king's accustomed bedtime, Louis prepared to rest. Cléry undressed his master and automatically started rolling the king's hair. That won't be necessary, Louis told him. As he laid down he asked Cléry to wake him at 5:00 A.M. The king slept soundly.

While the king slept the revolutionary government put the finishing touches on its preparations. Louis was to be executed in the Place de la Révolution, formerly the Place Louis XV, presently the Place de la Concorde. The guillotine, conveniently portable, had been erected by the carpenters under the watchful supervision of Sanson, the public executioner. The grim machine was set up between the pedestal that had, only a few months ago, held the statue of Louis XV, and the Champs-Elysées. The execution was to be carried out before noon. Louis would be fetched from the Temple at 8:00 A.M. to begin his last journey across Paris. The Executive Council of the Convention, headed by Garat, along with the Convention itself, would remain in session throughout the day, awaiting the official report of the king's death from the Commune's representatives at the scaffold. All this was in accordance with the specific instructions of the General Council of the Commune.

The Commune's security preparations were elaborate. Santerre was ordered to station enough troops at the entrances to the city "to prevent any crowd, of whatever nature it might be, armed or not, from entering or leaving the city." All the sections were ordered to be under arms at 7:00 A.M. No one was excused from duty except those functionaries who had other responsibilities. All forty-eight sectional committees were to sit in uninterrupted session throughout the day. The orders of the Commune were printed and posted on the walls of Paris during the night of January 20–21.

Santerre had arranged a major military operation. "Each section," wrote the former brewer, "will furnish twenty-five men, armed with muskets and sixteen cartridges, who know how to maneuver and whose principles are reliable. Each will be furnished with a card worn in the buttonhole, bearing his name, that of his section and of its president." These 1,200 men "will muster at the Temple at 7:30 A.M. precisely. Each chief commanding a detachment of twenty-five men will have a list of their names which he will give to the adjutant in service at the Temple." The muster roll would be called at the Temple and the officer in charge would have the authority to dismiss any man who did not want to serve at the king's execution. To assure tranquillity and allay any fears of another prison massacre, special details were assigned to patrol the prisons.

The escort bringing the king to the guillotine would consist of 100 men on horseback, fully armed, and drawn from the *gendarmerie*. The rear would be brought up by another hundred mounted men, drawn from the National Guard and the Military Academy. A large number of cavalry would be held ready at various staging areas throughout Paris. In addition to the 200 mounted guards there would be 1,200 foot soldiers to surround the coach carrying the king. These men, chosen for their patriotism, would be paced by 60 drummers under the command of a drum major. In all—the mounted men, the foot soldiers, the Temple guard, the sectional guards, the drummers—there would be between 8,000 and 9,000 armed men. Along the route, the same followed by the king for his two appearances before the Convention except that the procession would turn right down the present Rue de Rivoli instead of left toward the Manège, another 2,400 armed men would be stationed, drawn from the reserves, along with more than 6,000 men from the auxiliary corps and an additional 50 armed men from each section. Those not assigned to guard the route to the scaffold would be stationed in their respective sections, and each section was required to furnish, in addition to the troops on active duty, a reserve of 200 armed men to be stationed at the central meeting place of each section. This added another 9,400 men to the totals. Not included in these figures are the artillerymen, the troops stationed in barracks on alert, and those who lined the streets of the royal route. Altogether there were about 80,000 armed men on duty for Louis's march to the scaffold.

All troops not assigned to the escort took up their posts during the night of January 20. With the city bristling under arms it was an understatement of the *Annales patriotiques* to point out that on the eve of the "execution of the former king, one did not see the least movement in his favor." It would have taken an army to offer any significant threat. But the authorities were taking no chances: command of the entire operation was given to a professional soldier, General Berruyer. Commandant Santerre would be his second-in-command.

Louis was to be taken to the Place de la Révolution in the mayor's coach, accompanied by representatives of the Commune, a guard, and his confessor, Edgeworth. The public executioner, traditionally called "Monsieur de Paris," was ordered to wait with his assistants at the place of execution. Sanson, who took considerable pride in his work, was anxious to carry out his job without a hitch. The guillotine might be indifferent to its victims; the executioner was not. No Monsieur de Paris had ever had the honor of executing a king, and Sanson wanted precise instructions. He had written the Commune asking exactly when Louis would leave the Temple, when he was expected to arrive at the Place de la Révolution, and whether he would be brought thither by coach or "in the cart usually used for executions like this." Sanson, the ideal public servant, wanted his performance to be perfect.

Cléry was up before 5:00 A.M. on January 21. He waited for the clock to strike the hour before lighting the fire in Louis's room. The noise woke the king. "I slept well," he told Cléry. "I needed it. Yesterday exhausted me. Where is M. de Firmont?" The priest was in his own bed. "And you, where did you spend the night?" In a chair. Louis apologized for the discomfort he had caused his faithful servant. "Ah, Sire, can I think about myself at a time like this?" The king grasped Cléry's hand and shook it vigorously, with emotion and affection.

Cléry dressed the king and arranged his hair. While he was being coifed Louis carefully removed a seal from his watch chain, put it in his waistcoat pocket. He got up and placed his watch on the mantel. He removed his wedding ring, looked abstractedly at it for a moment or two, perhaps recalling only the touching moments in a difficult marriage, then put it in the same pocket with the seal. He changed his shirt, put on a white jacket he had worn the day before, took his coat from Cléry. Then he strode to the table, emptied the pockets of his briefcase, removed his lorgnette, tobacco pouch, and some personal effects. He put his coin purse on the mantel, next to his watch. Only then did he turn to Cléry and ask him to bring Edgeworth to the alcove. Cléry found Louis's confessor already awake and led him to the king. The two retired into the study.

Louis fell to his knees, resting on a little cushion Cléry had found in the Temple. He heard mass at 6:00 and took his first communion since August 1792. At 7:00 the king emerged from his study and called Cléry to give his final instructions: "Will you give this seal to my son . . . this wedding ring to the queen. Tell her that I am leaving her with a great deal of pain . . . This little package contains locks of hair of all my family. Give it to her too. Tell the queen, tell my dear children, tell my sister, that I had promised to see them this morning, but that I wanted to spare them the pain of such a cruel separation. How hard it is to leave without receiving their final embraces." At this the king broke down. Between sobs he begged Cléry to convey to his family the adieux he himself could not convey. He turned abruptly and reentered his study.

As soon as Louis left the room the guards made Cléry empty his pockets. They confiscated the ring, the seal, and the locks of hair. The council of guards at the Temple would decide whether Cléry would be allowed to fulfill his melancholy mission to the remaining members of the royal family. Fifteen minutes later Louis again emerged from his study. He asked Cléry to fetch him a pair of scissors. The valet passed the request to the guards. They demanded to know why the king wanted scissors, which were forbidden in the Temple. Cléry rapped at the study door and asked. The scissors were to be used by Cléry to cut the king's hair and thus spare him the humiliation of having his hair cut on the scaffold by the executioner. One of the guards carried the request downstairs. For a half hour the staff debated the king's request. The guard returned to Louis's apartment and told Cléry the request had been denied, then rapped at the study door and told the king, who replied: "I would not have touched the scissors. I wanted Cléry to cut my hair in your presence." The king did an about-face and returned to his study.

"My God," he told Edgeworth, "how happy I am to have my principles! Where would I be without them? With them even death appears sweet to me! Yes, there exists an incorruptible judge in heaven who will know how to give me the justice that men refuse me here."

When Santerre arrived, around 8:00 A.M., Louis was still closeted with his confessor. The commandant mounted to Louis's apartment, was admitted by Cléry, and confronted the king. "Monsieur, it is time to go." "I am busy. Wait for me there, I will be with you in a few minutes." He closed the study door and threw himself at Edgeworth's feet: "Everything is over. Monsieur, give me your final benediction and pray God that He will sustain me until the end."

Louis stood up, composed himself, reassumed his royal dignity, and left the study. Santerre repeated his grim announcement. Louis raised his eyes to heaven, nervously stamped his right foot, and repeated the simple phrase he had used to his family on the morning of August 10, 1792, when they left the Tuileries: "Let us go."

Cléry, standing just behind his master, next to the fireplace, offered the king his heavy coat. "I don't need it, just give me my hat." Louis took the three-cornered hat with its tri-color revolutionary badge, put it under his arm, shook Cléry's hand. "Messieurs, I wish that Cléry might stay with my son who is used to his care. I hope the Commune will grant this request." He handed some manuscript sheets to Jacques Roux: "I am charged only with conducting you to the scaffold," Roux announced and refused the pages. Jacques-Claude Bernard, the other representative of the Commune, accepted the sheets. They turned out to be Louis's last will and testament. Then, looking directly at Santerre, the king again said, "Let us go."

The king's departure from the Temple had been twice rehearsed, on December 11 and 26; on January 21 the king retraced his steps. Louis and the escort passed through the seven guardposts of the tower to reach the courtyard. The mayor's coach, surrounded by guards, was waiting. Louis mounted the coach without assistance, without looking back at his prison. Lieutenant Lebrasse and a sergeant sat facing the king; Edgeworth was at his side. During the procession to the Place de la Révolution Louis read the prayers for the dying and the penitential psalms, sometimes to himself, sometimes murmuring aloud. No one else in the coach said a word. There was no small talk, no discussion of Latin authors.

The January morning was cold, the air oppressively humid. It rained intermittently and a thick fog had settled. Not an unusual winter day for Paris. The march to the scaffold took an hour and a half. Except for the monotonous beat of drums there was complete silence. All the windows and doors of the houses and shops along the route were shut, by order of the Commune. The armed guards along the route stood four deep, motionless. What sympathy there might have been for the king went unexpressed, choked off by the immense concentration of troops. There were no taunts hurled at the king on his way to his passion.

But the elaborate precautions of the Commune had not entirely intimidated the royalists. During the night a handbill calling on the devout to save the king had been slid under doors. And Garrau told his colleagues in the Convention that he had seen a wall poster that made the same plea. As the coach carrying the king rolled out of the Temple courtyard someone in the crowd begged for the king's blessing. The mysterious, thaumaturgic powers of the king, for so many years an inherited ornament of the French monarchy, were still sought after so long as the king was alive. Near the Saint-Martin gate a young woman cried out in anguish from the crowd, an isolated, anonymous *cri de cœur.* At the intersection of the presentday boulevard du Temple and rue de Cléry—the latter the valet's posthumous reward for loyalty, an honor denied Robespierre or any of the important regicides—the Baron de Batz, leading four desperate adventurers, broke from the crowd: "Join us, all you who want to save the king!" The rescue, pathetically reminiscent of an earlier age of personal courage, failed. The guards immediately grabbed two of the paladins; the others disappeared in the crowd. Louis, absorbed in his prayers, had heard nothing; he did not even look up from his Bible. In front of the church Notre-Dame-de-Bonne-Nouvelle a man suspected of royalist designs was sabered and left for dead. Near the Madeleine, only a short distance from the Place de la Révolution, Beaugéard, one of the queen's former secretaries, tried to reach the king's coach. He was cut down and left in the street. The coach rolled into the mobbed square, dominated by the newly erected scaffold.

About twenty thousand people were jammed into the Place de la Révolution, and the steps leading to the Tuileries garden as well as the walls surrounding the garden were packed. Each of the streets that debouched into the great Place was guarded by cannon. The scaffold, its platform about six feet above the ground, stood almost in the center of the Place, approximately where the Obelisk stands today. The guards who ringed the structure held the crowds back and kept a path clear for the king's coach. The Commune, addicted to revolutionary symbolism, had chosen for the guillotine the place

LOUIS AT THE SCAFFOLD. An engraving by
Carlo Silanio, after a painting by Benazech. To the
king's left is Edgeworth, his confessor, giving the
king encouragement. The man on horseback with extended sword is Santerre. There are a number of inaccuracies in the engraving: there are too many steps
leading to the guillotine and the artist has put leaves
on the trees, in January! *Collection de Vinck,
Bibliothèque nationale*

THE KING IS DEAD. A popular print, artist unknown. The orientation of the scaffold (facing the Champs-Elysées), is correct. The figure remaining in the coach is probably Edgeworth; the soldier brandishing his sword is Santerre; the hangman showing Louis's severed head to the crowd is Sanson. The basket into which Louis's corpse was put can be seen on the scaffold. De Vinck considers this the most faithful rendering of the scene. Such popular prints, created by artists more interested in recording events than adhering to the rules of artistic expression, are often more immediate and charming than more self-conscious prints. *Collection de Vinck, Bibliothèque nationale*

where the crowd had stood in sullen silence as Louis was returned a prisoner from Varennes and where, even earlier, the royal cavalry had charged a crowd on its way to the Bastille on July 14, 1789, to commit its first act of revolutionary violence. Almost any public place in Paris would have served just as well as a reminder of the monarchical past and the revolutionary present. "The approach of the column was announced by a thundering roll of drums." The escort led the king's coach through the crowd and halted at the foot of the scaffold stairs. The king "was nearly concealed by the mounted gendarmes" surrounding the coach. It was 10:00 A.M.

Louis remained in the coach, talking in a low voice to Edgeworth. Then he opened the door and stepped down, unaided, "with a determined air." Edgeworth was at his side, holding the king's arm. "There he is, there he is," buzzed the crowd as the news passed back through the spectators packed into the Place de la Révolution. The executioners waited at the foot of the stairs. They started undressing the king, removing his coat and taking his hat. Louis insisted he be guillotined fully clothed. That was impossible. The hangman too had his rituals and was determined to make no exception, even for his most exceptional victim. Louis refused to let the executioners touch him. He removed his coat himself, and his collar, and handed them to Edgeworth. He stood in the bitter cold dressed in a plain white waistcoat, gray breeches and white stockings. The executioners tried to bind his hands behind his back. Louis shook them off. "Sire," said Edgeworth, "in this new outrage I see only a final resemblance between your Majesty and the God who is going to be his reward." Louis submitted. He mounted the stairs of the scaffold with a firm step.

Edgeworth remained at the foot of the stairs, uttering words of religious comfort to the king, as Sanson cut his hair. His face "very flushed," Louis walked to the left edge of the platform, looking around at the soldiers and the crowd. The drums beat their monotonous tattoo. Louis signaled them to stop with a nod of his head. For the last time the drummers obeyed their former king. There was silence. A few isolated voices from the crowd urged the executioner to do his duty. Sanson and his assistants remained rooted. Louis started to speak, in a clear, strong voice. "I die innocent. I pardon my enemies and I hope that my blood will be useful to the French, that it will appease God's anger. . . ." General Berruyer abruptly ordered the drums to roll; Santerre relayed the order. The king's last words were drowned out. The executioners quickly strapped the king to the plank, slid him through the "widow's window." The king uttered a frightful cry as the blade fell. Sanson's son grabbed the royal head out of the basket and held it up for the crowd. Royalist tradition insists that as Louis was being strapped to the plank he struggled to get free. "Son of Saint Louis," Edgeworth shouted above the drums, "mount to heaven." The king died with this apotheosis in his ears.

The thud of the guillotine blade released the tensions of the morning. "Long live the Republic! Long live liberty! Long live Equality!" the crowd chanted. Some tossed their hats in the air. The guards surrounding the scaffold waved their muskets and pikes. Some of the crowd ran to the scaffold, forcing their way through the crowd and the guards, to dip their handkerchiefs in the royal blood. These grim souvenirs passed as cherished relics in the nineteenth century.

It was all over at 10:22 A.M. The executioner exercised his official perquisites by selling some of the king's hair and his hair ribbon. The three-cornered hat with its revolutionary emblem was auctioned off from the scaffold. The king's brown coat, with its blue enamel buttons, was cut up and distributed to the crowd, who mobbed the scaffold trying to catch a piece of it. Some of the spectators formed a chain and danced around the scaffold, singing "La Marseillaise" with its heroic taunting of kings and courts.

The king's decapitated body was put in a wicker basket, his head between his legs. The basket was put in a *charrette*, a small open cart, and carried to the Madeleine Cemetery. The crowd continued its celebrating. At the cemetery the king's body was transferred to an uncovered wood coffin, covered with a double layer of quicklime, a layer of soil, and then lowered into a deep open grave which was immediately covered over. Santerre reported to the Commune that "the body was transported to the Madeleine with care and exactitude. It was buried between the bodies of those who died at the time of his marriage and the Swiss killed on August 10." Even in death the Commune was keenly attentive to symbolism.

The king's neighbors in his final resting place were the 130 victims of the panic that broke out on May 30, 1770, during the celebration of his marriage to Marie-Antoinette, and the 500 Swiss victims of the August 10 massacre at the Tuileries: the beginning and end of Louis's royal career.

The Commune not only imposed a revolutionary iconography on Louis's burial, it also sought to destroy all the traditional symbols of absolutism. The revolutionaries might scoff at the magical powers attributed to French kings, they might make obscene reference to the sacred crypt at Saint-Denis that held the remains of so many French kings, they might shoot the heads off the saints and monarchs that decorated the portals of Notre-Dame, but they were careful to obliterate the king's remains, give their contempt more than a propaganda value. The double dose of quicklime and the depth of the common grave were deliberately ordered. There was to be nothing left of France's last thaumaturgic king; nothing remained to be resurrected from the grave. In 1808, when Napoléon, anxious to monopolize all monarchical feeling in France, had the tower of the Temple razed to prevent possible pilgrimages to Louis's prison, the physical destruction of the monarchy and its martyr was complete.

CHAPTER XIII

The Memory of a King

JANUARY 21, 1793 – JANUARY 21, 1973

N THE AFTERNOON of January 21 the theaters opened as usual and the cafés and cabarets were crowded with Parisians. The topic of discussion was the execution. The deputies, in the Manège, harangued each other with brave words about justice and the republic, but the Convention was irreconcilably divided between regicides and *appelants*; and for the triumphant regicides, having voted the king's death now became the sine qua non of revolutionary respectability. To have fought at the Bastille, to have marched to Versailles, to have been in the Champ-de-Mars, to have invaded the Tuileries and the royal apartments, to have fought on August 10 provided proof of devotion and right principles; but to have sent the king to the guillotine was the necessary cap to a revolutionary career, a precondition for political participation and advancement. And the Parisians too were victorious. They had consistently supported the Mountain during the trial, and this support, articulated in the radical press, in sectional petitions, and in the constant threat of insurrection, had brought Louis to the scaffold. The Paris press continued its verbal struggle against the monarchy. "Today," wrote *Le Républicain*, "this great truth has been settled, that the prejudices of so many centuries had stifled. Today people are at last convinced that a king is only a man; and that no man is above the laws. Capet is no more. People of Europe, people of the earth, contemplate the monarchies. You see they are nothing but dust!" Carra, in his *Annales patri-*

222

otiques, celebrated "the indifference, the silence and the composure of the people." Had the Austrian Emperor, the Prussian king, George III of England been present, "they would have no doubt that their age is past."

But at the very moment Carra wrote these words the Prince de Condé, in his headquarters at Villingen, was attending a mass for the dead king. And when he was finished paying his respects to Louis he declared the young dauphin, Louis's son, the king of France. For the royalists the throne was not, could not, be vacant. Later in the week the Count de Provence wrote the Count d'Artois announcing their elder brother's death: "Whilst you shed tears for those near to us, you must not forget how useful their death will be for the country. Comfort yourself with this idea, and reflect that your son is, after myself, the heir and hope of the monarchy." The ambition Louis had excoriated in the Jacobins and his cousin, the Duke d'Orléans, lived on in his brothers. They had not helped Louis when he was alive; now they found the dead king a useful martyr for their own designs on the throne. But the royalists would have to wait more than twenty years to reap the benefits of Louis's death.

The revolutionaries, true to their conviction that everything concerning the trial was a matter for public concern, published the official report, the *procès verbal*, of the execution. The report, drawn up in the afternoon of January 21 and certified by two representatives of the Executive Council of the Convention, two representatives of the Department of Paris, and two representatives of the General Council of the Commune, transformed Louis's death into an inert lump of facts, a routine act of government:

> At ten hours and twenty minutes Louis Capet arrived at the foot of the scaffold and descended from the carriage. And at ten hours and twenty-two minutes he mounted to the scaffold. The execution was instantly carried out and his head was shown to the people.

From the moment of his death men were concerned with the legend of the dead king. The official witnesses of Louis's passion stripped it of all personal details. The king's interrupted speech, his disrobing, his haircut, the supposed last words ejaculated by Edgeworth, all disappeared from the official record. On January 24 the General Council of the Commune was embroiled in a heated debate over whether or not a detailed and accurate account of Louis's last days would be published. One council member proposed that all the guards in the Temple on January 19, 20, and 21 make reports of what transpired during those days. The Commune would then publish these materials. Hébert violently opposed the motion. It would be a mistake to enshrine the memory of the tyrant by publishing evidence of his courage and dignity in his final days. The only memory to be left to posterity should be that of the murderer of August 10, the conspirator who had called the European powers to avenge his fate. Hébert's arguments carried the day. The daily registers of Louis's imprisonment, kept by his guards, disappeared without a trace. They were last mentioned as extant in a letter of September 1817 from M. Lainé, the minister secretary of the interior, to Count de Pradel, director general of the king's household. If the royalists were going to make a cult of the martyred king they would have to do so without the help of the Revolution. Not only did the regicides bury in neglect anything that might be useful to the royalists, they also destroyed all the material remains of the monarchy, just as they had destroyed the king's physical remains. On September 24, 1793, the General Council decreed that "the bed, the clothes and everything that served for the housing and clothing of Capet will be burned in the Place de Grève." The order was carried out on September 29.

The king's last will and testament, the anecdotes left behind by those who had seen him or served him during his last days, would have to serve as the basis of a legend. The Church, so inept in dealing with the Revolution, so slow to act when it might have encouraged Louis, was equally slow in responding to his death. On June 17, 1793, Pope Pius VI, in secret consistory, declared Louis XVI a "royal martyr." His long and carefully argued *allocution* was published to all of Europe and translated into the vulgar tongues. Louis took his place with a small handful of monarchs such as Mary, queen of Scots, who had suffered death for purely religious reasons. The Pope's arguments, ignoring as they did all political matters, were not likely to appeal to any but the most pious Frenchmen, the most convinced royalists, the most cynical courtiers.

But the Restoration government was not deterred by the lack of information. The aristocrats, the priests, and Louis's brothers all came back to France together in 1814. For the next several years, following the unexpected interlude of Napoléon's Hundred Days, the Restoration refought the entire French Revolution, this time in words, decrees, sermons, and debates. High on the list of priorities for the restored Bourbons was giving Louis XVI the honors denied him by the regicides. But only after the symbolism and the hierarchies of the *ancien régime* had been reimposed on the nation, only after Frenchmen had paid homage to the "royal martyr" and savored once again the comforting resonances of a vanished world dominated by the privileged, would scores be settled with the regicides. First familial piety, then revenge. On May 14, 1814, Louis XVIII ordered a triumphal thanksgiving celebration in Notre-Dame. Immediately afterward he ordered a search for the remains of his brother. The Abbé Renard, one of the vicars present at the king's burial, was found, and using his evidence, along with the official reports of the Commune and Santerre, the Restoration believed it had found Louis's grave.

On January 19, 1815, the common grave was dug up and what the government insisted were Louis XVI's remains were exhumed. Mercier had written that the double dose of quicklime had "so destroyed him that it would be impossible for all the gold of the potentates of Europe to make the smallest relic out of his remains." Chateaubriand, the self-conscious embodiment of the Restoration, the creator of new myths for a despised monarchy, and one of the master spirits of a new aristocratic and reactionary romanticism, confirms Mercier's testimony. Chateaubriand stood in the rain as the grave was opened. But this man of so many words was more interested in rhapsodizing on the theme of his own feelings, so sensitively and self-indulgently fondled, and says nothing about what was found that day. Contemporary documents too are discreetly silent. Nothing that resembled the king, nothing that could be identified as the royal remains, had survived the Revolution's acts of oblivion. But on January 20 the king's supposed remains were placed "in a lead coffin [which was] inserted in a wooden bier to which was affixed a silver plaque carrying this inscription: 'Here is the body of the exalted, all-powerful and excellent prince

Louis, sixteenth of that name, by the grace of God King of France and Navarre.'" The next day a convoy, led by a specially built black hearse, bore the pathetic remains to their final resting place. The funeral procession left Paris at 9:00 A.M., following the rue d'Anjou, and arrived at the cathedral of Saint-Denis around noon. The coffin was laid in the magnificent crypt of the French kings in this first of the great Gothic cathedrals, a monument to Abbé Suger's sumptuous vision of his God. Later that day a splendid requiem mass was said for Louis XVI, with his brothers and *le tout Paris* present. It was the first of many such requiems celebrated in the nineteenth century.

And the creation of a useful cult and an accompanying legend did not stop here. On January 17, 1816, Louis XVIII issued a declaration: "All of France demands an expiatory celebration . . . The acts that we present to you, gentlemen, have not originated only in the chambers [of the government]. The mourning existed . . . in all French hearts from the sorrowful day when we lost he who wanted only to live to make us happy." The restored king proposed a monument expressing "the love of the French for so august, so saintly a victim":

I. The 21st of January of each year there will be, throughout the kingdom, a general mourning, on which we will fix the details. The day will be a holiday.

II. In conformity to the orders given by us on this subject last year, there will be, this same day, a solemn service in each church in France.

III. To expiate the crime of this sorrowful day, there will be erected, in the name of and at the expense of the nation, in whatever place it shall please us to designate, a monument, whose form will be determined by us.

IV. There will be equally erected, in the name of and at the expense of the nation, a monument to the memory of Louis XVII [the dauphin], Marie-Antoinette and Madame Elisabeth.

V. There will also be erected, in the name of and at the expense of the nation, a monument to the memory of the Duke d'Enghien.

The crown's proposal was adopted by acclamation in the Chamber of Deputies, which only proved that the Revolution had done its work well. No previous Bourbon king, not even Louis XVI himself, would have troubled or even considered submitting such a proposal to an elected assembly for approval. The king's will, sustained by the king's purse, would simply have ordered it done. No previous Bourbon king would have specified that the money come from the nation. No previous Bourbon king would have felt compelled to insist on his prerogatives in the matter. And no previous Bourbon king would have lumped together so many disparate elements in an attempt to forge them into a single patriotic cult. But the restored Bourbon monarchy was not the old Bourbon monarchy; it had neither the power, the prestige, nor the institutions necessary to rule absolutely. The regicides had been right: the kingship might survive a hundred assassinations, but not a single trial. The inclusion of the Duke d'Enghien, murdered by Napoléon, made it clear that this freshly minted cult had no deep roots, would not survive the Restoration itself.

The celebration of January 21 as a national holiday, a national day of mourning, lasted as long as the Restoration (1815–1830). The sacred text prescribed for the yearly memorial service was Louis's last will and testament, reprinted numerous times and frequently included in royalist memoirs of the Revolution. The testament was solemnly read from the pulpit each January 21, usually in place of a sermon, and the example of the restored Bourbons was an attempt to make the crypt at Saint-Denis an annual pilgrimage for the faithful. The July Monarchy (1830–1848), with Louis Philippe, the son of the Duke d'Orléans, on the throne, did not officially mark the day. Louis Philippe, of course, had no desire to remind his subjects that he was the son of a regicide father. But he was anxious to make his government a home for all Frenchmen and he left the Restoration laws on the books. The monument ordered by Louis XVIII was never built, and Louis Philippe let the project remain in limbo. Anyone wishing to celebrate January 21 was free to do so, but unofficially. The cult of the dead king continued to find adherents throughout the nineteenth century and suffered a revival in the early years of the twentieth at the hands of some French intellectuals who despised the Third Republic and sought to return to the Christian and monarchical past. Since the Second World War, Saint-Denis has become a working-class suburb of Paris, an ugly industrial sprawl on the northern outskirts of the city. Suger's magnificent cathedral, once dominating the landscape, is now hidden amid the houses and buildings thrown up by industrial France. It is visited only by dedicated tourists willing to take a tedious busride. And those who visit the royal crypt, green Michelin guide in hand, are probably unmoved by the reminder of Louis's passion.

January 21 is now marked quietly, so quietly that I found it difficult to locate the service in 1973. I had been reading about Louis's trial and death for more than a year, sometimes amused to see stamped on the collections of pamphlets from the regicides a handsome cachet declaring the book to be the property of the Bibliothèque royale. I wanted to pay my respects to the memory of a man I had come to know, who had absorbed so much of my time and interest. And I wanted to see his final resting place. I had dutifully followed Louis's posthumous career through the nineteenth century, from the first requiem in Paris, to the flamboyant pilgrimages to Saint-Denis made in his name in the twentieth century. I ignored the bemused tolerance of friends for my harmless obsession and made inquiries about the memorial ritual for the king.

The big Paris dailies, complacently republican, ignored the event. But the royalist newspaper, *La Croix*, carried a small announcement and invited the devoted to some seminars on Louis's death. The service was scheduled not for Saint-Denis, as I had hoped, but for the church of Saint-Germain-l'Auxerrois. The choice was fitting if not traditional. Saint-Germain-l'Auxerrois was the Paris church used by French kings when they resided in the capital. It is just across the rue du Louvre from the old palace of the Louvre. There has been a church on this site since the sixth century, as long as there has been a French monarchy. The original structure, burned by the Normans, was reconstructed in the tenth century by Robert the Pious. The tenth-century church fell into disrepair and a major reconstruction was begun in the sixteenth century. This renaissance church was badly damaged in 1831 during a popular demonstration and was restored to its present state later in the nineteenth century. It was cleaned during André Malraux's face-lifting program for historical monuments in the 1960s.

The church is a hodge-podge of styles, reflecting its difficult

history. The bell tower, in the Gothic style but of modern construc-
tion, still houses the bell that sounded the call to massacre Protestants on St. Bartholemew's Day in the sixteenth century. The revolutionaries had wanted it demolished for this very reason. It is not
a handsome church; too many hands during too many centuries
have left their mark on the building. The twelfth-century parts are
beautiful, the later additions less so. Much of the ornamentation,
both internal and external, was done in the sixteenth century and
seems meretricious in comparison to the older parts. And unlike an
authentic Gothic building, Saint-Germain-l'Auxerrois is squat,
horizontal rather than vertical in conception.

It was a winter day in Paris, damp, drizzling, cold, similar, I
mused, to the day of Louis's execution. The sky was overcast and
had that peculiar leaden look that seems unique to Paris and
which, by some alchemy, sets off the beautiful city to good advantage. There were about 150 people in Saint-Germain-l'Auxerrois. They were well-dressed and mostly middle-aged. These were
not curiosity seekers or tourists, but Parisians who had some feeling about Louis XVI and the monarchy and came to the church
during their lunch hour to hear the service. They thumbed through
the royalist pamphlets and newspapers set out on a card table at
the entrance to the church, then took seats in the small chapel
that had been created by hanging a cloth drop across the right
aisle. The altar was only a table, covered with a cloth and holding a small metal cross. The officiating priest was no local preacher.
He had been sent, probably by the bishop, to lead the ceremony.

Several seats in the front row had been left empty. French
friends explained that these were reserved for the Count of Paris,
the pretender to the throne, and his family. I have no idea if this is
true, if the Count of Paris ever appears at these memorial services.
In 1973, so said the gossip papers, he was miffed at his son's recent
marriage to an English model and had not been seen in public for
many weeks.

The service was bland and brief. There was no music and Louis's
testament was not read. No requiem mass was celebrated. The
priest deftly avoided saying anything about the Revolution, about
Louis's trial and death. He retailed none of the royalist anecdotes
about Louis's last days. By 1973 the martyred king had become

only another sinner. We were told that Louis's passion should serve as a symbolic reminder of our own sins; his death a memento mori for all. There was no pomp and circumstance and *le tout Paris* did not consider the observance worthy of their presence. It was almost a republican ceremony, austere and secular. Immediately afterward we all quietly left the church and went about our business in cold, rainy, republican Paris.

Epilogue

HE LEGACY of the king's trial and execution was mixed. It did not, as some Girondins argued (and some modern historians), begin the Terror. But it did, by removing the last remaining institutional prop of the *ancien régime*, set the Revolution on its republican course. The deliberate destruction of the executive branch of government, so dear to the constitution-makers of 1791 as one of the three necessary divisions of power, plagued the Revolution until it created a new executive with the Committee of Public Safety. The Revolution, it seemed, could not function without an executive.

The trial also sanctioned and encouraged new revolutionary forces, the Parisian radicals in uneasy alliance with the victorious Mountain. The regicides tried to put their victory into a revolutionary perspective. Robespierre thought Louis's trial the "most dangerous crisis of our entire revolution." Marat celebrated the "serene joy" that animated the people. For the first time he believed in the republic. Louis's execution was "one of those memorable events which are epoch-making in the history of nations. It will have a prodigious influence on the fates of Europe's despots and on the people who have not yet broken their chains." Marat was right. The French monarchy never again had the prestige, the power, the mysterious hold on the people that had once made French kings the greatest in Europe, the envy of their brother monarchs. Napoléon came close to approximating the power of the old kings, but he was an upstart and a military dictator whose throne rested on conquest rather than on the complex of interests and assumptions that bind a nation to its king. And the monarchies that survived the era of the French Revolution were haunted by the example of a nation bringing its king to justice.

For the royalists and conservatives of the nineteenth century

Louis's death was, as the brilliant Joseph de Maistre put it, "le grand crime." But de Maistre, and other intellectuals, who devoted their lives to cursing the French Revolution, had no extensive popular following. King-killing was held in less abhorrence after the Revolution than many were willing to admit. The regicides had pursued and destroyed royalty itself in the person of Louis XVI. Centuries of royalist propaganda had made the king inseparable from the monarchy, had made the king's two bodies into one. In a sense Louis fell a victim to the pretensions of his ancestors. He could not be punished without being killed and the nation could not have expressed itself in any other way but through the guillotine. When the historian Jean Jaurès wrote that kings "are never more than phantoms" once they have been tried and executed by their subjects, there were few indeed who would challenge him. The regicides had accomplished what they set out to do. Louis was not the last French king, but he was certainly the last king the revolutionaries would have been able to recognize as king.

"At last, my dear father," wrote the regicide Lebas to his father, "the tyrant is no more." The people, "delivered from the chief of the conspirators, shouted *Long live the Nation! Long live the Republic!* as his head fell." There were other regicides less delighted than Lebas. Rebecquy and Barbaroux, two deputies identified with the Girondins, wrote their constituents: "We voted for his death and against the reprieve that was asked for. As to the calumny spread against us, we are sending you a statement that we ask you to read carefully and to communicate to the twenty-four sections [of Marseille]." These regicides wanted only a hearing, not forgiveness. They had fulfilled their duty to the nation and were prepared to live with their actions. Brissot's *Patriote français* gives a nice summary:

> Whatever has been your opinion on this great affair, you can no longer have any doubt about the results. The representatives of the people have pronounced the death of Louis. Respect this decision, share among yourselves the responsibility that they have taken completely upon themselves. You, who have seen the greatest dangers attached to the execution of the tyrant and you who have seen no dangers, devote all your efforts—the former to forestall the evils you have foreseen, the latter to guarantee that they are not realized despite your expectations.

For the moment, a brief moment, the revolutionaries were united, or exhausted into unity. Had it been possible for the nation to solve the problem of the king in any other way, Carra assured his readers, it would have done so. "The conversion of a tyrant would have been preferable to his death," but Louis was beyond the efforts of the revolutionary missionaries.

There were only two points of near-unanimous agreement in the trial: Louis was guilty and he must answer for his guilt. This is the emotional and logical base for everything that happened. Reading the debates and the more than four hundred published *opinions* on the trial one is struck by the disproportionate amount of time given to those who wanted to save the king. There were, of course, in addition to the few royalists in the Convention, hundreds of deputies who wanted to keep Louis from the guillotine. But they were still a minority. Yet it was the regicides who had to convince and cajole and persuade throughout the trial, it was the regicides who had to fight off every legal novelty invented by the antiregicides. Why were so many anxious to spare Louis the death they all agreed he deserved?

The answer is not obscure. Louis was king, even after August 10. Jacobin passion and rationalism, Parisian impatience, paled before this potent fact. But once embarked on a trial, once convinced that there was only one solution to the problem of the king, the revolutionaries had no choice but to send him to the guillotine. The English revolutionaries more than a century earlier had discovered the same truth. "If we beat the King 99 times," said Manchester to Cromwell, "yet he is King still; but if the King beat us once, we shall all be hanged." "My Lord," Cromwell responded, "if this be so, why did we take up arms at first?" There were many in the Convention who asked themselves Cromwell's question. As Robespierre put it, you cannot have a revolution without revolution. The only possible answer was exactly this, and regicide was the consistent position of the Mountain. The Montagnards often overstated the case, resorted to extravagant threats and bizarre arguments, but remember, they had to move men's minds and hearts and exaggeration is often a useful political weapon. France had beaten her king ninety-nine times, and he remained king.

When the roll was called the deputies voted with Robespierre, with Saint-Just, with the Mountain, because they had taken up arms in the first place.

It is Robespierre, more perhaps than any other man, who sent Louis to the guillotine. Throughout the trial the voice of Paris radicalism, the ideologue of the Mountain, the tireless and compelling apologist for regicide and revolution, the man who struggled, in his unpleasant voice and carefully composed speeches, to impose his will on France, Robespierre, deserves the last word. "Formerly," he wrote, "when a king died at Versailles the reign of his successor was immediately announced by the cry: *The king is dead, long live the king*, in order to make it understood that despotism was immortal! Now an entire people, moved by a sublime instinct, cried: *Long live the Republic!* to teach the universe that tryanny died with the tyrant." After January 21, 1793, the revolutionaries, however reluctantly, chanted Robespierre's slogan: "The king is dead! Long live the Revolution!"

What of the survivors? Marie-Antoinette and Madame Elisabeth perished on the guillotine. The dauphin, removed from his mother's care, could not endure the emotional and physical hardships of imprisonment, neglect, and loneliness. He was made to testify against his mother, detailing a disgusting series of supposed sexual abuses, and the pathetic little boy eventually died in prison. A few royalists clung tenaciously and irrationally to the legend that Louis XVII was alive, but the restored Bourbons accepted and commemorated his death. All were victims then of the king's trial. Madame Royale was the only member of the royal family to survive, being exchanged for some revolutionaries who had been languishing in an Austrian jail. She returned to France with the victorious allies who put the Bourbons back on the throne, married the Duke d'Angoulême, and lived till 1851. Energetic, haughty, and pious, she exercised considerable influence over her uncles, Louis XVIII and Charles X. And she wrote her memoirs, an exercise in hagiography with little historical value. Cléry too survived, spending some time in England, where he wrote his memoirs, the most detailed and circumstantial account we have of Louis's imprisonment.

Of Louis's three lawyers, Tronchet and DeSèze survived, the

latter covered with honors by the restored Bourbons and eulogized at his death by the great Chateaubriand. Malesherbes, who deserved better, was guillotined during the Terror. The Girondins were purged from the Convention in June 1793 by the Mountain and the Paris Commune. Some escaped into exile and lived out the Jacobin dictatorship, returning to France after Robespierre's fall. Most, like homing pigeons, sought out their native towns and departments or wandered north to raise a counterrevolution against the Mountain. All were caught and beheaded, or hounded to suicide. Those captured in Paris were brought to trial in the autumn of 1793 and condemned. The trial of the Girondins was far less fair than the trial of the king.

Jacques Roux was driven to suicide in prison by his Jacobin persecutors. Danton was guillotined, the victim of his own personality, his own refusal to cooperate with the Jacobin government. Hébert too was guillotined when his lust for personal power became a challenge to the Jacobins. Marat was murdered in his bath by Charlotte Corday, a fanatic who claimed to be obeying divine commands. The supple Barère survived, but Robespierre, Saint-Just, and Couthon were guillotined in July 1794 when the Jacobin dictatorship fell to a coup d'état. And many of those who engineered the coup now climbed to the power denied them by the Committee of Public Safety. They entered the Thermidorian governments and enjoyed new, less radical, and more lucrative careers. A few retired from politics, gratefully returning to the obscurity whence they had been called in 1792.

When Napoléon seized power in 1799 the living regicides had another choice to make. Some buried themselves in obscure and safe bureaucratic posts with the armies of occupation and took up the duties of policing Napoléon's conquests. Having thrown off the yoke of monarchical government these regicides now found themselves oppressing the victims of a new French tyrant. They had become policemen. Napoléon himself, who had adroitly disentangled himself before being caught in the collapse of the Mountain, had no objections to using regicides to run his empire. He certainly had no interest in hunting them down so long as they either cooperated or remained silent. A man's past was less interesting to the emperor than his desire to serve the state and share in its rewards. "Despite their corrupted spirit," wrote Talleyrand, another experienced survivor, "it is enough that they can be useful to the state for the Emperor to have given them the means of serving it. He has not feared to use them, he has covered them with honors and fortune." Indeed he had; Napoléon was a practical man. When he sought a suitable match for himself he picked a niece of Marie-Antoinette and Louis XVI, Marie-Louise. When the new empress sat down, in 1810, to her first game of whist in France, she played with two regicides, Cambacérès (the arch-chancellor of the Empire) and Fouché (the chief of police). In all, 136 former deputies of the Convention served Napoléon; 129 were regicides.

The return of the Bourbons changed all this. When it became clear that Napoléon would be defeated by the allies the regicides tried to negotiate an amnesty with the returning dynasty. Article XI of the Charter under which France was to be governed was an act of oblivion for all those who had participated in the Revolution. But once Louis XVIII was on the throne he ignored the amnesty. The Restoration was determined to hunt down all the remaining regicides and drive them out of France. A king was not obliged to keep his word to revolutionaries. All the regicides were declared outlaws, and that indispensable regicide, Fouché, who remained in charge of the police during the Restoration, was charged with sending his former colleagues into exile. He showed some humanity in the task, personally sending many regicides passports and now and then some money, to those who were destitute. There is a story of an exchange of letters between Carnot and Fouché. "Where do you want me to go, traitor?" wrote Carnot to the regicide policeman. "Wherever you wish, imbecile."

Twenty-three years after their famous vote the regicides were forced into exile. Even the mighty who had served Napoléon, derisively called "magnates" by the remaining *conventionnels*, were forced to flee. Many ended up in Brussels, one of the few places in reactionary Europe that would take them in. It was a painful and sad end for an extraordinary generation of men, men who had seen France through her greatest crisis. Many declined quickly into senility, a few went mad, still others tried to maintain their dignity and their ideals. But in the pathetic little community of regicide exiles in Brussels it was difficult to live a normal life. Here and there, among individual Montagnards, a flicker of the heroic vitality of their youth and the days of the Convention could be seen. Some managed to keep the faith. These old men of the Mountain had consistently refused service with any government after the fall of Robespierre. They employed the forced idleness of exile to write their memoirs and recall, with fierce pride, the great days of 1792–1794.

Louis-Benôit Genevois, who sat for Isère, has left a fitting epitaph for the regicides, a declaration of faith in the rightness of the king's trial. As he lay dying in Geneva, in 1824, Genevois told his servant: "When I am dead and the Bourbons will have been dethroned, you will come to my grave and tap twice with your cane, and you will say: 'Monsieur, we have driven them out.'"

There is no record that Genevois's servant returned six years later to tap with his cane on his master's grave and announce that Charles X had been driven off the throne by another revolution. But perhaps he did.

The Third
Appel Nominal

The figures given in the text are those announced to the Convention on January 17, 1793, at the conclusion of the voting, by the president, Vergniaud. They are published in the *Archives parlementaires*, LVII, 99; *Le Moniteur*, XV, 228; and the *Procès-verbal* of the Convention, V, 288. These figures have a certain historical interest for they are the ones heard by the deputies and accepted by Louis and his lawyers, who maintained in their appeal that the king ought not to go to the guillotine by a majority of only five votes. Nevertheless these figures are inaccurate, and on January 18 Vergniaud, after consultation with the secretaries, declared the corrected vote, which the Convention ordered published as a separate pamphlet over the signatures of Vergniaud and the six secretaries (Salle, Valazé, Manuel, Le Sage, Bancal, and Gorsas): *Appel nominal: Extrait du procès-verbal de la séance permanente de la Convention nationale, des 16 et 17 janvier 1793, l'an deuxième de la République, sur cette question: Quelle peine sera infligée à Louis?* (Paris, Imprimerie nationale, 1793). Here are the uncorrected figures from the *Archives parlementaires* and *Le Moniteur*, followed by the corrected figures published by the Convention:

Uncorrected:

745	members of the Convention
1	dead
6	ill
2	absent without cause
11	absent on Convention business
4	not voting
721	voting members

319 voted some penalty other than death
366 voted for death
13 voted for unique conditional punishments
———
698 total votes

Clearly these figures do not add up. There were 749 eligible deputies rather than 745, and even with this error the totals do not add
up to 721 votes cast.

Corrected:

749 members of the Convention
  7 ill
  1 absent without cause
 15 absent on Convention business
  5 not voting
———
721 voting members

  2 for imprisonment in irons
286 for detention and banishment when peace is established,
    or for immediate banishment, or for solitary confinement,
    or for some combination of these punishments including
    death under certain specific conditions
361 for death without conditions
 26 for the Mailhe amendment
 46 for death with conditions attached (only after the expul-
    sion of all the Bourbons; only when peace was established;
    only when the constitution had been approved; and other
    variations)
———
721 total votes

This corrected tally was declared official by the Convention. These
figures are accepted by the nineteenth-century editors of the *Archives parlementaires*, LVII, 411, and *Le Moniteur*, XV, 235. Under the
rules of voting in the Convention a simple majority was needed:
361 was the simple majority and hence, however one analyzed the
rest of the votes, Louis was condemned to death. The Convention,
however, decided to count as regicide votes all those conditional
votes which were thought to imply death, that is, all conditional
votes in which the conditions could be detached from the vote for
death. Thus the 26 members who voted the Mailhe amendment
were counted with the regicides, whereas the 46 members who

voted for death with other conditions were counted with the non-regicide votes. There is a certain logic here, for the Mailhe amendment only called for a later consideration of whether there should be a reprieve for the king, whereas the other conditional votes demanded that certain things be done before Louis could be executed, and some of these conditions were impossible to fulfill (the expulsion of the Bourbons, for example, demanded the expulsion of the Duke d'Orléans from the Convention, a motion that had already been rejected by the deputies). Thus the totals become:

749 members of the Convention
721 voting members
387 for death
334 for some penalty other than death

In the last decade of the nineteenth century E. Belhomme set out to establish a reliable reconstruction of the voting in *Les Régicides* (Paris, 1893). Here are his figures (p. 7):

Belhomme:

749 members of the Convention
  7 ill
  1 absent without cause
 15 absent on Convention business
  5 not voting
___
721 voting members

  2 for imprisonment in irons
286 for imprisonment, detention, banishment
 46 for death with intrinsic conditions attached
361 for death without conditions
 26 for the Mailhe amendment
___
721 votes cast

Thus:

387 for death (including the Mailhe amendment votes)
334 for some penalty other than death
 28 not voting

Belhomme's totals agree with the Convention's corrected vote, although he corrects some errors in individual votes and supports the Mountain's contention that there had been some tampering with the votes. Belhomme singles out Gorsas, one of the secretaries and an intemperate Girondin journalist, as probably responsible—or at least under suspicion—for the tamperings. At any rate Belhomme's figures are accepted by an impressive collection of historians of the Revolution, including E. Seligman, whose *La justice en France pendant la Révolution, 1791–1794* 2 vols. (Paris, 1901, 1913) remains the best study of the subject (see II, 461); Georges Lefebvre, *La Révolution française*, 291; and Albert Soboul in *Le Procès de Louis XVI* (217–218)—as is his wont, Soboul cites the manuscript sources for the vote: the uncorrected figures are in the Archives nationales, C 245, dos. 332, p. 10 (copie); the corrected figures are in the Archives nationales, C 243, dos. 314, p. 53 (minute).

With such an impressive consensus there would seem to be no question that Belhomme's reconstruction is correct. Yet when one looks at the actual record of the session of January 16–17, 1793, and the various lists of analysis that were drawn up at the time, confusion again reigns. There is not a consistent listing of the deputies and their votes, and to compare the several lists with no principle of reconciling discrepancies other than personal preference or logical consistency does not get us very far. There are obvious mistakes—whether deliberate or accidental, Belhomme notwithstanding, is impossible to say—in the sources, and Belhomme himself forgets to include Antoine-Sauveur Boucher, who sat for Paris and voted for death, in his list of 361 regicides. There are also some problems with his list of the 26 deputies who voted the Mailhe amendment.

The only agreement to emerge from a comparison of the Convention's figures and lists with those later accepted or compiled by historians is on the 361 votes for death without conditions. And even here, in the most recent and scrupulous work on the Convention, Alison Patrick's *The Men of the First French Republic* (Baltimore, 1972), the author counts only 359 regicide votes (a problem that will be discussed in a moment). The central problem is one of judgment: in what category are various ambiguous votes to be counted? The Restoration, anxious to punish the Convention, included among the regicides all those deputies who had not definitively voted for some punishment other than death:

Restoration figures:

749 members of the Convention
721 voting members
361 for death without conditions
 26 for the Mailhe amendment
 46 for death with conditions
 22 who are in none of these categories but who voted against
    reprieve on the fourth *appel nominal*
___
455 regicides

The Restoration, paradoxically, made the king's condemnation the work of the overwhelming majority of the deputies rather than a few radicals. Royalist historians, or those hostile to the Revolution for one reason or another, have preferred to count the votes in such a way that the king appears to have gone to the guillotine by the smallest possible majority. Arthur Conte is one of these. His *Sire, ils ont voté la mort* (Paris, 1966), is hopelessly partisan, and he is anxious to excoriate the regicides and at the same time give the impression that the king died because of one vote:

Conte's figures:

749 members of the Convention
 28 not voting
721 voting members

361 for death without conditions
290 for some punishment other than death
 70 for death with conditions
___
361 regicides

Conte does not count the Mailhe amendment votes as regicide votes, and he is the only one I know of to do so. There is no source or authority for this analysis. These two examples represent the extremes possible, from 361 regicides (the simple majority) to 455 regicides (reached by dubious criteria).

Leaving aside these extreme interpretations, perhaps the best we can hope for is a consensus. It would be tedious and perhaps not very instructive to present a list of the 749 deputies with their votes as recorded at the time and later corrected. But a survey of the figures accepted by historians of the Revolution may be useful. In the nineteenth century Michelet accepted the figures given by the Convention in its corrected tally: 387 votes for death; 334 votes for some penalty other than death. Michelet counts the 26 Mailhe amendment votes as regicide and he makes no attempt to distinguish between the various nonregicide votes (see *Histoire de la Révolution française*, II, 175). Jean Jaurès, despite several inexplicable errors in simple addition and subtraction, also accepts these figures: 361 votes for death without conditions; 286 votes for imprisonment, banishment, and so on; 46 votes for death with conditions; 26 Mailhe amendment votes. Unfortunately this only adds up to 719 votes; but Jaurès then goes on to give his final totals: 334 votes for some penalty other than death, and 387 votes for death (including the Mailhe amendment votes), for a total of 721 votes (see *Histoire socialiste*, V, 155). Belhomme, Seligman, Lefebvre, and Soboul have already been mentioned, and there is no need to belabor the point by providing a monster list of all the historians of the Revolution.

I have compared the lists in the *Archives parlementaires*, *Le Moniteur*, the *Procès-verbal* of the Convention, the pamphlet published by the Convention, Belhomme, Seligman, Conte, and Patrick and have checked these figures against Kuscinski's *Dictionnaire des conventionnels*. My interest is only in the regicide votes, a purely arbitrary decision on my part. I accept as accurate the figures given by Belhomme: 387 regicides; 334 nonregicides. In the figures prepared by Patrick I find three discrepancies which I can only attribute to an oversight or a typographical error of that otherwise scrupulous and reliable historian:

> *Patrick's figures:*
>
> 749 members of the Convention
> 28 not voting
> 721 voting members
>
> 359 for death without conditions
> 289 for some penalty other than death
> 29 Mailhe amendment votes
> 44 for death with conditions

Patrick lists René-Jean Champigny-Clément (Indre-et-Loire) as voting the Mailhe amendment; Kuscinski lists him as voting for detention followed by banishment; all the other sources and authorities list him as voting for death without conditions. Patrick lists Jean-Baptiste Le Clerc (Maine-et-Loire) as voting for imprisonment; all the other sources and authorities list him as voting for death without conditions. If these two *conventionnels* are put with the regicides, as I think they should be, we have 361 votes for death without conditions. Patrick also has 29 Mailhe amendment votes, three more than anyone else: Champigny-Clément (already mentioned); Augustin-François Bouchereau (Aisne); and Augustin-Roland-Jean-André-Faustin Chédaneau (Charente). I can find no support in the sources or authorities for these votes. But if Bouchereau and Chédaneau, following the sources, are moved to the list of those who voted for death with conditions, we have 26 Mailhe amendment votes and 46 votes for death with conditions (instead of her original 44), and Patrick's figures agree with Belhomme's.

But consensus is not the best criterion for historical truth, although for the king's trial it is the best we have and are likely to have. What is more interesting is to see what these figures can tell us about Louis's trial and the men who condemned him.

Nearly 54 percent of the deputies cast regicide votes, and the figure of 387 votes for death explodes the royalist myth that the king went to the scaffold by only one vote. And the voting itself was free, even anarchic. Only three of the 83 departments were unanimously regicide: Haute-Loire, with seven votes; Ariège, with six votes; and Corrèze, with seven votes (six for death, one for the Mailhe amendment). There were three nonregicide departments: Basses-Pyrénées, with six votes; Hautes-Alpes, with five votes; Ardèche, with seven votes (four for imprisonment or banishment, three for death with conditions). Paris, the radical department par excellence, cast 21 regicide votes, three nonregicide votes.

There seems no useful geographical analysis that can be made, for regicides and nonregicides alike came from all corners of the nation. Similarly there is no evidence that any individuals were able to dominate their departments. It is not unusual to find the best-known members of a delegation voting one way and the rest another. No analysis by age or occupation or income gets us very far either. The voting was individualistic and often unpredictable. Perhaps the only interesting conclusion is Seligman's (II, 480) that "the entire Mountain, without a single dissident, voted for death." This may explain why the Girondins had so many difficulties as a faction in the Convention. Not only could they not vote consistently, but individual Girondins often voted erratically on the four *appels nominaux*—which raises the question of consistency.

Of the 361 deputies who voted unconditionally for death, 34 had voted for the appeal to the people on the second *appel nominal*. Some said that when the appeal failed to carry they were obliged to vote for death since Louis was guilty. Some may have sincerely intended to vote for death whatever the outcome on the appeal to the people. Some may merely have been expressing their trepidation about sending Louis to the scaffold on their own responsibility. Probably we shall never know. Anyhow, a very small percentage of the regicides (9 percent) had supported the appeal to the people.

Of the 46 who voted for death with intrinsic conditions attached, 27 had voted the appeal to the people (58 percent). This is easier to understand. These deputies were sincerely trying to save the king and doubtless saw the appeal to the people as a way of sparing him. It is difficult to make any very convincing suggestion about the remaining 19 deputies, who opposed the appeal and then voted death with conditions, that is, voted to spare the king.

Of the 26 deputies who voted the Mailhe amendment, 12 then voted for reprieve on the fourth *appel nominal*. This was a consistent vote since these deputies assumed that the Mailhe amendment meant that they could vote for death and then spare the king. Still, when their votes were counted with the regicides they raised no complaint in the Convention, or none at least that got into the record.

There remain some miscellaneous categories. The 22 deputies who had voted some punishment other than death later voted against reprieve. Again this makes little sense. If they had no desire to send Louis to the scaffold why then did they not vote reprieve when given the chance to do so? The Restoration, with some justification, grouped these deputies with the regicides, since a vote against reprieve meant approval of the verdict rendered on January 16–17; the king would be allowed to die. Only 11 of the 361 regicides voted for reprieve, another group of curious and inconsistent voters.

The most ambiguous group of voters, however, was the 46 deputies who voted for death with implicit conditions. Belhomme (pp. 20–21) thus analyzes these votes. Ten deputies, including Brissot and Louvet, voted for a reprieve until the acceptance of the constitution; and two of these added until peace. This was but another statement of the appeal to the people, for the constitution would have to be ratified and accepted by the people. These deputies were at least consistent in their refusal to accept the majority will and bring back the appeal to the people in a new form. Three other deputies voted for reprieve until peace, or until the end of the war. They apparently thought that once hostilities were over clemency would be possible and the death sentence could be reconsidered, although they did not say so.

Twelve deputies voted for reprieve until the Bourbons had been expelled, and the implications of this vote are discussed above. Seventeen voted for reprieve until such time as France was invaded; then the death sentence was to be carried out. This would make Louis a hostage, and it is precisely this macabre solution that Barère attacked when he argued against the appeal to the people, on January 4. Three deputies voted ambiguously for reprieve until such time as the Convention thought fit to execute the king. And, finally, Treilhard (Seine-et-Oise), a former president of the Convention, voted simply for reprieve "for the best interests of the Republic."

All of these votes express either a suspicious hypocrisy or else confusion, and as with so many such compromises these deputies earned the scorn of almost all shades of opinion: they had voted death without voting death; they had voted clemency without voting clemency. The Convention, I think, had no choice but to count these votes with the nonregicide votes, and none of the 46 protested this decision.

Beyond these simple observations we cannot go with any security. It is clear that regicide feeling was widespread in the Convention, certainly more widespread than the Girondins realized or were willing to admit. Regicide votes came from every part of

France, from every delegation save three, from every age group, every occupational group, every political persuasion. And this fact alone justifies the Jacobin insistence that Louis must die for the Revolution to live. This fact not only proves the Jacobins to have been the superior political tacticians of the Convention, it also proves that, although they were a numerical minority, they were able to express the will of the majority. Seligman perhaps puts the issue too dramatically when he insists that on January 17, 1793, the Mountain, almost in an instant, passed from the minority to the majority. Still, there is some truth in this view. Jacobin ascendancy in the Convention was still incomplete in January, but the king's death marked a major turning point in the Revolution.

A General
Note on Sources and
Authorities

Historians of the French Revolution habitually introduce their bibliographies with a warning that a comprehensive list of books, articles, and documents would require a considerably larger book than the one in hand. I see no reason to break the habit or belabor the truism. What follows is only a record of the sources I have used to tell the story of Louis's trial and death. References to secondary authorities have been kept to a minimum, mentioned only if they contain some useful documents, support a view of things I agree with, or present a contrary view. Sometimes I have given references to more than one edition of a work: a later edition might have good notes or a variant reading, or be more accurate, or have the virtue of being readily available. In general, however, let the reader beware, this is not an exhaustive list of sources, let alone of secondary authorities; rather it is the author's attempt to certify the reliability of his information while providing the reader with an aerial map of the territory.

Most of the materials for Louis's trial have been published, either by the Convention or by nineteenth-century compilers and editors. An indispensable guide to published sources is M. Tourneaux, *Bibliographie de l'histoire de Paris pendant la Révolution française*, I (Paris, 1890), chap. 6, "Procès et exécution de Louis XVI," 308–342. For additional published materials see the *Catalogue de l'histoire de France*, begun in 1855 by the Département des imprimés of the Bibliothèque nationale, in 14 vols., with supplements. Materials relevant to the trial are in series Lb[39], Lb[40], Lb[41], and Le[38] in the holdings of the Bibliothèque nationale. For Louis himself see G. Walter, *Répertoire de l'histoire de la Révolution française. Travaux publiés de 1800 à 1940. Personnes* (Paris, 1941), pp. 333–335.

Cartons 103–106 in the Archives nationales, the Rondonneau Collection (ser. AD I), contain numerous documents on the trial, but most of these have been published in the *Archives parlementaires* and I have used them in published form. For a guide to the manuscript sources see A. Tuetey, *Répertoire général des sources manuscrites de l'histoire de Paris pendant la Révolution française*, VIII (Paris, 1908), "Procès et exécution de Louis XVI," 103–167.

More than 400 pamphlets or opinions were published by deputies to the Convention in the course of the trial. Most of these were speeches either delivered to the Convention or written and not delivered but subsequently published at the expense of the government printing office. There is an excellent comprehensive list in Alison Patrick, *The Men of the First French Republic: Political Alignments in the National Convention of 1792* (Baltimore, 1972), pp. 382–392. The most convenient, and in many ways the most satisfactory way to follow the debates in the trial is in the *Réimpression de l'ancien moniteur*, 31 vols. (Paris, 1854). The relevant volumes are XIII, XIV, and XV. With a few exceptions, listed below, I have quoted the debates and the speeches from the *Moniteur*, and the interested reader can easily find the evidence in question in the issue of the *Moniteur* published the day *after* the debates in the Assembly. As a supplement to and control on the *Moniteur* (also organized by date), there is the *Archives parlementaires* . . . *Recueil complet des débats législatifs et politiques des chambres françaises* . . . *Première Série (1787 à 1799)*, 82 vols. (1867–1914; continued in 1961). The collection must be used with caution, especially the volumes published before 1907, since the first editors of the *Archives parlementaires* threw together all manner of contemporary materials that were not part of the debates. One may also consult the contemporary publication of this same material (the debates only) in *Procès-verbal de la Convention nationale: Imprimé par son ordre*, 72 vols. (Paris, 1792-an IV). For the debates at the Jacobin Society there is F.-A. Aulard's *La Société des Jacobins: Recueil des documents*, 6 vols. (Paris, 1889–1897). And there is a rich potpourri of documents of every kind, although the methods of organization or selection are elusive, put together by J.-B. Buchez and P.-C. Roux, *Histoire parlementaire de la Révolution française* . . . 40 vols. (Paris, 1834–1838). The relevant volumes for the trial are XIX–XXIV.

The contemporary newspapers are numerous and make fascinating reading. There is a good short account of the revolutionary press in Claude Bellanger, Jacques Godechot, Pierre Guiral, and Fernand Terrou, *Histoire générale de la presse française*, I, *Des Origines à 1814* (1969). The newspapers I have used follow (here again, I have not indicated issues or pages in the notes since it is easy to locate these sources by date; as with the *Moniteur*, the newspaper published the following day contained reports on the session in question). *Le Moniteur*, as already mentioned, is fundamental; in addition there are the newspapers of the political leaders of the Convention: J. P. Brissot's *Le Patriote français, journal libre*; M. J. Condorcet, et al., *Chronique de Paris*; Camille Desmoulins's *Les Révolutions de France et de Brabant*; A. J. Gorsas's *Le Courrier des départements*; J.-P.

Marat's *L'Ami du peuple* and *Le Journal de la République française*; René Hébert's *Le Père Duchesne*; J.-L. Carra's *Les Annales patriotiques et littéraires*; Maximilien Robespierre's *Le Défenseur de la constitution* and *Lettres à ses commettans*, in, respectively, his *Oeuvres complètes*, IV, ed. G. Laurent (1939), and V, ed. G. Laurent (1951); Louis-Marie Prudhomme, *Les Révolutions de Paris*; and J. A. Dulaure, *Le Thermomètre du jour*.

The memoirs of the revolutionaries are a particularly rich source. Whenever possible I have used the best scholarly editions, but all too often the student is thrown back on two massive nineteenth-century collections which must be used with caution. They were not carefully edited and apparently no attempt was made to compare variant readings or authenticate the manuscripts. One of these questions of authenticity is discussed by Elisabeth L. Eisenstein in her *The First Professional Revolutionist: Filippe Michele Buonarroti, 1761–1837* (Cambridge, Mass., 1959), pp. 64 and 181–197. The two collections are: Berville and Barrière, *Collections des mémoires relatifs à la Révolution française*, 60 vols. (1820–1828), and *Nouvelle Série: Avec Introductions, notices et notes par M. de Lescure*, 9 vols. (1875–1880).

There are several contemporary and near-contemporary collections of documents pertaining to the trial. A. J. du Gour, *Collection des meilleurs ouvrages qui ont été publiés pour la défense de Louis XVI, roi des Français*, 2 vols. (1793), contains 18 hard-to-locate pamphlets. Porcelin de Roche-Tilhac, *Le Procès de Louis XVI*, 7 vols. (1795), contains a number of speeches, but is not at all complete. *Le Pour et le contre: Recueil complet des opinions prononcées à l'Assemblée nationale dans le procès de Louis XVI* (1792), contains, as the title indicates, only those speeches delivered before the Convention, which are easily accessible in the *Moniteur*.

Where there exists a good scholarly edition for the speeches and works of a deputy, I have used it in preference to the versions in the *Moniteur*. Alas, there are all too few such editions. For Robespierre's speeches I have consulted, with pleasure, the splendid edition of Marc Bouloiseau, Georges Lefebvre, Jean Dautry, and Albert Soboul, *Oeuvres de Maximilien Robespierre*, IX: "Discours" (pt. 4), September 1792–July 27, 1793 (1958); for Danton, who normally spoke without notes, there are the ingenious reconstructions of André Fribourg, *Discours de Danton* (1910); and for Saint-Just there is the volume in the series "Idées" of his *Oeuvres choisies* (1968).

I have not included even a list of the numerous histories of the Revolution, whether in French or English; any interested student is doubtless familiar with the texts of Lefebvre, Aulard, Mathiez, Soboul, Furet and Richet and, in English, Thompson, Hampson, Sydenham, Palmer, and Cobban, to name but a few. There are, however, several general histories that I think stand apart from the numerous competent and scholarly treatments of the period. I want to pay brief homage to these men, who have influenced my thinking about the subject. Jules Michelet, *Histoire de la Révolution française* (1847–1853)—especially in the excellent critical edition prepared by Gérard Walter, 2 vols. (1939)—is perhaps the

most famous, and deservedly so, history of the Revolution. Michelet's inimitable style—some find it excessive and contrived—coupled with his exceptional intelligence and passion makes his work unique, a true classic. When Michelet began his great history there were still men alive who had lived through the Revolution, hence some of his information has the weight of source material.

M. Mortimer-Ternaux, *Histoire de la terreur, 1792–1794*, 8 vols. (1862–1869) is important for totally different reasons. The *Histoire de la terreur* is informed by a bilious and embittered spirit that despised radicalism and the Jacobins. Yet Mortimer-Ternaux's passion to excoriate his enemies out of their own mouths sent him in pursuit of all the documents he could find, and he was an indefatigable searcher. As a result his *Histoire* is a veritable mine of information, sometimes of documents that were subsequently destroyed by the *communards* in 1871.

Jean Jaurès, *Histoire socialiste de la Révolution française*, V: *La Mort du roi et la chute de la Gironde*, in the remarkable and handsome edition of Albert Soboul (1972), is another classic of revolutionary historiography. Jaurès was France's most extraordinary socialist leader and an intellectual of powerful capacity. His outstanding abilities and his intimate experience of French political life render his judgments compelling and stimulating. It is only with a good deal of trepidation that I have rejected the views offered by either Michelet or Jaurès, despite the exceptional advances in historical science since their day and our more scholarly view of the Revolution. Both works not only remain monuments to their authors' genius and to the ages in which they wrote, but they are, unlike so many antiques, useful to the modern historian who must wrestle with more information and ways of handling it than Michelet or Jaurès probably dreamed possible; and, more important, these are outstanding works of literature whose value is not to be measured in mere positivist terms.

For Paris during the Revolution there is an old but still excellent book, F. Braesch, *La Commune du dix août: étude sur l'histoire de Paris du 20 juin au 2 décembre 1792* (1911). Braesch wrote at a time when historians believed it their duty to load their texts with documents. Consequently Braesch has transcribed a number of manuscript sources that are not readily available, certainly not outside Paris. There is also a recent and beautifully illustrated book by Marcel Reinhard, *Nouvelle Histoire de Paris: La Révolution, 1789–1799* (1971). Reinhard, in addition to the standard biography of Carnot, *Le Grand Carnot*, has also written the most recent and the best book on August 10, 1792, *La Chute de la royauté* (1969), which contains a useful appendix of documents, some not otherwise available in book form.

There have not been many books on the king's trial. The standard work remains E. Seligman, *La Justice en France pendant la Révolution: 1791–1793*, 2 vols. (1901 and 1913). Alison Patrick's *The Men of the First French Republic*, mentioned above, is an excellent modern study of scrupulous scholarship that contains a series of tables and charts on the *conventionnels* and their

background, on voting patterns, on political alignments, that I have exploited and for which I am grateful. Arthur Conte, *Sire, ils ont voté la mort* (1966), is only about the voting on January 16–17, 1793, is absurdly partial, and is uncritical in its acceptance of questionable anecdotal evidence. Michael Walzer, ed., *Regicide and Revolution: Speeches at the Trial of Louis XVI* (Cambridge, Eng., 1974) is a collection (in translation) of a dozen speeches from the trial with a scintillating introduction which, however, I think is misleading. Finally, there is a dissertation by Ronald Lee Hayworth, submitted to Emory University in 1968: "The Trial of Louis XVI." Hayworth concentrates almost exclusively on politics, and although the dissertation is a bit wooden, he has some interesting things to say about the controversy over the king's inviolability during the trial and the responses of foreign governments to the trial.

For Louis himself and his imprisonment, the Marquis de Beaucourt has done all the students of the trial a service by collecting most of the relevant documents and memoirs in his *Captivité et derniers moments de Louis XVI: Récits originaux et documents officiels*, 2 vols. (1892). Baron de Vinck d'Orp, the greatest collector of prints from the revolutionary period—his magnificent collection was willed to the Bibliothèque nationale—has written a fascinating book, *La Meurtre du 21 janvier 1793* (1877). Although marred by the author's royalism, the book is completely reliable about the depictions of the execution, both contemporary and later copies and embellishments.

On the whole subject of political trials, especially in France, Jean Imbert has edited a useful collection of essays, *Quelques Procès criminels des XVIIe et XVIIIe siècles: présentés par un groupe d'étudiants* (1964); in addition see Paul Bastid, *Les Grands Procès politiques de l'histoire* (1962) and, for a more theoretical approach, Otto Kirchheimer, *Political Justice: The Use of Legal Procedure for Political Ends* (Princeton, 1961). Albert Camus has also written on the trial, with his customary elegance and intelligence, *L'Homme révolté*, translated into English as *The Rebel: An Essay on Man in Revolt*, trans. Anthony Bower (New York, 1956). There are two general books on kingship which I found stimulating: Marc Bloch, *Les Rois thaumaturges: Etude sur le caractère surnaturel attribué à la puissance royale particulièrement en France et en Angleterre* (1961), and Ernst Kantorowicz, *The King's Two Bodies: A Study in Medieval Political Theology* (Princeton, 1957). Both are brilliant, though in different ways.

The only readily available collection of documents on the trial is Albert Soboul's *Le Procès de Louis XVI* (1966). The collection contains most of the things one would expect—parts of famous speeches, excerpts from newspapers and other contemporary writings, and so forth—and also, since it was prepared by one of the outstanding social historians of the Revolution, some little-known documents on the food problem, on social questions, on the sections of Paris.

I have saved for the last not necessarily the best, but rather the most recent book, still in the process of being completed in a contemplated 8

volumes (3 have already been published). Claude Manceron's prodigious *Les hommes de la liberté*, a massive tableau of the generation of the French Revolution, when completed, promises to be a major, if anecdotal, history of the men who made the Revolution. It contains a wealth, literally a wealth, of information, all presented in an attractive style.

References

CUE TITLES

The place of publication, unless otherwise indicated, is Paris. The following cue titles have been used in the notes:

Beaucourt · *Captivité et derniers moments de Louis XVI, récits originaux et documents officiels, recueillis et publiés* by le marquis de Beaucourt, 2 vols. (1892)

Braesch · F. Braesch, *La Commune du dix août, étude sur l'histoire de Paris du 20 juin au 2 décembre 1792* (1911)

Buchez and Roux · J.-B. Buchez and P.-C. Roux, *Histoire parlementaire de la Révolution française, ou Journal des Assemblées nationales, depuis 1789 jusqu'en 1815. . . .* 40 vols. (1834–1838)

Jaurès · Jean Jaurès, *Histoire Socialiste de la Révolution française*: vol. 5, *La Mort du roi et la chute de la Gironde*, ed., Albert Soboul, 6 vols. (1972)

Michelet · Jules Michelet, *Histoire de la Révolution française*, ed. Gérard Walter, 2 vols. (1939)

Mortimer-Ternaux · M. Mortimer-Ternaux, *Histoire de la terreur, 1792–1794*, 8 vols. (1862–1869)

Patrick · Alison Patrick, *The Men of the First French Republic, Political Alignments in the National Convention of 1792* (Baltimore, 1972)

Seligman · Edmond Seligman, *La justice en France pendant la Révolution, 1791–1793*, 2 vols. (1901 and 1913)

Soboul · Albert Soboul, ed., *Le procès de Louis XVI* (1966)

PROLOGUE

I have taken details from several contemporary accounts to make a consistent whole. P.-L. Rœderer's *Chronique de cinquante jours: Du 20 juin au 10 août 1792* (1832) is the most detailed witness of events. Written forty years or so after the events, and after Rœderer had enjoyed a brilliant career under Napoléon, the *Chronique* views August 10 through the gilded mirror of autobiography and Rœderer appears the hero of the day in his own pages. Nevertheless, he was a reliable witness and most of the conversations come from his pages. I have supplemented Rœderer with the recollections of Etienne-Louis-Hector DeJoly, "Des Faits qui se sont passés au château des Tuileries dans la nuit du 9 au 10 août 1792, et dans la matinée du 10," first published by M. Montjoye, *Histoire de Marie-Antoinette-Josephe-Jeanne de Lorraine, archiduchesse d'Autriche, reine de France*, 3rd ed., 2 vols. (1816), and later, in a critical edition, as DeJoly's *Mémoires*, by Jacques Godechot, *Annales historiques de la Révolution française*, XVIII (1946), 289–382; also, G. Peltier, *Dernier Tableau de Paris: Ou Récit historique de la Révolution du 10 août, des causes qui l'ont produite, des èvenemens qui l'ont précédée, et des crimes qui l'ont suivie*, 3rd ed., 2 vols. (London, 1794), the earliest history of August 10; the letters of Domingo de Yriarte, the Spanish *chargé d'affaires* in Paris at the time, published by J. Chaumié, *Annuaire-bulletin de la Société de l'histoire de France* (1944), 129–258; *Procès-verbal de l'Assemblée nationale: Séance permanente du vendredi 10 août 1792* (1792); *Le Moniteur*, XIII; Mortimer-Ternaux, II. Modern accounts, with documents, are: Marcel Reinhard, *La Chute de la royauté* (1969), which I follow most closely in interpretation; A. Mathiez, *Le Dix août* (1931), informed by the author's usual vigor and aggressiveness; Philippe Sagnac, *La Chute de la royauté* (1909), balanced and still useful; and Braesch, painstakingly detailed. In my account I have deliberately suppressed some details—Louis reviewing the troops and Pétion's visit to the Tuileries, to name only two—to avoid cluttering the narrative flow, and have emphasized some concrete details of dress and speech drawn from the sources. The clearness of the night, the time and nature of the sunrise, are drawn from Rœderer, whose memory of these details is not contradicted by the other sources.

CHAPTER I

This account of the king's role in the Revolution is meant to be simply that, not a history of the Revolution. I have followed the standard modern accounts listed in my General Note. The text of the *séance royale* is in *Le Moniteur*, I, 92–96. For the opening of the Estates-General, Georges Lefebvre, ed., *Recueil de documents relatifs aux séances des Etats généraux, mai-juin 1789* (1953), I. For the *séance royale* see also Armand Brette, "La Séance royale du 23 juin 1789," *La Révolution française* (1891–1892), XXII, XXIII; and Pierre Caron, "La Tentative de contre-révolution, juin-juillet

1789," Revue d'histoire moderne et contemporaine (1904). In general I follow the views of Georges Lefebvre, *Quatre-vingt-neuf* (1939). There are two fairly recent biographies of Mirabeau, J.-J. Chevallier, *Mirabeau: Un Grand Destin manqué* (1947), and the Duc de Castries, *Mirabeau* (1960). The two quotations from Brissot on the necessity for war are from M. J. Sydenham, *The French Revolution* (New York, 1965), p. 91. Louis's "Déclaration du roi adressée à tous les français à sa sortie de Paris" is reprinted in Reinhard, *La Chute de la royauté*, pp. 437–452 and pp. 15–111 (along with the documents, pp. 453–470) on the flight to Varennes. Although modern historians discount the story of Drouet's recognition of the fugitive king from a coin, arguing that long before Drouet identified Louis his incognito had been exposed and the countryside roused by the presence of armed troops, I have included it as a charming piece of "revolutionary romanticism." The quotations from Chaumette come from *Mémoires de Chaumette sur la Révolution du 10 août 1792*, ed. F.-A. Aulard (1893). The quotations from Gouverneur Morris are taken from *The Diary and Letters of Gouverneur Morris*, ed. Anne Cary Morris, 2 vols. (New York, 1888). Vergniaud's growing radicalism is deduced from his *Opinion . . . sur la situation actuelle de la France: Prononcée le 3 juillet 1792* (1792). Madame Roland's letters are quoted from *Lettres de Mme. Roland*, ed. C. Perroud (1900–1902). Vergniaud is quoted from *Mss.: Lettres et papiers*, ed. C. Vatel, 2 vols. (1873). The call for Louis's dethronement is taken from *Arrêté de la section de Mauconseil pour la déchéance de Louis XVI* (July 31, 1792), reprinted in Soboul, pp. 34–36. For additional background: Braesch; Mortimer-Ternaux, I; and Buchez and Roux, XV, XVI, XVII. For Brissot his *Mémoires*, ed. C. Perroud, 2 vols. (1904); for Varennes, Mgs. Ch. Aimond, *L'Enigme de Varennes: Le Dernier Voyage de Louis XVI* (1936); for Marie-Antoinette's part in the flight to Varennes, Alma Soderhjelm, ed., *Marie-Antoinette et Barnave: Correspondance secrète, juillet 1791 –janvier 1792* (1934).

CHAPTER II

As above (Reinhard, Mortimer-Ternaux, Mathiez, Sagnac, Braesch, Mme. Roland, Brissot, Vergniaud). Also, for Alexandre's recollections, and quotation about "lions and tigers," "Fragments des mémoires de Charles-Alexis Alexandre: Sur Les Journées révolutionnaires de 1791 et 1792," ed. Jacques Godechot, *Annales historiques de la Révolution française* (April-June, 1952). For Santerre, "La Journée du 10 août par un révolutionnaire," *Revue de la Révolution*, VII, 1st semester (1866); for Barbaroux, his *Mémoires*, ed. A. Chabaud (1936), and his *Correspondance et mémoires de Barbaroux*, ed. C. Perroud and A. Chabaud (1923); for Chaumette, *Papiers de Chaumette*, ed. F. Braesch (1908); for Fournier, *Mémoires secrets de Fournier l'Americain*, ed. F.-A. Aulard (1890); also *Mémoires inédits de Pétion et mémoires de Buzot et de Barbaroux: Accompagnées de Notes inédits de Buzot et de nombreux documents inédits sur Barbaroux, Buzot, Brissot, etc.*, ed. C. A. Dauban (1866); Pétion, *Mémoires*, ed. C. A. Dauban (1866); Mme. Roland,

Mémoires, ed. C. Perroud, 2 vols. (1905). Danton's words come from the
Discours de Danton, ed. André Fribourg (1910); Robespierre's from *Lettres à
ses commettans: Oeuvres*, V. The pamphlet prepared by the Legislative is
*Exposition des motifs d'après lesquels l'Assemblée nationale a proclamé la convoca-
tion d'une Convention nationale* . . . (1792). For the fighting men involved,
J. Pollio and A. Marcel, *Le Bataillon du 10 août* (1881). Figures for casualties
are given in all the histories of the revolution of August 10. I have taken
mine from George Rudé, *The Crowd in the French Revolution* (London,
1958). For the petitions addressed to the Legislative on Louis XVI: Pétion,
"Pétition de la Commune de Paris à l'Assemblée nationale: Sur La Déchéance du roi"; "Adresse de la section de Henri IV à l'Assemblée nationale,
du 10 août, l'an 4ᵉ de la liberté"; "Adresse des canonniers du bataillon
de Saint-Mery à l'Assemblée nationale, du 10 août 1792." Also *Mémoires et
notes de Choudieu, réprésentant du peuple à l'assemblée législative: À La Convention et aux armées, 1761–1838*, ed. Victor Barrucand (1897). John Moore's
eyewitness account of the Tuileries on August 11 is from J. M. Thompson,
ed., *English Witnesses of the French Revolution* (London, 1938). For the work
of the Tribunal of August 17, E. Seligman, *La Justice pendant la Révolution*, I.
For the coup d'état at the Hôtel de Ville I have followed and blended
Sagnac, *La Chute de la royauté*, and Braesch. The figures on the September
Massacres come from Pierre Caron, *Les Massacres de septembre* (1935) and I
have followed his account. For the reorganization of government, P. Mautouchet, *Le Gouvernement révolutionnaire* (1912). For the various decrees,
Actes et décrets rendus par l'Assemblée nationale: Depuis le 10 août 1792. What
has survived of the debates in the Commune is preserved by M. Tourneaux, *Procès-verbal de la Commune de Paris* (1894). For information on the
election of deputies to the Convention: Dubois-Crancé, *Analyse de la Révolution française depuis l'ouverture des Etats-généraux jusqu'au 6 Brumaire an IV
de la République* . . . (1885) and his *Thermomètre du jour*; Buchez and Roux,
XX, XXI; Mortimer-Ternaux, IV; P. Mautouchet, "Le Mouvement élec-
toral à Paris en août-septembre 1792," *La Révolution française*, XLIV
(1903); Patrick, pp. 139–195, is a good survey of the elections; G. Dodu,
Le Parlementarisme et les parlementaires sous la Révolution (1911); and the newspapers, especially *Le Moniteur*, XIII. The statistics on the Convention are
from Patrick, pp. 247–294. The description of the Manège is from Dulaure,
Physionomie de la Convention nationale (1793). For the political differences of
the deputies, Patrick; Albert Mathiez, *Girondins et Montagnards* (1930) and
La Vie chère et le mouvement social sous la terreur (1927); M. J. Sydenham,
The Girondins (London, 1961) offers a view of the Girondins which Patrick
self-consciously set out to criticize; B. Melchoir-Bonnet, *Les Girondins*
(1969) is the most recent study in French. And finally, an indispensable
reference work, A. Kuscinski, *Dictionnaire des conventionnels*, 4 vols. (1916–
1919).

My treatment of the Jacobin-Girondin struggle in its origins is based on
the above, plus: R. M. Brace, *Bordeaux and the Gironde* (New York, 1947);

J. Guadet, *Les Girondins: Leur vie privée, leur vie publique*, 2 vols. (1861); C. Perroud, *Recherches sur la proscription des Girondins, 1793–1795* (1917), and his articles "Le Premier Ministère de Roland," *La Révolution française*, XLII (1903), and "Recherches sur le salon de Madame Roland en 1791," *La Révolution française*, XXXVI (1899); A. Aulard, "Evolution des idées politiques entre le 10 août et le 22 septembre 1792," *La Révolution française*, XXXVI (1899); A. Mathiez, "Les Girondins et la cour à la veille du 10 août," *Annales historiques de la Révolution française* (1931). For a useful survey of the treatment of the Jacobins and Girondins in the nineteenth century see G. P. Gooch, *History and Historians in the Nineteenth Century* (London, 1913).

In addition to Pierre Caron's standard study of the September Massacres, I have used: the newspapers; Buchez and Roux, XX; and J.-L. Tallien, *La Vérité sur les événemens du 2 septembre* (1792). The *Mémoires* of Barbaroux, Brissot, Buzot, Carnot, Choudieu, Pétion, and Mme. Roland are essential. In addition: P. C. F. Daunou, *Mémoires pour servir à l'histoire de la Convention nationale*, in A. H. Taillandier, *Documents biographiques sur P. C. F. Daunou* (1841); J. A. Dulaure, *Mémoires*, in L. Duchesne de la Sicotière, *Notice historique et littéraire sur Dulaure* (1862); Joseph Garat, *Mémoires de Garat*, ed. E. Maron (1862); Grégoire, *Mémoires*, ed. Hippolyte Carnot, 2 vols. (1837); J. D. Lanjuinais, *Fragment*, in J. F. Barrière, *Bibliothèque des mémoires*, XXX (1832); L. M. La Revellière-Lepaux, *Mémoires*, 3 vols. (1895); Louvet de Couvray, *Mémoires . . . sur la Révolution française*, ed. F.-A. Aulard, 2 vols. (1889); *Mémoires de S. A. S. Louis-Philippe-Joseph d'Orléans, duc de Montpensier, prince du sang* (1824); *Notes et souvenirs inédits de Prieur de la Marne*, ed. Gustave Laurent (1912); A.-C. Thibaudeau, *Mémoires sur la Convention et la Directoire*, 2 vols. (1824); Dumouriez, *Vie et mémoires*, ed. J. F. Barrière, 2 vols. (1848) (it is Dumouriez who characterized the Girondins as the Jesuits of the Revolution); Théodore de Lameth, *Mémoires*, ed. Eugène Welvert (1913); *Notes et souvenirs de Théodore de Lameth faisant suite à ses mémoires*, ed. Eugène Welvert (1914); Durand de Maillanne, *Mémoires sur la Convention nationale*, in *Mémoires sur les assemblées parlementaires de la Révolution*, ed. M. de Lescure, 2 vols. (1881). The quotation by Pétion is taken from his *Discours sur l'accusation intentée à Robespierre* (November 1792); the story of Danton's attempted *rapprochement* with Guadet comes from Michelet, who here follows Bertrand de Molleville, see Michelet, II, 160. There is a convenient list of the presidents of the Convention and previous assemblies in J. M. Thompson, *The French Revolution* (Oxford, 1966), pp. 527–530. For the Paris elections to the Convention see Patrick and a very good account in Norman Hampson, *The Life and Opinions of Maximilien Robespierre* (London, 1974), pp. 126–130. Louvet's *Robespierride* is in the *Moniteur* for October 30, 1792, and reprinted in pamphlet form: *Accusation intentée dans la Convention nationale contre Maximilien Robespierre* (1792). Robespierre's response is in his *Oeuvres*, IX, pt. 4.

CHAPTER III

There is a brilliant summary of the arguments on regicide in Michael Walzer, ed., *Regicide and Revolution*, pp. 1–46. For arguments concerning the inviolability question, Ronald Lee Hayworth, "The Inviolability Controversy in the Trial of Louis XVI," *Arkansas Academy of Science Proceedings*, XX (1966). The text of the constitution is in L. Duguit, H. Mounier, R. Bonnard, *Les Constitutions et les principales lois politiques de la France depuis 1789* . . . (1952), pp. 3–33. For the several reports delivered to the Convention on Louis's papers and procedures to be used against him: *Rapport de Louis-Jérôme Gohier . . . Sur Les Papiers inventoriés dans les bureaux de la liste civile . . . 16 septembre 1792* (1792); *Pièce trouvée dans une des secrétaires du cabinet du roi* (1792); *Rapport fait à la Convention nationale au nom de la Commission extraordinaire des ving-quatre, le 6 novembre 1792 . . . Sur Les Crimes du ci-devant roi, dont les preuves ont été trouvées dans les papiers recueillis par le comité de surveillance de la Commune de Paris, par Dufriche-Valazé* (1792); *Rapport et projet de décret présentés . . . Au Nom du comité de législation par Jean Mailhe, député du département de la Haute-Garonne* (1792). Gravelliers's petition is in the *Moniteur*, XIV, 147. John Moore's information is from Thompson, *English Witnesses of the French Revolution*. The story about Desmoulins's view of Saint-Just's *toilette* is taken from J. M. Thompson, *Leaders of the French Revolution* (London, 1929), 201; his speech is in *Oeuvres choisies*, 74–83. Also Marat, *Journal de la République française* and Brissot, *Le Patriote français*. On Paris in late 1792 Braesch and Mathiez, *Le dix août*, in particular, along with the general works mentioned above. The debates are in *Le Moniteur*, XIV, and some additional material in Buchez and Roux, XX, XXII. Chaumette's speech to the General Council is reprinted in Braesch, 840–842. The anecdote about how he came to change his name is taken from Buchez and Roux, XXII, 324. See also *Papiers de Chaumette*, ed. F. Braesch (1908). For Jacques Roux's speech, *Discours sur le jugement de Louis-le-dernier . . . par Jacques Roux* ("Extrait du registre des delibérations de l'assemblée générale de la section de l'Observatoire, du samedi, 1 décembre 1792"). Robespierre's December 3 speech is again from his *Oeuvres*. For the *armoire de fer* episode: the papers were printed in two publications of the Convention: *Troisième Recueil: Pièces imprimées d'après la décret de la Convention nationale le 5 décembre 1792, déposées à la commission extraordinaire des douze établie pour le dépouillement des papiers de l'armoire de fer*, 2 vols. (1792), and *Quatrième Recueil: Pièces imprimées d'après le décret de la Convention nationale du 5 décembre. Suite des pièces trouvées dans l'armoire de fer avec l'inventaire qui en a été fait à la commission chargée de l'examen desdites pièces* (1792). Roland himself explained to the Convention how he came to find the safe. Mme. Roland's justification for her husband is in her *Mémoires*. For the Jacobin reaction to the *armoire de fer* discoveries, Desmoulins, *Histoire des Brissotins: Ou Fragments de l'histoire secrète de la Révolution, et des six premiers mois de la République* (1793); René Levasseur, *Mémoires*, I, 80 (though not entirely his own work); Marat, *Journal de la*

République, and Aulard, *La Société des Jacobins*. Louis's letter to the Bishop of Clermont is document no. 69 in the *Troisième recueil*. Information on the pressure used by the Paris sections against Roland and the Convention is in Soboul, 87–88 (with references). I follow Jaurès' view of Buzot's motion to banish the Bourbons. See also Marat, *Journal de la République*, no. 80, "Les Renards rolandins et les dindons patriotes," and Robespierre, *Lettres à ses commettans*, in *Oeuvres*, V, 160–167. The story of Mirabeau's posthumous disgrace is in *Le Moniteur, XIV,* 660 (for the vandalism of his statue).

CHAPTER IV

For a physical description of the Temple and its tower, along with a floor plan of the destroyed tower, see A. de Beauchesne, *Louis XVII: His Life, His Suffering, His Death,* trans. W. Hazlitt, 2 vols. (London, 1853), I, 179–228; this work also contains an accurate account of the life of the royal prisoners in the Temple during their first month of imprisonment. Almost all the relevant documents and accounts concerning Louis's imprisonment have been collected and edited by Beaucourt. The recollections of Cléry, Verdier, and Mme. Royale, specifically referred to, come from Beaucourt, as does Mme. de Tourzel's anecdote about Louis being taken to prison. In describing Louis's day I have taken information from a variety of accounts, since no single source is complete, and put them together to form my composite picture. Cléry's recollections are the most complete and detailed and are published complete in a recent edition in the series *Le Temps retrouvé: Journal de ce qui s'est passé à la tour du Temple pendant la captivité de Louis XVI, roi de France, et autres mémoires sur le Temple* (1968). Cléry first published his *Journal* in London in 1798; an expanded edition appeared in Paris in 1814. In addition there is the *Récit des événements arrivés au Temple depuis le 13 août 1792 jusqu'à la mort du Dauphin Louis XVII* (1832), a collection of accounts that was eventually superseded by Beaucourt's two volumes. In 1892 appeared the first printing of the *Mémoire écrit par Marie-Thérèse-Charlotte de France: Sur La Captivité des princes et princesses ses parents depuis le 10 d'août jusqu'à la mort de son frère.* The following year an augmented and corrected edition, with notes by Louis XVIII, was published as the *Journal de Marie-Thérèse de France* (both are reprinted in *Le Temps retrouvé* volume). There are some additional details in Buchez and Roux, XXI, including discussions and decrees of the General Council, Manuel lecturing the prisoners, the king's illness, and the prayer Louis wrote for his son. Information on the lessons conducted in the Temple come from Cléry. The newspapers involved are *Révolutions de Paris, Annales patriotiques, Le Moniteur,* and *Le Courrier des départements.* On specific details of life in prison (all from Beaucourt, unless otherwise indicated): Verdier I, 239, gives the orders the guards received from the Commune; Cléry tells several anecdotes about the rudeness of the guards; Mme. Royale gives an account of the lessons; Lepitre, one of the guards, describes the workings of the Temple; Moëlle, another guard, adds some details; Hué describes his first view of Louis's apartment and also gives another version of the dauphin's nightly prayer. The decisions of the Commune regarding Louis's treatment are all in Beaucourt's second volume. Dorat-Cubières, one of the staff, made reports to the Commune which have survived and been published by Buchez and Roux, XXII. The conversation on hospitals in Paris is from the report of the *secrétaire-greffier* of the General Council of December 26, reprinted in Beaucourt, II, 233. The anecdotes about Louis's imprisonment that regularly appeared in the press are numerous; among others, *Le Moniteur* for October 10, November 10, and December 24, 1792, and Buchez and Roux, XXI, 302–307, 333–337. Hué, Cléry, and Malesherbes, all in Beaucourt, describe Louis's reading habits and taste. Lameth's anecdote is from his *Mémoires*, 211–212. Necker's evidence is from his *Réflexions présentées à la nation française: Sur Le Procès intenté à Louis XVI* (1792); Barbaroux's remarks are from his *Mémoires*, Carnot's from *Mémoires sur Carnot par son fils*, new ed., 2 vols. (1893); Sainte-Beuve's appraisal is from *Causeries du lundi* (1862), in his *Oeuvres*, XV, 343. G. Bapst, "L'Inventaire des livres de Louis XVI," *Revue française*, XXI, 532–533, supports the testimony of contemporaries on Louis's reading. The list of books requested from the Commune by Louis is in Beaucourt, II, 137–138, as is the session of the General Council for November 23, which discussed the request. Louis's ideas on tyranny are reported by Malesherbes, in Beaucourt, I, 320. The king's last will and testament is published, among other places, in Soboul, 236–240. There is a shrewd, if hostile, analysis of the king's character in Mme. Roland's *Mémoires*, 150.

CHAPTER V

Le Moniteur, XIV, for the debates; *Rapport qui a précédé l'acte énonciatif des crimes de Louis Capet, lu à la Convention nationale, au nom de la Commission des vingt et un, le 10 décembre 1792* (1792) completes the publication of the papers found in the *armoire de fer*. The act of accusation was published by Robert Lindet, *Attentat et crimes de Louis, dernier roi des français* (1792); the supporting documents are in the *Recueil des pièces justificatives de l'acte énonciatif des crimes de Louis Capet, réunies par la Commission des vingt et un . . .* (1792). The Convention also published as a separate pamphlet the record of the session, *Procès-verbal de la Convention nationale: Séance du mardi 11 décembre 1792 . . .* (1792). Louis's responses are the words he uttered at the time, taken from the transcript of the session. Barère's words are paraphrased. The security measures for Paris during Louis's trip to the Convention's bar were reported in *Le Moniteur*; for some additional details, see the newspapers of Brissot, Carra, Gorsas, and Marat. For the details of fetching Louis to the Convention, the conversations en route, and other such details, Beaucourt; also Durand de Maillanne, "*Mémoires*

sur la Convention nationale," in Mémoires sur les assemblées parlementaires de
la Révolution, ed. M. de Lescure, 2 vols. (1881); Papiers de Chaumette; Buchez
and Roux, XXI; "Le Procès de Louis XVI et la Révolution du 31 mai:
D'après La Correspondance de Blad, député à la Convention nationale,
avec la municipalité de Brest," La Révolution française, XXIX (December
1895); Oscar Browning, ed., The Despatches of Earl Gower, English Ambassador at Paris from June 1790 to August 1792: To Which Are Added The Despatches of Mr. Lindsay and Mr. Monro and the Diary of Viscount Palmerston
in France during July and August 1791 (Cambridge, England, 1885), p. 258
for Monro's report; Théodore de Lameth, Mémoires, pp. 264–265. The view
that Louis had decided on the general contours of his defense when he
was interrogated is my own. Most students of the trial do not give him
much credit for his defense, prefering to think it was imposed on him by
his lawyers. This interpretation fits in with most of Louis's previous political blunders, but occasionally in his career he could and did make up his
own mind, and he was not a stupid man, although his views were generally narrow. The anecdote about Valazé contemptuously turning his
back on the king comes from Barère's Mémoires . . . Publiés par Mm. Hippolyte Carnot et David (d'Angers), 4 vols. (1842–1844).

CHAPTER VI

The debates are from Le Moniteur, XIV. The letters of refusal or acceptance from the lawyers are also printed here, along with letters received
from various people volunteering their legal services. Malesherbes's letter
is part of the permanent display at the Musée des archives, also reprinted
in Le Moniteur. Marat on Malesherbes is from his Journal de la Révolution
française, no. 82; all the documents on giving the lawyers access to Louis,
searching them, deciding to let Louis have pens and paper are reprinted
in Beaucourt. On the Duke d'Orléans, Annales patriotiques, December 11,
1792, prints his letter; Buchez and Roux, XXI, reprints his Lettre de Louis-
Philippe-Joseph au conseil provisoire de la Commune . . . asking to change his
name. For Buzot's attack, Discours . . . sur la famille des Bourbons . . . 16
décembre 1792 (1792) and his Mémoires. Desmoulins's analysis delivered to
the Jacobin Club on December 16 is reprinted in Buchez and Roux, XXI;
Marat's opinion of the duke is in the same volume, see pp. 415ff; Monro
to Grenville is from The Despatches of Earl Gower . . . p. 258. For the responses of the sections: Adresse de la section des Gardes-Française à la Convention nationale (1792); and for Faubourg-Monmartre, Extrait du procès-
verbal de l'assemblée générale du 23 décembre 1792 (1792). On Louis's lawyers,
Edmund Biré, Les Défenseurs de Louis XVI (Lyon, 1896). For the remarkable
legal school of Bordeaux, Henri Chauvot, Le Barreau de Bordeaux de 1775 à
1815 (1856). The argument that the Girondin attack on the Duke d'Orléans
was the beginning of the end for the faction, that the precedent they themselves introduced led them to the guillotine, is from Michelet.

CHAPTER VII

The debates are from *Le Moniteur*, XIV. Louis's analysis of his plight is recorded by Malesherbes, reprinted in Beaucourt, I, 290. For the details of Louis preparing his defense: Cléry in Beaucourt and Cubières's report to the Commune on December 21, 1792, in Buchez and Roux, XXII. Malesherbes's and Louis's response to DeSèze's peroration are in Beaucourt. The details of fetching the king from the Temple for his final appearance and the conversations that took place in the coach during the trip are in Beaucourt, II. DeSèze's *plaidoyer* is available in several places. I have used the edition immediately issued by the Convention and signed by two secretaries (Osselin and J. A. Creusé-Latouche), *Défense de Louis: Prononcée à la barre de la Convention nationale, le mercredi 26 décembre 1792, l'an premier de la République, par le citoyen DeSèze, l'un de ses défenseurs officieux* (1792). The version given in *Le Moniteur* is only a fragment. Buchez and Roux also print the entire text, XXII, 2–57. The text of the constitution can be found in Duguit, Mounier, Bonnard, *Les Constitutions et les principales lois politiques . . .* (1952); and the relevant clauses are in chap. 2, "De La Royauté, de la régence et des ministres," sects. I (descent of the crown), II (inviolability), V–VII (conditions under which abdication is presumed), VIII (conditions under which the king can be tried after abdication). Louis's last speech to the deputies is in *Le Moniteur*, XIV, 847–848, and, another version, in Buchez and Roux, XXII, 57–58. I have followed the *Moniteur* version. For reactions to Louis's appearance before the Convention: Thompson, *English Witnesses of the French Revolution* (Oxford, 1938); Beaucourt, II; *Despatches of Earl Gower*, 267; and *Le Moniteur* in the regular column "Commune de Paris." For contemporary evaluations of the *plaidoyer* and DeSèze's performance: Choudieu, *Mémoires*, 257–258; the *secrétaire-greffier*'s report to the General Council of the Commune, the evening of December 26, is in Beaucourt, II, 232 (this same report also contains details of Louis's trip back to the Temple); Marat, *Journal de la République française*, no. 86; Brissot, *Patriote français*, no. 1234; Gorsas, *Le Courrier des départements*, no. 37. The *plaidoyers* for the king sent from exile are: Jacques Necker, *Réflexions présentées à la nation française: Sur Le Procès intenté à Louis XVI* (1792); Lally-Tollendal, *Plaidoyer pour Louis XVI* (London, 1793); Bertrand de Molleville, *Dénonciation de prévarications commises dans le procès de Louis XVI: Adressées à la Convention nationale* (London, 1793); Louis de Narbonne, *Déclaration de M. Louis de Narbonne, ancien ministre de la guerre, en France: Dans Le Procès du Roi* (London, 1793). There is an extensive list of others in Edmund Biré, *Les Défenseurs de Louis XVI* (Lyon, 1896). The anonymous pamphlet referred to is *Lettre à monsieur DeSèze, défenseur officieux du roi* (n.d.). For a brief analysis of Necker's *Réflexions*, David P. Jordan, "In Defense of the King," *Stanford French Review*, I, 3 (Winter 1977), 325–338.

CHAPTER VIII

Saint-Just's speech is in his *Oeuvres choisies*, 92–102; Robespierre's in *Oeuvres*, IX; all the other debates are from *Le Moniteur*. Barbaroux's comment on the origins of the appeal to the people is in his *Mémoires*, 158–159. The speeches discussed are: J. B. Salles, *Opinion . . . Dans L'Affaire du ci-devant roi*; J. Serre, *Opinion . . . sur la question suivante: La mort de Louis intéresse-t-elle le salut de la république?* Buzot, *Opinion . . . Sur le Jugement de Louis XVI*; Rabaut-Saint-Etienne, *Opinion concernant le procès de Louis XVI*; Biroteau, *Discours . . . Sur le Jugement de Louis Capet*; Vergniaud, *Opinion . . . Sur le Jugement de Louis*; Gensonné, *Opinion . . . Sur le Jugement de Louis*; Pétion, *Opinion . . . sur le roi*; Lequinio, *Opinion . . . Sur la Défense de Louis XVI*; Barère, *Discours . . . Sur le Jugement du procès de Louis Capet*. Napoléon on the appeal to the people, made on June 12, 1816, is quoted in Gérard Walter, ed., *Actes du tribunal révolutionnaire* (1968), 162. For other responses: Joseph de Fiévée, "Mémoires," in *Mémoires sur les journées révolutionnaires et les coups d'états*, ed. M. de Lescure, 2 vols. (1875); Dubois-Crancé, *Analyse de la Révolution française*; Gorsas, *Le Courrier des départements*, XVIII; Brissot, *Le Patriote français*, no. 1249. Vergniaud's appraisal of the appeal to the people is in *Réponse de Vergniaud, député de la Gironde, aux Calomnies de Robespierre, député de Paris: Prononcé à la Convention nationale le 10 avril 1793* (1793). Chauvot, *Barreau de Bordeaux*, 97, has a good description of Vergniaud's oratorical style. Fabre's appraisal of Barère's speech before the Jacobins is quoted in Robespierre, *Oeuvres*, IX, 212. I follow Jaurès, V, 103, on the success of Barère's speech.

The Haute-Loire letter, along with a couple of others, are in *Le Moniteur*, XV, 68, 72, 80; for the affair in Rouen, *Le Moniteur*, XV, 314, 140; the letter to the Convention announcing the troubles is reprinted by Soboul, 179–180. For an account of the episode and an analysis see Cl. Mazauric's communication to the Société des études robespierristes (December 1965), "A Propos De La Manifestation royaliste de la Rougemare (11 janvier 1793): Royalistes, modérés et jacobins à Rouen." For *L'Ami des lois* see *Le Moniteur*, XV, 109, 124, 30, 119. The play itself is *L'Ami des lois: Comédie en 5 actes en vers* (1793); and a modern account of the play and its impact is in Marvin Carlson, *The Theatre of the French Revolution* (Ithaca, 1966), 143–148. The letter sent by Boze to the king is reprinted in C. Vatel, ed., *Vergniaud: MSS., lettres et papiers*, 2 vols. (1837), II, 120ff. On Dumouriez's schemes, *Le Moniteur*, XV, 10; XVI, 640. Danton's judgment of Dumouriez is from Jaurès, V, 117–118, "A capable military leader but in politics a worn-out nag." Also Dumouriez, *Vie et mémoires*, ed. J. F. Barrière, 2 vols. (1848). For Spanish attempts at corruption, Albert Mathiez, "Les Tentatives de corruption de l'Espagne pour sauver Louis XVI," *Annales historiques de la Révolution française*, III, 179–183. Ocariz's letters to Spain are published by Alfred Chabaud as an appendix to his edition of the *Mémoires de Barbaroux* (1932). Danton's schemes, uncovered by Mathiez, who was passionately interested in discrediting him, are detailed in "Danton, Talon, Pitt et la mort de Louis XVI," in *Etudes robespierristes* (1918); *Danton et la paix* (1919), chap. 3; "Danton: Agent de la liste civile," *Annales révolutionnaires* (1914); "Danton et la mort du roi, d'après un document inédit," *Annales révolutionnaires*, XIV, 335–337. The conversation between Talon and Charles Lameth is reprinted by Gustave Rouanet, "Danton et la mort de Louis XVI," *Annales révolutionnaires* (1916). For Tom Paine's scheme, *The Diary and Letters of Gouverneur Morris*, II, 118–119; the speech itself, "Reasons for Preserving the Life of Louis Capet," is in *The Writings of Thomas Paine*, ed. Moncure Daniel Conway, 3 vols. (London, 1895). Miles's letters to Pitt are in *The Correspondence of William Augustus Miles on the French Revolution, 1789–1817*, ed. Rev. Charles Popham Miles, 2 vols. (London, 1890), I, 398–400. See also Choudieu, *Mémoires et notes*; Théodore de Lameth, *Mémoires*; and the *Adresse des citoyens de la commune de Rouen à la Convention nationale sur l'appel au peuple* (1793). The jibe on obscure deputies known only to the paymaster is by the terrorist Carrier, although I cannot recall the source.

CHAPTER IX

The figures are from Patrick. The debates, as always, from *Le Moniteur*. Additional information is from Seligman, II. My view of the appeal to the people and the tactics of the antiregicides follows Jaurès, V, 24, 67, 69, 75, 88, 128, 145–146. For the conduct of business in the Convention, *Rapport sur l'ordre des travaux de l'Assemblée nationale: Fait Au Nom du comité de législation, par M. Hérault, député de Paris* (January 25, 1792). *Archives parlementaires*, LVII, for the figures announced to the Convention. The pamphlets issued by the Convention on the voting are: *Appels nominaux . . . sur ces trois questions: 1. Louis Capet est-il coupable de conspiration contre la sûreté générale de l'état? 2. Le Jugement de la Convention nationale contre Louis sera-t-il soumis à la ratification du peuple? 3. Y Aura-t-il un Sursis, oui ou non, à l'exécution du décret qui condamne Louis Capet? . . . Liste comparative des cinq appels nominaux faits dans les séances des 15, 16, 17, 18 et 19 janvier 1793 . . .* (1793). Also, *Correspondance et mémoires de Barbaroux*, published by Cl. Perroud with Alfred Chabaud (1928), 286–287; Brissot, *Mémoires*, II, 252; Buzot, *Mémoires*, ed. C. A. Dauban, 56; Lebas, *Correspondance*, 20–21; and E. Seligman, "Le Compte des voix dans le procès de Louis XVI," *Bibliothèque de la Société d'histoire moderne* (1911). Mallet du Pan is quoted by Jaurès, V, 69. The formal decree concerning procedures in the voting is in *Archives parlementaires*, LVII, 63.

CHAPTER X

Garat's report on the state of Paris is in *Archives parlementaires*, LVII, 339; Chambon's letter is in *Le Moniteur*, XV, 181. Brissot's description of January 16–17 is in *Patriote français*, no. 1256; Mercier's is in *Paris pendant la Révolution (1789–1798): Ou Le Nouveau Paris* (1962), 294–295; the story about

Duchastel carried in on a stretcher to vote is also from Mercier. Garat's second report on Paris is in *Le Moniteur*, XV, 226. On suspicions of bribery in general and Mailhe as a recipient, M. A. Baudot, *Notes historiques sur la Convention nationale* (1893), 207; Jaurès, V, 133. The anecdote about Vergniaud's vote is from J. B. Harmand, *Anecdotes relatives à quelques personnes, et à plusieurs événemens remarquables de la Révolution française*, new ed. (1820), 84–85. For a discussion of Harmand's reliability, see Alison Patrick, "Regicides and Anti-regicides in January 1793: The Significance of Fouché's Vote," *Historical Studies* (University of Melbourne), XIV, 55 (October 1970), 341–360. The anecdote about the response of Louis's lawyers is in Poujoulat, *Histoire de la Révolution française*, I, 396. The story is also told by Edmund Biré (*Les Défenseurs de Louis XVI*), who follows Poujoulat, 151. Louis's letter to the Convention, along with the remarks of Malesherbes and Tronchet, are in *Le Moniteur*, XV, 229ff. As always the debates are from *Le Moniteur*, XV. See also, E. Belhomme, *Les Régicides* (1893); Eugène Welvert, "Un Prêtre Régicide, Chasles," *Revue des questions historiques*, no. 94, vol. 56, 548–554.

CHAPTER XI

The debates are from *Le Moniteur*, XV. For the English version of Tom Paine's speech, "Shall Louis XVI Have Respite?" see *The Writings of Thomas Paine*. Romme's diary is quoted by Alessandro Galante Garrone, *Gilbert Romme: Histoire d'un révolutionnaire, 1750–1795*, trans. Anne and Claude Manceron (1971), 288. Danton's remarks are from Théodore de Lameth, *Mémoires*; Louis's reactions to the news of the voting is from *Le Courrier français*; Louis on his cousin, Philippe-Egalité, is from Edgeworth's recollections, reprinted in Beaucourt, I, 320. See also, "Le Procès de Louis XVI: D'Après Les Papiers inédits du conventionnel Delbrel," *Revue bleue*, no. 93, vol. 52, 227–233. For reactions to the voting: A.-C. Thibaudeau, *Mémoires sur la Convention et le Directoire*, 2 vols. (1824), I, 11; Levasseur, *Mémoires*; *Mémoires de Carnot par son fils*, I, 296; *Mémoires de Garat*, ed. E. Maron (1862); and *Mémoires historiques sur le XVIIIe siécle, et sur M. Suard*, 2d ed., 2 vols. (1821); Brissot, *Patriote français*, no. 1245; Dubois-Crancé, *Analyse de la Révolution française: Depuis L'Ouverture des Etats-généraux jusqu'au 6 Brumaire an IV de la République, suivie du compte rendu fait par Dubois-Crancé de son administration au ministère de la guerre* (1885), 113; Marat, *Journal de la République française*, no. 101. The figures on voting are from Patrick. The Restoration antiregicide legislation is in Duguit, Mounier, and Bonnard, *Les Constitutions et les principales lois politiques de la France . . .* (1952).

CHAPTER XII

Lebas's letter is quoted by Jaurès, V, 169, n. 12. The proclamation of the Provisional Executive Council of the Convention is in *Le Moniteur*, XV, 232; the preparations of the Commune, extracted from the *procès-verbal* of the

General Council, are in Beaucourt, II, 253, 273; Santerre's preparations, along with the orders he issued, are in Edmund Dutemple, ed., *Ordres du jour inédits de Santerre* . . . (1875), 8–10 (which includes the General Council's orders to Santerre), and 12, 19–20 ("Suite de l'ordre du dimanche 20 janvier 1793 . . . Quatre heures de relevée"). The figures for the number of troops involved in the execution are drawn from this source. Malesherbes's announcement of the vote is reprinted in Beaucourt, I, 292, as are details of Louis's preparations for death (I, 291), his thoughts on his approaching ordeal (I, 175), his reading of Hume (I, 175), his last supper (I, 181), his farewell to his family (I, 185), his last day (I, 186–187), his final words to Cléry (I, 192), his farewell to the Temple (I, 189), and his remarks to Edgeworth (I, 326). Mme. Royale's account is also in Beaucourt, I, 18–19. There are two versions of Santerre's arrival to fetch Louis, both of which agree substantially: Beaucourt, I, 329 (Edgeworth's) and Buchez and Roux, XXIII, 331 (taken from *Procès des Bourbons* (1798), II, 151). Sanson's letter to the Commune is reprinted in Beaucourt, II, 298. For other anecdotes: *Révolutions de Paris*, no. 185; Marat, *Journal de la République française*, no. 105; *Annales patriotiques*, no. 23; Thibaudeau, *Mémoires*; Garat, *Mémoires historiques* . . . ; for the weather, P. de Vaissière, *La Mort du roi* (1910), 59. Louis's letter to the Commune is in Buchez and Roux, XXIII, 341; the description of the coach arriving at the scaffold is by J. G. Millingen, in Thompson, *English Witnesses of the French Revolution*, 228. On the drumroll that drowned out Louis's last words see *Ordres du jour inédits de Santerre*, 22, and, another version, Choudieu, *Mémoires*, 278. There is some controversy over the famous "mot" of the Abbé Edgeworth: see Beaucourt, app. IV, and vol. II, pp. 367, 369; and Louis Combes, "Le Mot attribué à l'abbé Edgeworth de Firmont," in *L'Amateur d'autographes* (June 1, 1865), IV, 161–167. I follow the version of Combes on what Edgeworth said. Santerre's letter announcing where Louis is buried is reprinted by Beaucourt, II, 304. In addition: Arnaud de Lestapis, *La Conspiration de Batz, 1793–1794* (1969); Pierre-Joseph Joly, "Une Relation inédite de la mort de Louis XVI," *Revue Champagne et Brie*, LXXXXV, 2d ser., VII, 237–240; A. Aulard, "L'Exécution de Louis XVI et la presse française," *Revue française*, LXXXII (1929), 65–76, 153–162; Baron de Vinck d'Orp, *Le Meurtre du 21 janvier 1793* (1877); François-Louis Bruel, *Un Siècle d'histoire de France par l'estampe, 1770–1871* (1909); and the great collection assembled by Baron de Vinck d'Orp, *Collection de Vinck: Un Siècle de l'histoire de France, 1770–1871*, 248 vols. The original *procès-verbal* of the execution (reprinted in Beaucourt and Soboul) is in the Archives nationales, A.N. C182, dos. 103, p. 3 (this is a photocopy; the original is on display in the Musée des archives). The newspaper accounts are: *Le Républicain*, no. 22 (also in Buchez and Roux, XXIII, 300); *Annales patriotiques*, nos. 21, 22; Marat, *Journal de la République*, no. 105; Brissot, *Patriote français*, no. 1259; Robespierre, *Lettres à ses commettans*, *Oeuvres*, V. Also Mercier, *Nouveau Paris*, 80–82; Lebas, *Correspondance inédite*, 21–22; Barbaroux, *Correspondance et mémoires de Barbaroux*, ed. C. Perroud and A. Chabaud (1923), 293; Walzer, *Regicide and Revolution*, 85; *Testament de Louis XVI, dernier roi des Français: Ses Derniers Paroles sur l'échafaud et le procès-verbal des commissaires nommés par le conseil exécutif pour assister à son exécution* (n.d.). Interpretations of the meaning of Louis's trial and death are many; here is a sample of contemporary opinion on which I have drawn: *Mémoires de Meillan: Député par le département des Basses-Pyrénées à la Convention nationale* (1823), 13–15; Levasseur, *Mémoires*, I, 100ff; Lebas, *Correspondance*; *Mémoires de Louvet de Couvrai sur la Révolution française*, ed. F.-A. Aulard, 2 vols. (1889); Paul Mautouchet, "Une Lettre de Condorcet sur le procès de Louis XVI," *Révolution française*, LXIV, 220–224. And in addition to all the authorities cited above, see also: Paul Bastid, *Les Grands Procès politiques de l'histoire* (1962); V. Pierre, "Le Clergé constitutionnel dans le procès du roi," *Quinzaine* (January 16, 1898); E. Léotard, *La Condamnation de Louis XVI devant l'histoire* (Lyon, 1888).

EPILOGUE

Chateaubriand, *Mémoires d'outre-tombe*, ed. Maurice Levaillant, 2d ed. (n.d.), pt. 3, 1st epoch, bk. 5 *Exhumation des restes de Louis XVI*. The *procès-verbal* of Louis's burial is reprinted in Beaucourt, II, as is the order of the General Council of September 24, 1793, on the disposal of Louis's possessions. The Abbé Renard's deposition is in *Le Moniteur* for January 21, 1815, as is the *procès-verbal* of the removal of Louis's remains to Saint-Denis. The former is also reprinted in Pierre de Vaissière, *La Mort du roi* (1910), 152–153. The pope's speech is *Allocution de notre très-saint père le pape Pie VI, dans le consistoire secret, du lundi 17 juin: Au Sujet de l'assassinat de sa majesté très-chrétienne, Louis XVI, roi de France* (Rome, 1793). For the celebrations of January 21 in the nineteenth century: *La France en deuil: Ou Le 21 janvier* (1815); J. Mathieu, *Célébration du 21 janvier depuis 1793 jusqu'à nos jours* (Marseille, 1865); and the contemporary newspapers throughout the years, under January 21–22. On the subsequent careers of the regicides: E. Belhomme, *Les Régicides* (1893); Eugène Welvert, "Les Conventionnels régicides après la Révolution," *Revue historique*, LXXXXVII, 64, 298–326; Baudot, *Notes historiques*; A. Kuscinski, "Les Conventionnels en exil," *Revue française*, LXXXXI, 20, 121–137; and finally that marvelous reference work, A. Kuscinski, *Dictionnaire des conventionnels*.

Index

Acte énonciatif, 65, 77, 78, 102–105, 108, 120, 128, 132, 133. *See also* Commission of Twenty-one
Albertier, 106
Alcudia, Duke of, 156
Alexander, Charles-Alexis, 34, 35, 36, 37, 79
Angoulême, Louis, Duke d', 80, 234
Angoulême, Marie-Thérèse-Charlotte, Duchess d'. *See* Marie-Thérèse-Charlotte de France
Anville, Bourguignon d', 92
Appeal to the People, 142, 143, 144, 146, 147, 150–164, 167, 168, 173–178, 184, 185, 192, 200, 201
Appelants, 201, 202
Appels nominaux: first *appel nominal*, 171–172; second *appel nominal*, 172–176; third *appel nominal*, 178, 182–191, 194, 200–205; fourth *appel nominal*, 195, 196–199; mentioned, 163, 166, 168–169, 170, 172, 178, 194, 195, 198, 200, 204, 205, 246
Archives parlementaires, 170n, 239, 240, 244
Armoire de fer, 71–73, 74, 76, 102, 104, 129, 137, 152
Artois, Charles-Philippe, Count d', 16, 80, 82, 223, 234
Audrien, Yves-Marie, 129
August 10, 1792, Revolution of, xi, xiii, xv, 16, 38–39, 42, 44, 51, 52, 57, 59, 61, 63, 66, 67, 74, 76, 78, 103, 134, 135, 151, 152, 206, 222
Azéma, Michel, 156

Bailly, Jean-Sylvain, 25
Bancal, Jean-Henri, 165, 168, 196, 197, 239
Barbaroux, Charles-Jean-Marie, 38, 51, 62, 63, 64, 85, 103, 144, 165, 196, 232
Barère, Bertrand, 77, 108–111, 136, 149–151, 165, 171, 173, 174, 185, 186, 197–198, 235, 247
Basire, Charles, 57
Bastille, Fall of the, 16, 19, 39, 42, 54, 108, 219, 222. *See also* Fête de la fédération

Batz, Jean-Pierre-Louis, Baron de, 218
Bayle, Pierre, 86
Beaugeard, Nicolas-Joseph, 218
Belhomme, E., 241, 242, 244, 245, 247
Bergoeing, François, 176, 186, 198
Bernard, Jacques-Claude, 207, 217
Berruyer, General, 214, 220
Bertezène, Jean-Etienne, 188
Besenval, Pierre-Joseph-Victor, Baron de, 125
Biroteau, Jean-Bonaventure-Blaise-Hilarion, 143
Bossuet, Jacques-Bénigne, Bishop of Meaux, 86, 88
Boucher, Antoine-Sauveur, 242
Bouchereau, Augustin-François, 245
Bouillé, Louis-Joseph-Amour, Marquis de, 24, 27
Bourbotte, Pierre, 77
Boyer-Fonfrède, Jean-Baptiste, 166, 167, 176, 186, 198
Boze Affair, 151–153
Boze, Joseph, 151, 152
Breteuil, Louis-Auguste le Tonnelier, Baron de, 24, 73
Brutus, 150
Brissot, Jacques-Pierre, 29–30, 30–32, 51, 68, 122, 139, 143, 146, 147, 152, 159, 165, 176, 182, 183, 196, 198, 199, 232
Brunswick Manifesto, 41
Buffon, Georges-Louis, 85
Burke, Edmund, 18
Buzot, François-Nicolas-Léonard, 51, 75, 76, 101, 121, 122, 143, 144, 185, 196

Caesar, 67
Cahiers de doléance, 126, 192
Calon, Etienne-Nicolas de, 72
Cambacérès, Jean-Jacques-Régis de, 173, 199, 236
Campan, Jeanne, 82
Carnot, Lazare-Nicolas-Marguerite, 84, 152, 203, 236
Carra, Jean-Louis, 34, 165, 188, 222, 233, 242
Casenave, Antoine, 196, 197
Chabot, François, 76

Chambon, Aubin Bigore du, 195
Chambon, Nicolas, 106, 107, 108, 112, 128, 130, 153, 155, 179, 180
Champ-de-Mars, Massacre of, 109, 222
Champigny-Clément, René-Jean, 244, 245
Charante-Inférieur, Department of, 176
"Charitas," Papal Bull, 23
Charles I, King, 113, 114, 115, 191, 206
Charles IV, King, 156
Charles X. *See* Artois, Charles-Philippe, Count d'
Chasset, Charles-Antoine, 175
Chateaubriand, François-René, Vicount de, 125, 225, 235
Chateauneuf-Randon, Alexandre-Paul, Count de, 190
Chaumette, Pierre-Gaspard (Anaxagoras), 33, 69–70, 105, 111
Chazal, Jean-Pierre, 188
Chédaneau, Augustin-Roland, 245
Choudieu, Pierre-René, 138, 156
Cicero, 52, 85, 92
Civil Constitution of the Clergy, 19, 23
Cléry, Jean-Baptiste, 87, 90, 91, 92, 93, 94, 96, 97, 128, 205, 206, 207, 209, 211, 212, 215–218, 234
Collot d'Herbois, Jean-Marie, 101
Colonge, 80
Commission of Twenty-one, 77, 78, 103, 120, 124. See also *Acte énonciatif*; Lindet, Jean-Baptiste-Robert
Commission of Twenty-four, 62, 63, 64, 77, 129. *See also* Valazé, Charles-Eléonor Dufriche-
Committee of Public Safety, xvi, 103, 231, 235
Committee on Legislation, 69, 73, 77. *See also* Mailhe, Jean-Baptiste
Commune, The: censors king's reading, 85; closes *The Friend of the Laws*, 155; demands quick trial, 74; General Council of, 69, 82, 85; forbids king to see his family, 120; obliterates king's memory, 224; restrictions on king's lawyers, 119, 121; rules on prisoners, 94–95, 96–97, 98, 99; transfers king to Convention, 105; Vigilance Committee of, 61; preparations for execution, 206–207, 209, 210, 213, 217, 218–219, 220–221; mentioned, 8, 19, 35, 39, 40, 41, 43, 50, 53, 54, 56, 69, 79, 139, 235
Condé, Louis-Joseph de Bourbon, Prince de, 223

Condorcet, Jean-Antoine-Nicolas Caritat, Marquis de, 101, 146, 175, 196
Constitution of 1791, 26–28, 58, 115, 117, 130, 131, 133. *See also* Louis XVI, views on constitution
Conte, Antoine, 171
Conte, Arthur, 243
Convention Assembly: composition of, 45–47; attitude toward Paris, 71; rejects delay in execution, 210; vote on king, 239; voting described, 168–170; mentioned, xi, xv, 43, 44, 47, 48, 52, 57, 59, 60, 61, 64, 65, 66, 69, 101, 102, 118, 119, 120, 121, 124, 129–134, 136, 143, 146, 148, 150, 151, 154, 172, 173, 178, 179, 186, 194, 199, 204–205, 222
Corday, Charlotte, 235
Cordeliers Club, 20, 32, 36, 106, 123
Coren-Fustier, Simon-Joseph, 143
Corneille, Pierre, 85, 92
Coulombeau, Claude, 97, 107, 111
Couthon, Georges, 162, 165, 196, 235
Criminal Code of 1791, 101, 102, 113, 115, 116, 118, 120, 124, 133, 139, 164
Cromwell, Oliver, 233

Damiens, Robert-François, 58
Danton, Georges-Jacques: his coup d'état, 35–36; calls France to arms, 41; tries to reconcile factions, 51; mentioned, xv, 38, 50, 52, 57, 69, 72, 156–157, 181, 188, 199, 201, 235
Daumier, Honoré, 183
Daunou, Pierre-Claude-François, 164
David, Jacques-Louis, 149
"Declaration of the king," 28
Declaration of the Rights of Man and Citizen, 17, 109
Defermon, Jacques, 129, 165
Dejoly, Etienne-Louis-Hector, 7, 8
Deleyre, Alexandre, 186
Dennelle, Marguerite, 52
Desacy, Claude-Louis-Michel, 185
Desbouillons, Pierre, 37
DeSèze, Raymond, 124–125, 127, 128, 130–136, 138, 139, 141, 142, 145, 186, 191, 234
Desmoulins, Camille, 50, 67, 76, 122
Diderot, Denis, 46, 86
Drouet, Jean-Baptiste, 26, 62, 156
Dubois-Crancé, Edmond-Louis-Alexis, 158, 200, 201
Duchastel, Gaspard-Severin, 189
Ducos, Jean-François, 176, 186, 198

Ducreux, Joseph, 83
Dufriche-Valazé, Charles-Eléonor. *See* Valazé, Charles-Eléonor Dufriche-
Dumont, André, 193
Dumouriez, Charles-François Duperrier, General, 155, 156, 159
Duplantier, Jacques-Paul, 186
Durand-Maillane, Pierre-Toussaint, 122

Edgeworth de Firmont, Henry Essex, 209–212, 214–217, 219, 220, 223
Elisabeth, Philippine-Marie-Hélène, Madame, 1, 5, 6, 8, 79, 81, 91–95, 209, 210, 212, 226, 234
Engerran, Jacques, 145
Enghien, Louis-Antoine, Duke d', 226, 227
Estates-General, 11, 13, 14, 15, 20, 108, 132, 136

Fabre d'Eglantine, Philippe-François-Nazaire, 151
Faubourg-Montmartre, Section, 123–124
Fersen, Axel, count de, 24, 25, 31
Fête de la fédération, 19, 32
Fouché, Joseph, 236
Fournier l'Americain, Claude Fournier-l'Héritier, 34, 37
Francis II, Emperor, 30
Friend of the Laws, The, 154–155, 179
Froger-Plisson, Louis-Joseph, 174

Garat, Joseph, 179, 180, 203, 208, 209, 210, 213
Gard, Department of, 188
Garnier, Captain, 37
Garrau, Pierre-Anselme, 186, 189, 197, 218
Gasparin, Thomas-Augustin, 151, 152
Genevois, Louis Benôit, 237
Gensonné, Armand, 143, 146, 152, 176, 179, 186, 189, 198
Gerdret, 8
Gironde, Department of, 185–186
Girondins: "inner sixty," 48, 49, 51; basic politics, 49–51; view of trial, 58–60; tactical errors of, 159–160; strategy on voting, 162–163, 166–168; demand two-thirds vote, 180; mentioned, 47, 48, 49, 51, 52, 53, 55, 56, 58, 59, 63, 64, 65, 68, 69, 73, 75, 76, 78, 103, 121, 123, 125, 134, 140, 143, 144, 148, 150, 151, 152, 153, 154, 155, 158,

159, 161, 162, 164, 166, 167, 169, 174, 175, 176–177, 182, 190, 193, 195, 198, 200, 202, 235
Givey, J. B., 115
Gorsas, Antoine-Joseph, 139, 158, 189, 190, 239
Gouges, Marie-Olympe Aubry, Olympe de, 119
Goupilleau, Jean-François-Marie, 71
Grangeneuve, Jean-Antoine, 176, 186, 198
Gravilliers, Section, 71
Great Fear, The, 16
Grégoire, Henri, 101
Grenville, William Wyndham, Lord, 112, 122, 140
Guadet, Marguerite-Elie, 51, 151, 152, 176, 185, 186, 192, 198
Guffroy, Armand-Benoit-Joseph, 196

Hardy, Antoine François, 140
Harmand, Jean-Baptiste, 185
Haute-Garonne, Department of, 170, 183, 184
Haute-Loire, Department of, 153
Hautes-Pyrénées, Department of, 186
Hébert, Jacques-René, 70, 155, 174, 224. See also *Père Duchesne, Le*
Helvétius, Claude-Adrien, 86
Hérault de Séchelles, Marie-Jean, 65
Hervilly, General d', 37
History of England. See Hume, David
Horace, 85, 92
Hué, François, 84, 85
Huguenin, Sulpice, 35
Hume, David, 86, 206

Indre-et-Loire, Department of, 176
Isnard, Henri-Maximin, 202

Jacobin Club of Paris, 20, 32, 36, 52, 55, 72, 106, 122, 123, 151
Jacobins: basic politics, 48–51; view of trial, 58–60, 115–116; strategy on voting, 162–163, 166–168; challenge impartiality, 169; mentioned, 29, 47, 48, 49, 50, 51, 53, 55, 56, 58, 59, 61, 68, 69, 71, 74, 75, 76, 78, 103, 121, 122, 123, 125, 140, 142, 146, 150, 151, 152, 155, 161, 162, 164, 166, 167, 169, 172, 175, 176–177, 182, 187, 190, 193, 196, 198, 200, 202, 204
James (Temple guard), 95
January 21, 1793, 227–228

Jaurès, Jean, xiii, xv, 172–173, 184, 232, 245
Jay, Jean, 186
Jeanbon Saint-André, André, 143, 147
Jemappes, Battle of, 64, 78, 188
Jesuits, 87, 89, 209
June 20, 1792, 1, 7, 32, 114, 129, 222

"La Carmagnole," 64
Lacaze, Jacques, 176, 186, 198
Laclos, Choderlos de, 75
Lacombe-Saint-Michel, Jean-Pierre, 152, 195
Lacroix, Jean-Michel, 196
Lafayette, Marie-Joseph-Paul, Marquis de, 7, 23, 25, 27, 32, 73, 114
La Fontaine, Jean de, 86
Lalande, Joseph-Jérôme, 171
"La Marseillaise," 33, 64, 220
Lamballe, Marie-Thérèse de Savoie-Carignan, Princess de, 1, 79, 81, 96
Lameth, Théodore de, 84, 115, 119
Lanjuinais, Jean-Denis, 121, 173, 174, 180, 181, 184, 195
Lasource, Marc-David Alba, 202
Lebas, Philippe-François-Joseph, 177, 208, 232
Lebrasse, Lieutenant, 217
Le Clerc (Temple guard), 95
Le Clerc, Jean-Baptiste, 245
Lefebvre, Georges, xi, 242, 244
Legendre, Louis, 108, 169
Legislative Assembly, xv, 7, 9, 27, 29, 32, 39, 40, 43, 44, 56, 57, 61, 62, 72, 79, 81, 110, 134, 151, 168
Lehardy, Pierre, 181, 184
Lemoine (valet de chambre), 25
LeMonnier, Doctor, 98
Leopold II, Emperor, 30
Lepeletier de Saint-Fargeau, Louis-Michel, 202
Lequinio, Joseph-Marie, 143, 147
Lesage, Denis-Toussaint, 239
Levasseur, René, 156
Lazowski, Claude-François, 34
Leyris, Augustin-Jacques, 188
Lindet, Jean-Baptiste-Robert, 102–103, 104, 132. See also Acte énonciatif; Commission of Twenty-one
Loir-et-Cher, Department of, 186
Lonqueue, Louis, 46
Louis XIV, King, 19, 80, 83, 88, 93, 97, 107
Louis XV, King, 7, 44, 46, 58, 83, 213

Louis XVI, King: character of, 5, 6, 8, 18, 83–84, 90–91, 126; views of monarchy, 11, 13, 14, 18, 90; séance royale, 14, 15; views of society and state, 14–15, 137–138; views on reform, 15; rejects Mirabeau's scheme, 23; suspended, 26; views on constitution, 28, 73; June 20, 1792, 32; August 10, 1792, 36–37; views on religion, 73, 87–89, 211; portraits, physical description, 82–83; reading habits, taste, 85–87, 129; views of Voltaire, Rousseau, 85; last will and testament, 89–90; life in prison, 90–96, 98–100; educates his children, 92; taste in food, 93; en famille, 94, 212; courage, 95–96; hostility to Commune, 98; illness, 98; on his fate, 100; appearance before Convention, 106–108, 112, 128–129, 136; tactics in trial, 112–115; his defense, 127–128, 130–137, 141–142; last letter to Convention, 191; hears sentence, 205–206; opinion of Philippe-Egalité, 206; prepares for death, 206, 210, 212–214, 215, 216–217; requests delay, 208; last meal, 211; final wishes, 215–216; to scaffold, 217–219; execution, 219–220; last words, 219–220; burial, 220–221; declared royal martyr, 224; body exhumed, 225; state funeral, 225–226; mentioned passim
Louis XVII (The Dauphin), 1, 10, 79, 86, 87, 91–95, 97, 212, 223, 226, 234
Louis XVIII, King, 16, 125, 200, 210, 223, 225, 226, 227, 234, 236
Louis Philippe, King, 99, 183, 227
Louvet, Jean-Baptiste, 51–53, 54, 62, 63, 121, 123, 148
Loysal, Pierre, 166

Mably, Gabriel Bonnot de, 86
Mailhe amendment, 183–185, 189, 190, 194, 200, 204, 240, 241–246
Mailhe, Jean-Baptiste, 63–65, 66, 68, 100, 183, 184, 185, 189, 194, 195, 204. See also Committee on Legislation
Maine-et-Loire, Department of, 176
Maistre, Joseph de, 232
Malesherbes, Guillaume-Chrétien de Lamoignon de, 89, 118, 119, 125, 127, 128, 130, 186, 191, 205, 206, 235
Mallarmé, François-René-Augustin, 168
Mallet du Pan, Jacques, 173

Malraux, André, 228
Manchester, Edward Montagu, Earl of, 233
Mandat, Antoine-Jean Gailliot, Marquis de, 4, 5, 8, 35
Manège: description, 44–45
Manuel, Pierre-Louis, 63, 80, 165, 168, 183, 189–190, 239
Marat, Jean-Paul, xvii, 25, 51, 52, 54, 60, 75, 77, 115, 119, 122, 139, 151, 154, 155, 162, 195, 196–197, 231, 235
Marie-Antoinette, Queen, xii, 1, 6, 8, 10, 24, 25, 31, 63, 79, 91, 92, 93, 94, 95, 97, 99, 211, 212, 216, 218, 226, 234, 236
Marie-Louise, Empress, 236
Marie-Thérèse-Charlotte de France (Madame Royale), 1, 10, 79, 91, 92, 93, 95, 209, 211, 212, 234
Marseillais Battalion, 33, 36, 37, 38, 106
"Marseillaise, La," See "La Marseillaise"
Mary, Queen of Scots, 114, 224
Mercier, Louis-Sébastien, 182–183, 190, 225
Merlin de Thionville, Antoine-Christoph, 61, 76
Michelet, Jules, xiii, xv, 205, 245
Miles, William Augustus, 157
Mirabeau, André-Boniface-Louis Riquetti, Viscount de: physical description and life, 21–22; corruption, 22; plan for saving monarchy, 22–23; reputation destroyed, 72–73, 76–77; mentioned, 23, 30, 32, 88, 98, 100, 109, 153, 157
Moëlle (Temple guard), 107, 108, 111
Moisson, Commander, 37
Monro, Colonel, 112, 122, 140
Montesquieu, Charles de Secondat, Baron de, 46, 85, 93
Moore, John, 38
Morisson, Charles-François-Gabriel, 66, 68, 171
Morris, Gouverneur, 32, 157, 197
Mortimer-Ternaux, M., xiii, xv
Mauconseil, Section, 33

Napoléon, 118, 125, 158, 200, 203, 221, 225, 227, 231, 235
Necker, Jacques, 16, 84, 85
Neuf Sœurs (Masonic Lodge), 171
Newspapers: Ami du peuple(L'), 21; Ami du roi(L'), 21; Annales patriotiques et littéraires, 96, 155, 165, 210, 214, 222–223; Croix (La), 228; Chronique de Paris, 54, 80; Journal de la République française, 155; Journal du diable, 21; Journal royaliste, 21; Moniteur universel (Le), 55, 127, 170n, 239, 240, 244; Patriote français (Le), 21, 68, 115, 139, 232; Père Duchesne (Le), 155; Point du jour (Le), 21, 149; Républicain (Le), 222; Révolutions de France et de Brabant, 21; Révolutions de Paris, 21; Sentinelle (La), 52; Thermomètre du jour (Le), 54
Noël, Abbé, 157
Noël, Jean-Baptiste, 171, 172

Ocariz, Chevalier d', 156, 188
Orléans, Duchess d', 183
Orléans, Duke d'. See Philippe-Egalité
Ovid, 86

Paine, Thomas, 156, 157–158, 165, 196, 197
Paris, City of: law of May 21, 1790, 18; sections, 18, 19; delegation to Convention, 187
Paris, Count of, 229
Pâris, Philippe-Nicolas-Marie de, 202
Patrick, Alison, xiii, 252, 245
Penières-Delzors, Jean-Augustin, 193
Pétion, Jérôme, 5, 6, 35, 50, 59, 65, 66, 75, 76, 79, 81, 101, 115, 116, 123, 143, 147, 175, 185, 198
Phaedrus, 86
Philip the Fair, 80
Philippe-Egalité, 60, 75–76, 121, 122, 124, 125, 145, 158, 159, 162, 172, 187, 206, 223, 227, 241
Philippeaux, Pierre, 76
Philosophes, 87, 88, 118
Piques, Section, 73
Pitt, William, 157, 210
Pius VI, Pope, 23, 224
Poissonière, Section, 82
Pons, Philippe-Laurent, 174
Pradel, Count de, 224
Prelude, The, 53
Provence, Count de. See Louis XVIII
Prudhomme, Louis-Maris, 99, 106

Quinette, Nicolas-Marie, 77, 164

Rabaut-Saint-Etienne, Jean-Paul, 143, 144
Racine, Jean, 85, 92
Rebecquy, François-Trophime, 232
Reflections on the French Revolution, 18

Renard, Abbé, 225
Restoration, The: defines regicides, 200–201, 203; honors Louis XVI, 225–227; creates royal cult, 226–227
Réunion, Section, 154
Rewbell, Jean-François, 122
Robert the Pious, 228
Robespierre, Maximilien: August 10, 1792, 38; attacked by Louvet, 52–53; responds, 53–54; speech of December 3, 1792, 74; scorn for king, 119–120; on king's defense, 139; speech on appeal to the people, 148–149; calls for immediate execution, 195; on the trial, 205, 231, 234; mentioned, xv, xvi, xvii, 50, 51, 55, 60, 62, 63, 76, 101, 103, 118, 122, 134, 143, 144, 147, 149, 150, 154, 158, 162, 167, 169, 188, 189, 192, 196, 218, 233, 234, 235
Robespierride, 52–53, 72. *See also* Louvet, Jean-Baptiste
Roederer, Pierre-Louis, 5, 6, 7, 8, 9
Rohan, Cardinal de, 117
Roland, Jean-Marie, 50, 51, 59, 60, 69, 71, 72, 73, 122, 147, 152
Roland, Manon-Jeanne Phlipon, Madame, 25, 50, 51, 72, 147
Ronsin, Charles-Philippe, 40
Rossignol, Jean-Antoine, 35
Rouen, 154
Rousseau, Jean-Jacques, 46, 85, 86, 130, 131, 140
Roux, Jacques, 70–71, 207, 217, 235
Royale, Madame. *See* Marie-Thérèse-Charlotte de France

Sainte-Beuve, Charles-Augustin, 85
Saint-Antoine, 1, 6, 34, 35, 38
Saint-Cloud, flight to, 25, 109
Saint-Germain-l'Auxerrois, 228–229
Saint-Just, Louis-Antoine de, xvii, 46, 47, 66–67, 67–68, 74, 132, 142, 143, 150, 162, 175, 194, 234, 235
Saint-Marcel, 1, 6, 34, 35, 38
Salles, Jean-Baptiste, 143, 144, 239
Sanson (Executioner), 215, 219
Santerre, Antoine-Joseph, 34, 36, 37, 93, 108, 111, 130, 179, 196, 207, 213, 214, 216, 217, 220, 225
Séance royale (June 23, 1789), 14, 16, 18, 23, 28, 192
Seine-et-Marne, Department of, 174
Seligman, E., xiii, 242, 244
Seneca, 129

September Massacres, 41–43, 44, 50, 53, 54, 57, 60, 76, 95–96, 179, 196
Serre, Joseph, 143, 144
Sieyès, Emmanuel-Joseph, Abbé, 12
Simenon, Georges, xi
Simon (Temple guard), 95
Soboul, Albert, xi, xii, xiii, 242, 244
Sourdat, 119
Spain, interference of, 156, 184, 185, 188
Suger, Abbé, 226, 228
Swiss Guards, 7, 35, 36, 37, 38, 39, 40, 41, 104, 220

Tacitus, 89
Talleyrand, Charles-Maurice de, 236
Tallien, Jean-Lambert, 71–72
Talon, Antoine-Omer, 73, 109
Target, Guy-Jean, 117, 118, 119
Tasso, 86
Tellier, Armand-Constant, 174
Templar Knights, 80, 81
Temple, The: description, 80–81
Tennis Court Oath, 13
Terence, 86
Thibaudeau, Antoine-Claire, 203
Thierry, Marc-Antoine, 129, 137
Third Estate, 23, 138
Thomas à Kempis, 85, 86
Thuriot, Jacques-Alexis, 117, 196
Tourzel, Louise-Félicité de Croy d'Havré, Marquise de, 1, 8, 40, 79, 81
Tourzel, Pauline-Joséphine de, 8, 79, 81
Treilhard, Jean-Baptiste, 166, 175, 195, 247
Tribunal of August 17, 1792, 40
Tronchet, François-Denis, 117, 118, 119, 125, 127, 128, 130, 191, 234
Tuileries: conquest of, 36–38
Turgot, Anne-Robert-Jacques, 86
Turreau de Linières, Louis, 140

Valazé, Charles-Eléonor Dufriche-, 62, 64, 72, 100, 108, 111, 129, 239. *See also* Commission of Twenty-four
Valmy, Battle of, 43–44, 64
Varennes, flight to, 24–26, 28, 44, 62, 73, 79, 104, 109, 121, 129, 156, 205, 219
Vendée, Department of, 176
Vergniaud, Pierre-Victurnien, xv, 143, 144, 145, 146, 148, 149, 150, 151, 152, 158, 165, 166, 167, 169, 171, 172, 175, 176, 185–186, 188, 190, 191, 194, 195, 198, 199
Villette, Charles-Michel, 178

Virgil, 86
Voltaire, 46, 85, 86
Voulland, Jean-Henri, 188

Wadelaincourt, Antoine-Hubert, 171
Walzer, Michael, xiii
Westermann, François-Joseph, 34, 37
Wittinghof, General, 108
Women's March on Versailles (October
    5–6, 1789), 17
Wordsworth, William, 53

Designer: Al Burkhardt
Compositor: G & S Typesetters
Text: VIP Palatino
Display: VIP Garamond
Printer: Maple-Vail Book Mfg. Group
Binder: Maple-Vail Book Mfg. Group